Culture Wars

Critical Social Thought
Series editor: Michael W. Apple
Professor of Curriculum and Instruction and of Educational
Policy Studies, University of Wisconsin-Madison

Already published
Critical Social Psychology Philip Wexler
Reading, Writing and Resistance Robert B. Everhart
Arguing for Socialism Andrew Levine

CULTURE WARS

School and Society in the Conservative Restoration 1969-1984

Ira Shor

Routledge & Kegan Paul
London and New York

First published in 1986

Reprinted 1987

by Routledge & Kegan Paul Ltd
11 New Fetter Lane, London EC4P 4EE

Published in the USA by
Routledge and Kegan Paul Inc.

in association with Methuen Inc.
29 West 35th St., New York, NY 10001

Set in Times, 10 on 12pt
by Input Typesetting Ltd, London
and printed in Great Britain
by T. J. Press (Padstow) Ltd,
Padstow, Cornwall

Library of Congress Cataloging in Publication Data

Shor, Ira, 1945–

Culture wars.
(Critical social thought)
Bibliography: p.
Includes index.
1. Educational sociology—United States.
2. Education—United States—Curricula.   3. Politics and
education—United States.   4. Conservatism—United States.
I. Title.   II. Series.
LC191.4.S54   1986   370.19   85-2305

British Library CIP data also available

ISBN 0-7102-0637-2
      0-7102-0649-6 (pb)

The great educational experiences of the last ten years have been the civil rights, anti-war and women's movements.

Ronald Gross (1972)

The era of alienation did not end with the close of the Vietnam War.

S. M. Lipset and William Schneider (1983)

It is astonishing that so few critics challenge the system . . . The people are better than the structure. Therefore, the structure must be at fault.

Theodore Sizer (1984)

Contents

Series editor's introduction

In *Ideology and Curriculum* I argued that in order to understand how education functions socially we needed to situate it within the class, race and gender dynamics that exist in our society. This required us to recognize how the kinds of facts, skills and values that schools organize and select are related to how students are organized and selected, and then stratified economically and culturally. Thus, we should always ask a series of questions about the knowledge that schools teach and the ways they go about teaching it. 'Whose culture?' 'What social group's knowledge?' 'In whose interest is certain knowledge being taught in our educational institutions?'[1]

These kinds of questions point to a particular way of thinking about schools, one that is caught by the title of Ira Shor's new volume, *Culture Wars*. In this perspective, our educational system provides an arena in which different groups with different conceptions of what is important to know, and often different power, fight it out, so to speak. The culture that ultimately finds its way into the school is the result of these battles, compromises, and what has been called 'accords.' However, these accords can only be temporary. Given the fact that the economy is often in crisis, that power does shift in government, and that ideological tensions in the larger society are often exacerbated (and are now growing rather rapidly), educational policy and what happens inside school buildings are constantly subject to these battles. And sometimes these can be quite intense. Questions of schooling, then, become intensely political.

One need only look around to notice that this politicization has become much more visible. We are witnessing a large number of attacks on schools, especially from right-wing critics. Censorship is growing, and there are clear attempts to define what counts as important knowledge only that which meets the needs of 'reindustrialization' and 'rearmament.' At the same time, there is a movement in a majority of states in America to standardize and control both the processes and outcomes of teaching, thus taking as many aspects of teaching as possible out of the teacher's control and placing it in a framework of an inappropriate industrial logic. The ultimate effects of this may be the deskilling of teachers and a loss of any substantive vision of what education can be besides simply socialization to existing norms and values.[2] When coupled with the pressure to institute voucher plans and tax credits that might nearly dismantle the public school system and leave it only for the poor and disenfranchised,[3] these tendencies would be both a pedagogical and social disaster, I believe.

There has been a remarkable offensive – one combining big business and finance, and conservative political and religious groups – aimed at delegitimating democratic discourse and restoring 'authority.' This is occurring in government, in the media, in the paid and unpaid workplaces of men and women, and elsewhere.

By and large, what is going on is the recurrent conflict between property rights and person rights in our economy.[4] In essence, it is the rights of profits and the market versus the rights of equality and justice that are at stake. Conflicts between these two sets of rights are not new; they are a constitutive part of our political economy. At issue, though, are not merely abstract conceptions of rights, but economic, political and cultural power.[5] In education, especially, what is also at stake are the conditions under which teachers will labor, the kinds of knowledge our children will learn, and ultimately whether we will have an educated citizenry that can raise the ethical and political questions so necessary to keep democracy a vital living force or instead a quiescent population more interested in personal gain than the social good.

It is important to realize, however, that just as the conflict between property rights and person rights is not new, so too has education always been a contentious element in this conflict. Historically, as David Hogan has so nicely demonstrated, class politics, for example, played a dual role in education. Debates over education and what it should be about were part and parcel of struggles both between working-class and more powerful groups and within these groups from the beginning of mass popular education in the United States. Just as importantly, struggles over the form, content and aims of education helped create class, race and gender politics in this country and elsewhere. That is, education was not just a response to the different goals by various contending groups. It played a major role in helping to form these groups into powerful collective forces.[6] Thus, education needs to be seen as both a cause and an effect of ideological, political and economic movements. It has always, then, been caught up in the politics of inequality in the larger society.

Over the past two decades, scholarship on what I have been discussing – on the relationship between our formal institutions of education and the structures of inequality – has made immense progress. In a relatively short period of time, we have moved from a position that basically saw education as an isolated phenomenon concerned only with passing on the supposedly neutral culture of 'all of us' to a situation in which it has become increasingly clear that schools as institutions and the curriculum, teaching and evaluation that go on inside them favor specific portions of the American population. Education may be a public good, but a large segment of that public is less well served than others.

In examining our schools critically, however, we must be very careful not to assume that they are simply tools for the recreation of class, race and gender inequalities. This is not the case. Some incredibly talented and committed people work in these institutions. Furthermore, there are ideas and practices within many of our educational institutions that are progressive, that signify very important victories by teachers, people of color, women and others in making schools more formally democratic in their content, processes and results. It is exactly these progressive elements that are currently under attack. By tracing out the recent history of what he identifies as the three major periods of this attack, Shor helps us understand both how and why it came about. In so doing, he enables us to recognize how situated the school indeed is in the politics of the surrounding culture. But it is also the way he does this that is just as helpful.

While our understanding of the relationship between education and class, race and gender is becoming even more impressive, a considerable portion of the theoretical and empirical research on this is simply inaccessible to a broad audience. It is inaccessible in two ways. Much of it is published in academic journals or scholarly books, thereby making it a subject of considerable debate among a segment of the professional educational community but less than totally visible to others. Perhaps even more crucial is the fact that this research has been carried on in something of a private language. It has been noted for its involved theoreticism and, often, the abstract nature of its arguments. This is truly unfortunate if the ultimate aim of such research is to have an impact on how we all think about and act upon schools. *Culture Wars* is a partial remedy to this situation. It is clearly political in that it sees that schools have been a target for a 'conservative restoration,' a restoration that has an impact not only on education but on our economy and our entire polity. Yet it is also politically clear. Shor illuminates the political choices before us in a language that shows exactly what is at stake if we are to defend the gains that have been made in education against those who would turn the school and its teachers and students into appendages of industry and conservative forces.

Many people have criticized the emerging right-wing tendencies within education. While such criticism is important, to say the least, it is just as significant to articulate an alternative program to those being advocated by conservative elements in industry, government and by right-wing groups. It is to Shor's credit that not only does he provide a clear political history of these tendencies, but he describes a number of the principles and practices that could be used to create a more politically and pedagogically democratic educational experience.

Even though *Culture Wars* devotes most of its time to documenting the considerable success of the conservative restoration, it is not a pessimistic book. Not only are there suggestions for renewing and expanding the democratic and critical tradition in education, there is also a very real sense that seeds of discontent are being planted right now within restoration politics that will grow as time goes on and this retrogressive movement weakens. Thus, as a totally instrumentalist view of schooling gains strength in this period, as students and others look on education as only something that is useful for getting a job or getting ahead, cynicism will also gain strength. Just as in earlier periods when temporary accords led to new crises, so too will the growth of cynicism be hard to contain during the conservative restoration.

Shor sees the possibility, hence, of a different kind of 'restoration' growing within the current 'search for order,' if only we can learn from what has happened in the recent past. He puts it this way while at the same time summarizing a number of the arguments in the book.

Cynicism can be as politically unmanageable as open rebellion. The historic transition from protest culture in the 1960s to 'the culture of narcissism' in the 1970s only posed new and more widespread crises. The reversal of the 1960s arrived at the predicament of the 1980s through many mechanisms inside school and out. In three major waves of school reform, restoration policies revealed the importance of curriculum in culture war. Career education in the early 1970s, and the back-to-basics Literacy Crisis a few years later, both contributed to an alienation and decay which alarmed official commissions in 1983 as they launched a third reform effort. This epic search for order began in 1969 with a society in upheaval and a school system breeding dissent. Fifteen years later, neither education nor any other major institution was working to anyone's satisfaction. When the new restoration eventually retreats, culture war will open for another age of opposition whose success rests on learning from the culture wars of the past.

While Shor does not overtly say this, the message of *Culture Wars* reminds us of something else, the importance of collective memory.[7] Part of the task of the educational community is to keep alive the traditions of democratic economic, political and cultural alternatives so that they can be drawn upon when that time of conservative retreat comes. For those readers who wish to see such democratic alternatives emerge in their legitimate place in political and educational discourse once again, this task of collective memory is the challenge we must take up.

Michael W. Apple
The University of Wisconsin-Madison

Notes

1 Michael W. Apple, *Ideology and Curriculum* (Boston: Routledge & Kegan Paul, 1979), pp. 15–16.

2 See Michael W. Apple, *Education and Power* (Boston: Routledge & Kegan Paul, 1982). We need to remember that teaching, especially elementary school teaching, is largely 'women's work.' What we may be actually witnessing is the recurrence of a long line of attempts to gain outside control of women's labor. For further discussion of this see Michael W. Apple, 'Work, Gender and Teaching,' *Teachers College Record*, 84, No. 3, Spring 1983, pp. 611–28.

3 I have discussed the educational and political implications of voucher plans and tax credits at greater length in Apple, *Education and Power, op. cit.*

4 Frances Fox Piven and Richard Cloward, *The New Class War* (New York: Pantheon, 1982), p. 41.

5 Apple, *Education and Power, op. cit.*

6 David Hogan, 'Education and Class Formation: The Peculiarities of the Americans,' in *Cultural and Economic Reproduction in Education*, ed. Michael W. Apple (Boston: Routledge & Kegan Paul, 1982), pp. 32–78.

7 See, for example, Raphael Samuel (ed.) *People's History and Socialist Theory* (Boston: Routledge & Kegan Paul, 1981).

Foreword
by Paulo Freire

I came to know Ira Shor through reading his first, very excellent book, *Critical Teaching and Everyday Life*. Later, we began a correspondence that, although rather infrequent, laid the foundation for a series of meetings during which we both deepened our understanding of general educational problems and, also, experienced the birth of a frank and brotherly friendship. It was with great satisfaction, therefore, that I accepted the invitation to write a few words to present to his readers his new, and also excellent, book *Culture Wars: School and Society in the Conservative Restoration 1969–1984*.

This book is equal in importance to *Critical Teaching*. In it, Ira Shor competently describes various changes of emphasis in certain educational objectives occurring while what he calls the 'conservative restoration' begins to take the place of the protest movements of the 1960s. Or, put another way, he describes the conservative restoration as the response of certain powerful forces, attempting to confront and overcome what they saw as not only explicit but also implicit in the protest movements. The fact is that within the crises of the 1960s, there was a clear, strong discrediting of established authority which, in its turn, necessarily had to find an efficient form of action against the popular forces that were both judging and threatening its image. Thus the authority that was being challenged turned toward conservative reform in the schools and in the wider society.

Culture Wars interprets school politics after 1969 as an attempt to use the curriculum to intervene in crises that were global in nature. In his analysis of official efforts to adjust the curriculum so that it would conform to dominant political needs, Shor calls attention to three principal phases of school reform. The first, from 1971–5, focussed on vocational issues and stressed career education. The second, from 1975–82, was related to language competence and was seen as a literacy crisis. Finally, the third revolves around the strong demand of authorities for more discipline, greater attention to academic subjects, and computer training – all a part of the anxious pursuit of something called 'excellence.' Actually, all of these represent political attempts by the establishment to counteract the denunciations of the 1960s. Whether they took place within the schools or in the larger society, these attempts show very clearly the political nature of education, even though this is denied, on the one hand innocently, on the other hand, cleverly, by those who are either naive or very astute.

A critical, rigorous reading of this book is a profound experience. The reader's curiosity is stimulated to follow closely the author's reflections on the facts presented. The obvious point referred to above becomes even more clear: each of the principal phases of school reform corresponds to a specific political intention in the interest of safeguarding the establishment.

A careful study of this book is well worth the effort.

Paulo Freire
Sao Paulo, June 1984

Acknowledgments

I want to thank a number of people who improved this book. Fred Pincus and I have had a two-person seminar in higher education for several years. Our thoughts have mingled, and for this book he offered me much helpful criticism. Without his sustained advice, I would have had a much harder time writing *Culture Wars*. Bertell Ollman was another critic who read successive drafts and helped me understand how to shape the book's arguments. His reviews of each chapter made them into stronger presentations. Earlier versions of the book were read by Mark Schulman, Dick Ohmann, Tom Heaney and William Alexander. They graciously plowed through rough drafts and sent me detailed suggestions on what to keep, what to throw out, what to polish and what to refine. Arthur Maglin also studied the manuscript and gave me sage advice on how to even out the political critique from chapter to chapter. He also sent me weekly clippings of articles on education and thus kept my finger on the pulse of school issues even while I was buried away typing. Joel Cohen read a synopsis of the book's argument, and told me line by line which points were not well-constructed. My thanks also to Carman St John Hunter for translating Paulo Freire's preface.

I want to thank the Guggenheim Foundation for supporting my research with a Fellowship that helped me take time off to write the final draft.

Lastly, Paulo Freire's work has inspired me for over a decade. I still learn with him about creatively engaging the limits we face in school and society.

Ira Shor

New York City
January 1985

1 The hinge of 1969
Authority makes war on the 1960s: the theme of 'settling for less' in school and society

Young people rarely challenged the legitimacy of their parents', or their university's, or their government's authority. They are questioning it now!
> Charles Silberman, *Crisis in the Classroom* (1970)

By the early 1970s . . . corporations were beginning to recognize the threat to their own power and privilege . . . .
It would have been astonishing if corporations had not fought back – both on their own and through their influence over government policy.
> Bowles, Gordon and Weiskopf, *Beyond the Wasteland* (1983)

Within the span of a single student generation, the prophecies of 'youth revolution' and 'the greening of America' and fears that totalitarian leftist student groups might shut out intellectual freedoms have been disproved.
> Richard Freeman, *The Overeducated American* (1976)

A period like the sixties can have a devastating effect on learning and schooling.
> Jay Sommer, Teacher of the Year, 1981

Experimental colleges and programs so prevalent in the 1960s are largely invisible today, when we need more than ever what they were designed to provide.
> Allen Davis, William Newell, *Chronicle of Higher Education* (1981)

The university helped compass its own downfall in the 1960s . . . . It willingly abandoned the one doctrine indispensable to its moral integrity – academic neutrality.
> Arnold Beichman, *New York Times* (1983)

1

Surprise upheavals and long reactions

Just before 1970, a new literature on the death and rebirth of
education burst on the scene. That year, the works of such critics
as Kohl, Kozol, Dennison, Leonard and Herndon were joined by
Charles Silberman's massive *Crisis in the Classroom*.[1] He began
his influential tome with a message patently clear at the time:
'Ours is an age of crisis.' Silberman portrayed the snowballing
upheaval of the 1960s in the words of a business colleague:

> 'The American situation deteriorated from serious to critical.
> Cambodia, Kent State, the killings of blacks in Georgia and
> Mississippi, along with all the protests and counter-protests
> and counter-counterprotests that stemmed from these,
> plunged the nation to a level of bewilderment and fear that it
> had not reached in the depth of the great depression.'[2]

With the sense of crisis everywhere, it seemed natural to pose
education as part of the social drama rather than as an isolated
debate on effective teaching. Not only were the fates of schooling
and society radically linked, but the pace of events convinced
many that a great historical change was in the offing. Perhaps a
new society itself was about to dawn in learning and in economics,
in this age of aquarius. Ivan Illich was then the brilliant prophet
of 'deschooling.' At the moment Silberman wrote in favour of the
progressive renewal of mainstream schools, Illich denounced large
official structures and called for self-directed learning. He
predicted the inevitable and imminent demise of public education
in the face of the new consciousness spreading through society:

> The disestablishment of schools will inevitably happen – and
> it will happen surprisingly fast. It cannot be retarded very
> much longer and it is hardly necessary to promote it
> vigorously, for this is being done now. What is worthwhile
> is to try to orient it in a hopeful direction.[3]

The walls of Jericho seemed to be crumbling as great visions
clashed with each other as well as with the status quo. The decline
of these Utopian hopes was as breathtaking as their sudden
arrival.

The legendary eruption of protest culture in the 1960s still
haunts life in the 1980s even though the Philistines remain in

charge of Jericho. Those who saw the upheavals still feel lingering effects despite the conservative 'big chill' of the 1970s. Yet, few knew then that the 1960s were coming, including some astute radical thinkers. One who became a mentor to student activists, Herbert Marcuse, wrote in 1964 about the thwarting of opposition.[4] He considered consumerism, mass culture and official tolerance of some dissent as bulwarks against radicalism. Another sharp critic, C. Wright Mills, wrote then about liberal intellect being 'overwhelmed' in a conservative age.[5] McCarthyism settled like a glacier over any optimism for fundamental social change. Even an establishment historian like Diane Ravitch agreed in her study of postwar education that no great upheavals were on the horizon when the 1960s began:

> Riding the crest of exuberant growth, thinking of themselves as leaders of vital and socially dynamic institutions, college and university officials had no reason to anticipate the era of crisis that lay before them. . . . In a time of unbounded optimism, no one could have predicted that many of America's campuses would come under siege in the late 1960s.[6]

Ravitch admitted that public schools back then had unsolved problems, but she saw bristling confidence in higher education as the 1960s opened. The eruption came fast, seemingly from nowhere. School and society have not been the same since.

The surprising activism of the 1960s included massive protests against the Vietnam War, demands for race and sex equality, the formation of radical caucuses inside unions and academic professions, countless small dissenting publications, and the spread of alternate education ideas. This grass-roots movement posed immediate and long-term threats to authority. It put business, schooling and the government on the defensive. In response, a conservative restoration emerged after Richard Nixon's tight 1968 election victory. He and his retinue had some cause for alarm. In October 1969, they watched from their Watergate windows as the gigantic Moratorium Against the War in Vietnam paraded below. The sight of so many red flags and banners led colorful Martha Mitchell to declare it another Russian Revolution. Something would have to be done.

In economics and in education, the Nixon Administration began turning back the tide of activism. It began the first of several chilling recessions which ushered in the hard times of the 1970s. In schooling, the Nixon program included a vast national plan called 'career education.' Curriculum was tilted in the direction of work discipline and job-training. Perhaps that would cool the ardor of youth. If not, careerism was followed in the mid-1970s by a 'Literacy Crisis' and a 'back-to-basics' movement. Perhaps those programs would put some noses to the grindstone. In 1983, while some key insiders like Ravitch continued criticizing the 1960s, a new crisis of 'mediocrity' was officially declared, and a new war for 'excellence' was launched. The radical and Utopian excitement of education in the 1960s became mediocrity and austerity by the 1980s. How did such a transition occur?

One road to the school crises of the 1980s was the 'legitimacy crisis' of the 1960s, worsening in the 1980s. Evidence of mass alienation from school and other institutions abounds. A major survey by Lipset and Schneider (1983) found confidence in society at an all-time low.[7] The many school crisis reports of 1983 pleaded for national consensus.[8] Reagan's Secretary of State blamed the Beirut debacle on dissent at home.[9] In 1984, one school head accused long-haired teachers and the end of dress-codes from the 1960s of undermining discipline.[10] Another big-city school chief lost her right to bar anti-war groups from school while she allowed in army recruiters.[11] Paulo Freire's liberatory ideas spread[12] while another professor's essay on teaching Vietnam to students in the 1980s drew heated replies in a major journal.[13] From the conservative side, one academic wrote the university's epitaph in 1983, killed by the egalitarian excesses of the 1960s.[14]

The battles of the 1960s kept fading at the same time that the issues refused to go away. Resurgent conservatives after 1969 showed success and failure in dealing with the crisis from below. After the eruption, came their restoration.

Nixon's horse

Before the smoke of the 1960s cleared, durable Richard Nixon took over as first champion of the conservative cause. He began turning the tide against mass movements while disastrously crippling the credibility of the authorities. His failures were bad omens for building a new conservative consensus in the 1970s. Even before the Watergate fiasco, Nixon lacked the charisma and legitimacy to spread a strong reactionary revival.

Nixon limped into office on a plurality, claiming to speak for 'the silent majority.' His quiet horse became the noisy 'moral majority' in Ronald Reagan's 1980 victory. By the 1980s, political issues had made a long swing towards conservatism. Yet, the word 'majority' in two campaigns is telling. It signalled the long restoration search for a national consensus as powerful as the protest culture of the 1960s. Such popular support never emerged for the right as it consolidated power through the 1970s. After a decade of restoration, Christopher Lasch observed in 1979 the frustration of the new order:

> Hardly more than a quarter-century after Henry Luce
> proclaimed 'the American century,' American confidence has
> fallen to a low ebb. Those who recently dreamed of world
> power now despair of governing the city of New York. Defeat
> in Vietnam, economic stagnation, and the impending
> exhaustion of natural resources have produced a mood of
> pessimism in higher circles, which spreads through the rest of
> society as people lose faith in their leaders.[15]

Lasch saw that 'A pervasive distrust of those in power had made society increasingly difficult to govern.' This predicament helps explain Reagan's aggressive posture, after 1980, to impose a consensus refusing to form.

Declining liberalism and radicalism also gave Reagan more running room than Nixon enjoyed. The 1960s was a tough medium limiting the advance of conservative policies in Nixon's first term. The economic recession engineered in 1971 helped cripple mass activism but it also crippled loyalty to the system imposing hard times. In the transition years from left to right, 1969–72, conservative culture faced some awesome tasks. The 1960s was a hard act to follow and a difficult culture to replace. There were global melodramas, youthful idealism, fat times in an expanding war economy, rising aspirations, a growing sense of power among the disaffected. An autonomous discourse invented from below put the establishment on the defensive. At the grass roots, there was a subversive emergence of action and communication. This new vocabulary validated the demands and the language modes of historically dominated groups – minorities, women, the young, senior citizens, native Americans, gays, the handicapped. An enormous postwar generation was coming of age when democratic dissent and questioning authority were popular themes. The ideological challenges by protest vocabulary were matched by economic challenges. The material expectations of organized and unorganized masses of people exceeded the routinely unequal distribution of wealth.

Something had to be done fast to adjust downwardly political and economic life. Something had to be done fast to silence the daily talk, the rally speeches, the many teach-ins, the underground publications, the guerilla theaters, the radical films, the experimental courses, the alternate programs, the many small groupings, through which the themes of dissent spread along with unsupervised organization. The voice of authority had to move from the defensive to the offensive. The reinvention of official rule fell to a man with little appeal or imagination, Richard Nixon. He was followed by inept and bland leaders in Gerald Ford and Jimmy Carter. The federal executives were thus weak partners in the conservative forces reversing the 1960s. Until picturesque Ronald Reagan taught Washington how to whistle 'Dixie' and chew gum at the same time, it was up to big business and the ultra-conservative churches to divert the tide away from protest culture and towards a Golden Age of restoration.

On the road to more disorder: right-wing kings of swing

Disorder and alienation are two ongoing signs of conservative failure documented in the Lipset-Schneider study and in the laments of school 'mediocrity' in 1983. But there were others throughout the current restoration. The continuity of opposition between the 1960s and the 1980s was not broken in the way the conservative 1950s broke the link between the 1930s and the 1960s. In the 1970s and 1980s, 1960s' veterans and new activists kept alive protest actions. Despite the conservative climate, a maturing left reshaped itself. If the 1960s had included more activists from the 1930s, it could have been less of a Children's Crusade. In the very tough conservative medium of the 1970s and early 1980s, visible activism showed itself around environmental, anti-nuclear and women's issues. Some dissident threads from the 1960s matured into consequential theories – feminism, neo-marxism, liberatory education, holistic health care. The evolution of alternate media in documentary film, people's theater and political art was dramatic also. Still, the swing to the right has been the dominant direction of recent politics. It was severe enough to disintegrate mass movements and to reverse notable gains from the 1960s. Trade unions since that time have accepted worse and worse contracts. Affirmative action and civil rights enforcements have been weakened. Urban renewal of housing for low- and middle-income families gave way to gentrification. In education, increased student electives and experimental courses from the 1960s were reduced by more required classes in traditional subjects. Women's and minorities' programs have been put under budgetary and administrative pressures to rejoin regular academic departments. The open door to college was restricted by rising tuition and by entry/exit exams making it harder to go on to a four-year degree from a community college. The most notable reversal of egalitarianism in the 1970s came at the City University of New York. It abandoned its 129-year-old policy of free tuition in 1976, fired hundreds of junior faculty hired for the open admissions experiment, and imposed a skills-testing program.[16]

In education, as in any other part of society subjected to restoration, there is a conservative ideology underlying the reversal of the 1960s: that ideology intervenes against the democratic distribution of wealth and power. Policy-making power and money are redistributed upward in a restoration. The conservative language for this reversal pits 'quality' against 'equality.' Restoration policy promotes itself as the defender of 'excellence' and 'high standards.' Such political vocabulary dominates discussion in a conservative period. It helps authority disguise the real intention of strengthening hierarchy. To restore the domination of the old order, the results of the egalitarian era are judged from the top down and found to be dismally inferior to the quality of learning before the changes were made. However, the debate never allows the words 'hierarchy,' 'domination,' 'power,' to enter the discussion. The standards of the elite are posed as undebatable, the only language in which to judge the situation, a universal rather than a class-specific evaluation.

One restoration voice who spoke this universal language was

Robert Ebel. In 1978 he saw ruins all around us in education, thanks to egalitarianism:

> Evidence of decline in educational achievement in recent
> decades is beyond question. . . . The schools have taken no
> strong action to resist or reverse the decline. They have not
> set high standards of achievement in learning and worked
> hard to get their pupils to reach those standards. . . . Has
> commitment to democratic equality made schools identify
> excellence with elitism? Does some deficiency in excellence
> among teachers themselves limit their inclination to
> encourage excellence?[17]

Ebel was speaking to an audience at the Educational Testing Service (ETS), the organization marketing the nation's most famous standard exam, the Scholastic Aptitude Test (SAT). He denounced the progressive pedagogy which tends to use fewer of the tests busily marketed by ETS. The testing business and the billion-dollar textbook industry certainly have a big stake in class-room pedagogy. They have a lot to lose if students and teachers write their own materials and do their own internal evaluations of learning. The huge dollar purchases of schools are one commercial dimension to the shape of curriculum. In the scope of a grand culture war, standard testing and mandated texts involve the domi-nance of official ideology, the construction of consciousness in each new generation of students, and the displacement of oppo-sition voices. In supporting the restoration pedagogy of lectures, tests and texts, Ebel suggested two key conservative themes which echoed from one end of the restoration to the other: equality is in competition with excellence and the individual student and teacher are to blame for the current school decline. These conservative claims needed ample test scores to make them cred-ible. If scores on traditional tests were lower, then obviously non-traditional students and non-traditional teaching were the culprits.

In using test scores to indict egalitarianism and to support 'excel-lence,' Ebel reversed the 1960s' tendency to name the system as the source of school and social problems. Ebel and other resto-rationists read test results as proof of severe *personal* deficiencies in students and teachers. Experimental methods allowed such decay to happen. The system was no longer the problem assaulted from so many sides in the 1960s. Rather, the old system was the best solution to the problem of decline. The old way of doing things used to produce excellence, and now it is time once again to restore its dominance and universalize it for everyone.

The claim of gross personal failure at the bottom and of excellence at the top justified austere measures by the authorities to put the house in order again. Ebel's charge that progressive/egalitarian education gave us 'two generations of warm-hearted but soft-headed pedagogy,'[18] echoed in the great crisis year of 1983. *Fortune* magazine offered a cover story on the latest school debacle, blaming John Dewey and his followers for the rise of social reform over excellence in education.[19] A month after that, *Time*'s own cover story on the new reform wave zeroed in on the experimental years of the 1960s, virtually repeating Ebel's earlier claims:

> There is no question that expectations for curriculum and standards dropped over the past 20 years. In many schools, the art of diagramming sentences went the way of *Wuthering Heights* and survey literature courses were transformed into cotton candy electives like 'Expressions of Love.'[20]

At almost the same moment, Ebel's themes of personal teacher/student failure in the collapse of standards were supported once more by Arnold Beichman in the *New York Times* magazine.[21] In a conservative jeremiad, Beichman denounced the 1960s, the decade of social relevance and personal courses, the source of the new 'dark age' descending on the university. Years earlier, these themes had been anticipated in a 1977 *Christian Science Monitor* feature story by a university dean, who declared educational decline to be the legacy of the radical 1960s.[22] Ravitch later agreed in anti-1960s parts of *The Troubled Crusade* (1983).

Another articulate voice of restoration themes was Steven Cahn. He connected egalitarianism, the 1960s, and class-leveling as the triple threat to academic excellence. In a reprinted essay, Cahn singled out one leader of the 1968 upheavals at Columbia University, Mark Rudd, the same figure Beichman mentioned in his own attack on the protest era. Cahn's appropriately-titled restoration essay, 'Restoring the House of Intellect,' declared that

> During the 1970s, faculties were in retreat, fulfilling Mark Rudd's hope that students would take control of the

university. The time has come to reverse that trend. Strong faculties that claim their rightful authority and use it wisely will receive more than the respect of their students; they will earn the gratitude of the nation.[23]

Cahn was part of the national trend to return rightful authority to its shaken throne. Like other restorationists, he saw the collegiate malaise as 'a hangover of the 60s.'

He quoted Jacques Barzun's queasy dismay with the students of the 1950s, the last decade when traditionalists were on the warpath over schooling. Back then, Barzun wrote

what is observable at the end of 16 long years of an ordinary education: no knowledge that is precise and firm, no ability to do intellectual work with thoroughness and dispatch. Though there are college graduates, many of them cannot read accurately or write without travail and doubt, cannot utter their thoughts with fluency or force.[24]

Cahn worried over how much worse the situation is now than earlier, and what Barzun would say about educational decay today. Barzun did manage to become an eminence grise of two decades of restoration when *Newsweek* sought his expert commentary on its media darling of 1975, 'the Literacy Crisis.' Barzun declared, 'We have ceased to think with words. We have stopped teaching our children that the truth cannot be told apart from the right words.'[25]

Cahn's theme of 'restoring the house of intellect' and Barzun's notion of 'the right words' are an ideal restoration marriage. Traditional academics could restore their authority only if their words were once again accepted as the only right ones, the universal language all of us should speak. This was an urgent project because opposition ideas were successfully competing with the knowledge of the authorities. The language-rich 1960s put official knowledge on the run by identifying the academic authorities with the illegitimate power of the government and corporations. The universities were hardly neutral 'ivory towers,' but were rather knee-deep in research useful to the military and paid for by the corporations. In the battles over the Vietnam War, iconoclastic students and teachers saw the universities helping business and the Pentagon outfit the war machine. The innocence of higher education was exposed even more by the discovery of its racial, sexual and class inequalities. 'The right words' were drowning in a flood of dissenting words. Outlaw ideology advanced as official knowledge retreated – marxism, feminism, libertarian and progressive education, the critique of domination, anti-imperialism, egalitarianism. Authoritative knowledge and traditional education lost their credibility in the advance of radical revelations.

The loudness of opposition language in the 1960s forced the conservatives to come forward even louder in their attempt to reimpose their once-universal standards. The three major resto-ration reforms discussed in this book – career education, the Literacy Crisis, and the demand for academic excellence – were each thrust onto school and society with massive communications crusades. 'The right words' had to be retaught if the authorities were to regain their legitimacy. The 'wrong' words of radical opposition had to be obscured, to hide what the 1960s had illumi-nated, to opaque domination in society, to conceal even education's role in reproducing dominant ideology.

Teaching 'the right words' and displacing the wrong words are the dual essence of culture war. That double process goes on wherever ideas are transmitted – curriculum, mass media, public spectacles, church, etc. The early restoration confronted a formi-dable discourse of radical ideas from the protest era – we shall overcome, one man/one vote, civil rights, black power, equal rights, peace now, power to the people, make love – not war, open access, free schools. Traditionalist forces gradually regained the initiative by repressing opposition and by promoting a new vocabulary. On the one hand, radical teachers were often fired, political leaders harassed, and the dissident press sabotaged.[26] In terms of educational reversal, school language filled in the 1970s with conservatizing words like career, survival, illiteracy, tests, accountability, competence, quality, excellence and high tech. To make the transmission of authority even more secure, Standard English was forcefully prescribed against the idioms of non-traditional groups entering college – white colloquial, black bi-dialectical, hispanic bilingual. The language of everyday life and the language of the left were declared illegitimate.

From a traditional point of view, it looked as if the Ivory Tower was becoming a Tower of Babble thanks to the 1960s. All kinds

11

of barbarian tongues, leveling schemes and political demands were threatening the King's English. Campuses were once peaceful places in the good old days, when no one looked too carefully at the war research done in the labs. Now, everyone was asking how many blacks were in the student body and how many women were professors. Even the high schools were in revolt. Could a new voice of authority restore the comfortable silence of a lost Golden Age?

Silence is golden

Conservative dreams of a Golden Age before the 1960s came to the attention of Richard Ohmann early in the 1970s' Literacy Crisis. *Newsweek*'s 1975 cover story on the new American morons made talk of illiteracy fashionable. Word spread that schools had abandoned the basics and had renounced high standards. The aging SAT was trotted out so often it became a household word, proving by its declining scores that civilization was in danger. Ohmann was one of the first critics of this suspicious exercise. He examined the shaky evidence behind Literacy Crisis claims and smelled an unmistakable nostalgia in the air in 1976:

> It should not be surprising that among those falling over each other to assign blame for 'the' decline in literacy, conservative feelings are often in evidence. There's a tendency to indict the movements of the 1960s. Mass education and open admissions come under attack for lowering standards.[27]

Ohmann discovered that some test scores had been rising during this period, some remained stable, and some had declined. A special conference on test score declines had been convened a year earlier by the National Institute of Education, and its report offered more evidence of a very mixed picture.[28] A broad reading of test scores made the Literacy Crisis a fiction, if not a hoax, in Ohmann's words. As an opposition voice, Ohmann had some impressive credentials when he tilted with the restoration crusade. He was a scholar on the English language, on English education, a literary critic, and the author of the just published *English in America* (1975). From 1968–78, he was the editor of *College English* magazine, the higher education journal of the National

Council of Teachers of English. His dissent on the Golden-Age illiteracy camp was joined by others as the debate took wing. But the political initiative of the age rested with the conservatives. Their formulation of the Literacy Crisis was the right word at the right time. It was followed by a back-to-basics movement even more committed to Golden-Age ideology. The false reading of test scores will be discussed later on in Chapter 3 which is devoted to the Literacy Crisis, one of the more squalid episodes of the restoration. It demonstrated the partisan rather than universal nature of 'standards.' The 1960s were equally partisan, but on the side of egalitarianism – an angel or a devil, depending on your ideology.

The dybbuk of the 1960s also troubled the President of the American Federation of Teachers, Albert Shanker. In a 1982 speech to a local school district in New York, he announced contrarily that American public schools were both the envy of the world and places where parents feared for their children because of violence and drugs.[29] Shanker said that 'Somewhere around 1960, though, something in our attitudes towards teachers and schools changed.' The 1960s, he declared, brought a widespread loosening of standards and a bias against teaching a specific set of values. He was disturbed at the cultural relativism encouraged by the protest period. Criticism of traditional schooling was as widespread as criticism of the whole social order. It was a tough time for authority. Like Barzun, Shanker harked back to a Golden Age when the right words of an official culture were lingua franca in the realm. This theme of a universal course of study embodying a singular dominant culture took shape in the restoration as a 'core curriculum.' That core of knowledge emanated from the center of authority outward to the periphery. It is based in Standard English, a traditional reading list, and cleansed versions of history (the 'American Heritage'). The 'core curriculum' idea rejects the ideological diversity of the protest era. It is one school-form for imposing conservative consensus.

That consensus was strong in the 1950s. Its breakdown in the 1960s worried corporate circles as well as the President of the second largest teachers' union. Anti-business and anti-military values on campus grew to the point where corporate and military recruiters were often under siege when they came looking for personnel. Dow Chemical drew out the most passionate protests because it made the napalm used in Vietnam. Other values appeared then as long-term threats to the business way of life: environmentalism, cooperatism, affirmative action, occupational health and safety, and anti-consumerism. Concerns for the earth's resources, for communal work and living, for consuming less, for sexual and racial equality, for healthy work conditions, were interferences to corporate power. Protest culture loomed as a precursor to socialism. 'Equality, ecology and peace' was an agenda incompatible with the business-military enterprise. Too many people were studying foreign policy, hiring practices, job injuries, pollution and product-safety. This kind of mass literacy was unacceptable to the authorities. Knowledge was out of control.

The business world moved in a number of ways to absorb the challenge. Consumerism helped draw some autonomous threads back into the center. Dressing-down was displaced by dressing-up. The absorption of denim as a fashion fabric helped ease this transition, as did such ingenious fashion ploys as the 'no-bra' look of the early 1970s. The 'new age' health food interest spawned a new growth industry. A spin-off into exercise made jogging shoes and athletic suits a new intersection for glamor and consumerism. The vitality of high-tech helped here, in the successive marketing of electronics like CB radio, VCRs, quadraphonic, walkman stereo, video-discs and the personal computer. It became increasingly hard to afford these toys as unemployment and the cost of living rose in the 1970s. The aging student rebels were forced to grow up in housing markets, consumer markets and job markets all firmly controlled by business. The new generation of students came of age when corporations were busily restoring their good name through new products as well as through media campaigns and through school curricula.

Advertisements for itself: business sells business values

On one major communications front of the restoration, big corporations bought expensive advertising space in mass-circulation magazines and newspapers. They ran advocacy copy praising business as a responsible pillar of American life. These communiqués also pushed pro-corporate policies like deregulation of natural gas prices and of airline fares. In election years, corporate advocacy tried to drum up support for voting, but the two major parties were slow to recover. Almost half of all adult voters stayed home in November, confirming Henry Steele Commager's observation on the dismal leadership of the last decades.[30]

Mobil Oil was a creative player in the advocacy game. It spent some $21 million in 1978 alone on such advertising.[31] Its messages and those of other multi-national giants often appeared on the expensive op-ed (opinion-editorial) pages of the *New York Times*. Comforting and upbeat news of business progress came our way, in a decade when energy prices soared despite abundant supplies of everything from coal to natural gas to oil. The communications over-kill of these ads signaled an aggressive corporate rebound from the 1960s, into the new hardball world of the 1970s. The opposition could not compete at this level of media and was simply out-broadcast. However, the limits of power, money and media were displayed by a growing anti-nuclear movement and by the disaster at Three Mile Island in 1979. Nuclear power plants became economic and political albatrosses hanging on the necks of government and business, one of their largest failures in the restoration.

More successful were new corporate ventures in curriculum. Business had always been deeply involved in education, especially in the debates on vocational training, which will be examined in the next chapter. The challenge of the 1960s required a new ideological campaign through curriculum in the 1970s. In one response to campus radicalism a number of corporations endowed business institutes and chairs at various universities. This collegiate invasion drew the attention of the *New York Times* as a second decade of restoration began in 1981:

Though money for higher education is as tight as ever, in most sectors, a rising market has been developing in recent years in one of the quieter corners of university life: business financing of chairs, or institutes, devoted to the study of private enterprise. Since the country's first private enterprise chair was established at Georgia State University in 1963, more than 40 colleges and universities have followed the trend, asking corporations for money to help get the message of

15

American business across. . . . The private-enterprise chairs
and institutes arose originally because of what business
perceived as a proliferation of radical and Marxist ideas in
academic circles in the 1960s.[32]

The importance of such campus advances was suggested by one
corporate consultant in the *Wall Street Journal*: 'What is being
taught in the universities today will be the generally accepted
concept ten years from now.'[33]

Given business advocacy in media and institutes in higher
education, and the strong career thrust of the early 1970s, it is all
the more remarkable for opposition ideologies to have matured
in this conservative era. The growing legitimacy of a neo-marxism
resulted in a *U.S. News* cover-story in January 1982. It declared
that 'At a time when the conservative views of Ronald Reagan
prevail in Washington and across much of America, a small but
fervent group of radical leftist professors is expanding its foothold
on the nation's campuses.'[34] If you consider how the McCarthy
purges of the 1950s chased the left from schools, colleges, media,
arts and trade unions, you will get some feel for the weakness of
the current conservative consensus. Even in the 1920s, Upton
Sinclair complained that schools were graveyards for radical
teachers.[35] Many dissident teachers were also fired in the late
1960s and 1970s. But the new conservative age co-existed with
the low-profile development of radicalism.

The high-profile business effort to marginalize the opposition
went far beyond ads, institutes and chairs. Pro-corporate films
were produced and distributed cheaply to public schools.[36] The
work ethic itself took shape in a national reform called career
education. The promotion of careerism in schools and colleges
was designed to distract students from their discontent. In addition
to tilting all of curriculum towards occupationalism, business
culture increased its presence through 'Adopt-a-School' programs.
This business-school linkage, begun in the 1970s and accelerated
in the comprehensive crisis of 1983, allied a corporation with a
school, a college, a district or a whole city system. Curriculum
materials and business personnel were offered to the classroom.
Students and teachers were invited to make on-site business visits.
Excess machinery and supplies were donated from the company
office to the school. Each linkage made the influence of business

over curriculum more secure, thus providing the business world with a closer supervision of content and ideas. It also enhanced the public service image of private enterprise. This mode of re-legitimizing the established order had some appeal to overworked and underpaid teachers. They would be grateful to receive prepared lessons on ready-to-go ditto masters (spirit duplicating machines). If the college president, school principal, district super-visor or mayor had mandated the linkage, then the teachers would have to go along with the plan. A good many teachers also share the partisan loyalties of business-prepared materials. Studying the 'Adopt-a-School' program in several big-city systems, Sheila Harty observed a great deal of big business activity:

> Our 1977 surveys found that 64 per cent of *Fortune's* 500 top
> industrials and 90 per cent of the major trade associations and
> electric utilities provide materials free. 29 per cent of *Fortune's*
> *500*, 47 per cent of trade associations and 53 per cent of
> utilities design these materials for classroom use grade k-12
> with teacher guides and mimeo stencils. . . . Teaching aids
> on the 'energy crisis' distributed by local utilities, for example,
> become vehicles for nuclear power promotion.[37]

Harty concluded that 'under business's tutelage, knowledge becomes a means to an end, quantitative, pragmatic and market-able. The result is an anti-intellectualism that creates a trade-school mentality . . . a numbing of critical inquiry into the uses of power in society and the source of ethical value in life.'[38] The anti-intellectual thrust of restoration reform was so successful in the 1970s, that by 1983 a 'Thinking Crisis' was declared in education.

Critical inquiry and ethical values played key roles in the protest culture of the 1960s. The rise of mass movements politicized larger and larger areas of society. Again, there was too much of the wrong kind of literacy.[39] Thus, it made sense for business to restore itself by numbing the critical potential of curriculum. Trade-school pedagogy is the most anti-intellectual and depolitic-ized form of education. It had always been business's curriculum-of-choice for the mass of students. They are offered limited tech-nical schooling, or, as Dewey said, trained like animals instead of educated like human beings.[40]

Thus, the business invasion of curriculum after the 1960s sought to secure certain outcomes and to prevent others. Education's content was injected anew with 'the right words.' This injection fortified school's purpose in transmitting the work ethic, some marketable skills, and minimum literacy in Standard English. Such a treatment also interfered with unorthodox ethical and critical studies. Those kind of studies had been driven into some parts of the liberal arts. Only an elite used to get a serious exercise of liberal intellect, but after the mass expansion of higher education in the 1950s and 1960s, liberal study was available to far greater numbers of students. The grand scale of higher learning at that time fed into the social criticism of protest movements. The activism of even immature students proved very damaging to the legitimacy of business, government, the military and schooling. There was so much problematic material being discussed and acted on from the bottom up: an immoral war in Vietnam, racism and sexism despite constitutional guarantees of equality, poverty in the richest nation on earth. Education was breeding dissident politics, and politics was where ethics and knowledge intersected. It is no wonder, then, that liberal study and protest culture declined together in the 1970s as careerism and trade-school curriculum advanced the cause of business.

From Wall Street to the bible belt: a holy alliance for God and profits

Big business was not the only force on the offensive in the restoration. It was joined by a field of religious and political allies. An aggressive alliance of centrist and rightist forces combined to close the 1960s' opening to the left. From the center to the right, each restoration group had a stake in the re-legitimation of authority. Those groups included religious fundamentalists, space-age corporate technocrats, state planners, mainline politicians, college and school administrators, think-tank trustees, union leaders, media marketers, conservative intellectuals and fashion moguls. With the waters rising fast in 1969, they raced for the ark two-by-two, Nixon at the helm.

The grand restoration alliance was glued together by a grand common enemy, the spreading protest culture of the 1960s. A rebellious house needed order and a generation of liberal accommodations needed a dose of austerity. However, the factions of the restoration had some conflicting interests. These conflicts became more apparent as the floor fell out from under liberalism in the 1970s and as protest action withdrew to the margins.

One key difference among restorationists was the bible agenda of the religious right and the secular agenda of the political center. This split between scripture and the constitution will be discussed further in the coming pages because it influenced the three major phases of education reform. Another split was between business and trade union elements. Private enterprise needed to stop the growth of anti-business ideology, but it also needed to reduce the price of labor and increase the cost of living (inflation), as means of securing higher profits. Trade union leaders were uncomfortable with the spread of rank-and-file caucuses in the 1960s and could rule more easily once mass activism subsided. But they became increasingly unable to negotiate contract increases as the power of business grew in the restoration. Business faced a profits squeeze in the 1970s which led to an aggressive anti-labor policy.[41] The economic austerity of the 1970s and the 1980s had a political bonus insofar as workers and students were in retreat, forced to cope privately with hard times. The unionized Northeast lost jobs to cheap-labor, anti-union areas in the South, the West and abroad. Wealth was transferred from the public sector to the private sphere, from education and social services to the military and to business. Labor leaders long-used to supporting the corporate order found that order undermining their role. They could not deliver the goods.

Restoration life was also difficult for politicians. They had participated in the quelling of mass movements only to find conservative public life unmanageable. The new economic austerity provoked workers in their jobs, citizens at election time, and consumers when they made purchases. The high cost of living, the scarcity of jobs and housing, the decay of public services undercut the politicians, who were held accountable for why nothing worked any more. Austerity was the common policy of both major parties, which shielded the corporations from blame as both Democrats and Republicans lost credibility. They maintained power by inertia and by a media monopoly on political debate, but a low percentage of voters appeared each November.

While the business austerity undermined the credibility of union

leaders and politicians who supported restoration, it also weakened the authority of school administrators and teachers.
Traditionalists on the education front who welcomed a swing to
the right were themselves unsettled by the return of order. The
two key destabilizing contradictions in this lunge for stability
concerned budget and curriculum. As wealth drained from the
public sector to the private sector, education and social services
had a depression imposed on them in the 1970s. Constant budget
cuts in schools and colleges forced administrations to order firings,
hiring freezes, service reductions, tuition increases at the collegiate
level and work-load increases. Teacher pay began falling behind
the inflation rate. At the same time, the conditions of schools
and public colleges became shabby. Such harsh and deteriorating
circumstances repelled students from taking education seriously. It
also demoralized teachers. The austerity extended from economics
into pedagogy, as occupationalism and back-to-basics put the
noses of teachers and students to the grindstone. Austerity
through curriculum proved as uninspiring as austerity through
budget-cutting. By imposing dismal conditions, conservative
policy sabotaged the chance for strong conservative consensus.
The authorities in education found the lower grades (especially
high school) and the community colleges less and less manageable.
Union leaders found it harder to influence rank-and-file voting on
contracts and on major-party candidates at election time. Political
leaders found the electorate more volatile.

The bi-partisan reversal of the 1960s used austerity in ways that
made public disorder inevitable. The public sector had been the
primary arena for egalitarian gains, radical dissent and liberal
policy. The rise of restoration meant the rise of private interests
in the economy and in education. As public college tuition went
up, private universities became more competitive. As public allo-
cations to higher education declined, public college facilities
decayed, thus making private campuses ever more attractive. As
school budgets fell, their deteriorating facilities also encouraged
those parents, who could pay, to take their kids out. Some colleges
began awarding scholarships on the basis of merit rather than
need, thus confirming the elite direction of policy in the 1970s.
De-funded public education became dispirited. Thus, it lost the
initiative as a base for protest culture. Organized opposition
retreated to the margins. Taking its place was aggressive authority

at the top and unorganized alienation at the bottom, the politics of restoration. The positive power of austerity met the negative power of student resistance.

How right was the restoration?

Some ventures of the restoration sabotaged conservative consensus, some achieved success in pushing society to the right, and some were significant reversals of protest culture. Economic austerity not only cooled the public sector as an arena of liberal-left advance, but it also sank the fortunes of small private colleges which could not keep up with the costs of doing business. The schools that went under sent their pupils to those that could make it through, producing an overall strengthening of private education. The private colleges were a political and religious haven from the liberalizing effects of public policy, as they were less unionized and less subject to requirements for affirmative action, integration, ideological diversity and compensatory programs. The boldness of private education in taking federal money without accepting the liberal impact of federal law advanced into the 1980s when Grove College successfully argued in court that federal aid did not obligate the entire institution to follow government regulation but only the specific parts receiving money.[42]

Private institutions were not only able to accept tax money but were also able to pursue religious, racial and sexual policies not acceptable in public units. The advance of conservative culture into public education was just as notable. Busing was discredited as a means of 'forced' integration. Equally ominous was the spread of censorship and of 'creation science' into public schools. An Arkansas judge in 1982 ruled against the validity of 'creationism' as a scientific equal to evolutionary theory, so the bible approach to curriculum suffered a setback there. But the religious, conservative censorship of textbooks and library books, as well as curriculum, kept moving ahead into the 1980s.[43] Sociologist Fred Pincus surveyed the damage from right-wing censors during the restoration period:

Several schools were bombed and several people were shot in

21

the struggle over school books in Kanawha County, West
Virginia in 1974. Schoolboard members in Levittown, N.Y.,
removed 11 'offensive' books from high school libraries in
1976 after being pressured by a conservative parents' group.
Senior citizens in Warsaw, Indiana, burned 40 copies of a
book that had been banned by the local school board in 1977.
The State Commission of Education in Texas banned five
standard dictionaries from the public schools in 1976 because
they included the definitions of certain objectionable words.[44]

Sex, dirty words, non-traditional life-styles and dissident politics
outraged conservative censors. Their vigilance over library books,
classroom books and even dictionaries swept some very popular
authors into their nets – Kurt Vonnegut, Arthur Miller, Mark
Twain, Bernard Malamud, Piri Thomas, and even Shakespeare.
A court ruling in the famous Island Trees (N.Y.) school district
in 1983 made it unconstitutional to prevent students from reading
books in a library, but it left untouched the power of schoolboards
to refuse to buy blackballed books.

Two conservative book-chasers achieved stardom in this squalid
arena – Mel and Norma Gabler of Texas. They began their ideological warfare in 1961 but came of age in the reactionary tide of
the 1970s. They run a book-screening network that pressures state
education departments which centrally adopt books for classroom
use. According to a *New York Times* profile of this couple, the
trouble with most texts is

> that they are written from the perspective of people who do
> not believe in God. . . . This perspective, they say, is a
> religion called secular humanism, which permeates every
> aspect of contemporary society, and teaches youngsters to
> lie, cheat and steal. . . . They are against having the story of
> Robin Hood taught in school because, they claim, it sanctions
> stealing. They take issue with a textbook that reads, 'The law
> that allowed slavery in America was wrong, so people could
> break the law,' because they say it encourages insubordination.
> They seek to remove a book that encourages youngsters to
> imagine themselves as sit-in protesters of the 1960s on the
> grounds that doing so teaches rebellion.[45]

To them, secular humanism opens the door to cultural relativism, which in turn encourages dissent and non-traditional values. Instead of monogamy, heterosexuality, religious faith, patriotism and obedience, school breeds opposition politics and alternate life-styles. Their effort on behalf of tradition was the most conservative version of the core curriculum. The bible was the universal standard for learning.

From the fundamentalist Gablers to the centrist Shanker to the traditionalist Barzun, the core curriculum transmits an official value system disguised as universal knowledge. If curriculum does not transmit dominant ideology, it will produce a generation unsatisfactorily socialized. For the re-socialization of the young after a protest episode like the 1960s, one wing of the restoration drew on the authority of scripture while the other leaned on secular knowledge held by academicians. The purpose was the same – to restore a hierarchy of power threatened by egalitarian movements. The church-restorationists defended a tradition farther back in time than the university experts. In this uneasy alliance of heaven and earth, the secular wing did not support censorship, because it posed as the protector of constitutional rights. Instead of outright book-banning, core-curriculists simply excluded outlaw ideology from the universal knowledge all should possess. Textbook studies by Fitzgerald, Anyon, Griffin and Marciano exposed the official laundering of history.[46] *The Paideia Proposal*, so widely discussed in the reform wave after 1983, similarly excluded 'unofficial' history in the foundational reading lists, leaving out egalitarian, abolitionist, feminist and narrative documents.[47]

Book-banning can have a conservative impact even if a whole text is not removed from a library or curriculum. The billion-dollar textbook industry was busy in the restoration learning what words were acceptable in the new conservative age. If a whole book was not scrapped, chapters would be rewritten to purge references to evolution or to politics outside the mainstream, or to sex. The Gabler home-ground of Texas was the single largest book-buying school system in the country. If the Gablers could get a book removed from a Texas purchase order, then other states which centrally adopted texts for classroom use would get the message, along with the publishers who produce them.

Hard-core text censorship from the religious right or soft-core exclusion from the academic center joined a larger matrix of

political repression. That matrix included the elimination of dissident programs and faculty from the 1960s. The pressure on
compensatory, women's and minority programs from the protest
era accelerated in the restoration. Some exemplary firings of
faculty served notice on the risky business of protest politics or
of experimental teaching or of too ideological a stance. Still,
censorship and firings were often divisive, sloppy and provocative.
They invited opposition protest, expensive litigation, and even
mass sympathy for the book, author or teacher axed. Public readings of banned books gave the opposition a rallying point in
conservative times. Strong feelings exist for free speech. Enough
people view repressive firings, book-bannings and program liqui-
dations as intolerant power-mongering. Many students often
admire the teacher being fired and many will only become more
eager to read the books declared unacceptable. Such messy acts
of repression weaken the consensus sought by restoration forces
at the right or at the center. Each swipe at outlaw ideology helps
the opposition make friends. If only the books or programs or
teachers had been overtly communist, it would have been easier.
Gone were the simple days of the 1950s when the Golden Age
had the Red Menace to kick around.

Rest in peace, Red Menace

The New Left of the 1960s did not like communism. Its political
style was out of sync with the old left. In language and action,
the freshness of protest culture in the 1960s was simultaneously
its strength and weakness. The self-invented radicals were
untamed but also inexperienced. The explosion outside the limits
of old left and establishment politics included anti-authority as
well as anti-Soviet feelings. Newer revolutions in China, Cuba
and Vietnam had romantic appeal. But the unschooled ingenues
of the 1960s were very American in their Utopian, populist and
non-organized upheaval. The government did what it could to
find communist conspiracies in the student, black and women's
movements.[48] Yet, the simple fact kept surfacing that no one
seemed to be in charge, certainly not the old left of the 1930s or
the minions of the Kremlin.

The anti-communism of the New Left and the counter-culture

of the 1960s posed some formidable problems for the restoration. Without a singular Red Menace, conservatives were forced to cast around for names of the enemy. This communications dilemma resulted in one wing of the restoration taking the offensive against 'secular humanism,' a formulation uncomfortable to the center, which saw itself as both secular and humanist. Centrists who came up with fuzzy pronouncements on 'the right words,' did no better by their cause. While both center and right were threatened by the egalitarian thrust of the 1960s, only the far right could comfortably attack such an American ideal as 'equality.' The consensual vocabulary which eventually emerged sought 'excellence,' 'standards,' 'competence,' 'accountability' and 'quality.' Not only could such words mean a hundred different things to a hundred people, but the excessive emphasis on 'minimums' left the elite academic center high and dry as the defender of 'excellence.' In its communications searches, the restoration was displaying its own disabled conservatism. The presence of a revolutionary threat in the absence of communism was a condition of the 1960s which made it harder for the restoration party to cohere. Cracks remained for opposition culture after the period of protest ended.

As long as opposition culture did not cohere into a single party or gather around one ideology, it could not be decisively smashed by a conservative counter-attack. Egalitarian resistance was simply everywhere and nowhere at the same time. This created mutual incoherence on both the left and the right. The conservative forces had far more organized power but they were unable to focus it terminally on the diffusive protest culture. This protected the continuity of opposition from the 1960s to the 1980s and helped disable the conservative drive for consensus.

In the short run during the transition phase from the 1960s to restoration, traditionalists from the center to the right, secular to religious, had a system to protect against the threat from the left. That was reason enough for them to find common ground. As the egalitarian opposition waned, the restoration camp faced its own internal divisions, most apparent in the center-right split of the great school crisis in 1983. That story will be told in Chapter 4. It is important to note here that the restoration could not mop up pockets of radicalism from the non-communist 1960s in the way it scrubbed political life in the McCarthy era. Left ideas emerging from the 1960s confounded the restoration by maturing in the age

25

of Reagan. By Orwell's legendary year, conservatives had still not constructed the strong national consensus first sought by Nixon.

The dollar menace

The absence of one big union on the left in the 1960s continued to limit its power afterwards while also protecting it from purges like 1919 and the 1950s. The historic passing of the Red Menace cheated restoration forces of anti-communism as a way to build pro-business, pro-military consensus. Yet the more disabling and enabling feature of the recent conservative revival has been the economic crisis. The restoration after the 1960s was the first reactionary period in this century to coincide with an economic crisis.

The 1920s and 1950s were fat times when expanding production kept profits high. The domestic demand for labor was strong. Internationally, the US dominated world economics disrupted by war. These two decades restored traditional authority shaken by two insurgent labor episodes – the pre-World War I era and the depression 1930s. The repression of militant labor after both World Wars was eased by fat times. Expanding economies were buoyant ways to reduce unrest. A horn of plenty accompanied the fist of authority.

Hard times are different. In the 1970s, the restoration had to impose 'settling for less' on the population. This helped reverse the ardent 1960s while disabling the growth of conservative consensus. On the one hand, young people and new families had a harder time surviving the recession. On the other hand, the mainstream of society could not afford to absorb them into comfortable careers and settled establishment lives.

The restoration was thus gaining and losing ground at the same time, dispersing mass resistance while unable to bring it back into the American Way of Life. From the plus side, trade unions as well as student and minority movements grew weaker. Management transplanted factories to low-wage areas, imposed wage and benefit cuts, recovering profits by reducing labor costs. Each new contract year brought smaller increases until negotiations in the 1980s became dominated by 'givebacks,' or how large the decrease was from prior concessions. The transfer of wealth from the wage package to business profits was no different than the de-funding of education and social services in the public sector. The umbrella of economic crisis was a very large shield under which to pursue this reversal. Cuts in what is often referred to as 'the social wage' of public programs, as well as cuts in the real wage you earn at a job, were simply more acceptable against a backdrop of national economic decline.

The vocabulary of the new austerity became sadistic. Debates arose on cutting out the fat, or whether we were cutting to the bone, or into the bone as well. Human sensibility begins at the skin, so there is no part of the body numb to a knife. The barbaric cutting of pounds of flesh dis-cultured education by eliminating the 'fads and frills,' the dispensable arts and electives in music or dance, for example. The new cultural minimum called for cost-effective career training and back-to-basics. At the college level, the liberal arts drew fire as a frivolous luxury, in a society where there was suddenly too little of everything, except college graduates.

Hard times depressed the Utopian esprit familiar in the 1960s. Prosperity, a low rate of inflation and unemployment, cheap housing, low-cost books, etc., supported a happy-go-lucky student life from which a communal resistance flowed. Economic crisis in the 1970s quickly burdened people with money woes and job hunts. Fierce competition for courses and programs, scholarships and loan money, seats in a dental school, jobs and apartments, all made students into each other's enemies rather than into a unified group fighting for 'power to the people.' The same economic decline privatizing people failed to regather the divided pieces into a consensus on the right. The austerity was strong enough to fragment protest culture but the economy was too weak to distribute the good life. Young people were kept adrift for years in a declining economic twilight zone, not left, not right, floating in the middle of the road. Rising career worries accompanied diminishing activism, as the doors were closed to secure mainstream lives and to radical social change. However, the centrist drift in student opinion appeared to be ending in the 1980s as political causes heated up on campus.[49]

Economic depression lasted long after it served a purpose of disintegrating opposition and disciplining aspirations. This indicated a long-term predicament for official culture. In too many corners of life there was unemployment, low wages, menial work, high rents, crime, drugs, alcoholism, and the spectacle of the rich and powerful spending their way from midnight to dawn. In daily life, routine decisions became irritating tangles – to stay in school or to drop out and go part-time while taking any kind of low-paid job; to go on to graduate school or to stop at the bachelor stage; to study psychology or literature instead of a technical career in business or computers; to move to a different region far from your roots or to stay put and squeeze your connections; to marry now and have a kid or to wait until you found good work and could afford a mortgage; to divorce now or to stick it out until you could lay aside some cash for a move; to keep the jalopy on the road or to sell it and take the bus instead; to turn up the thermostat or to put on an extra sweater; to go away for a quiet week or to use the dough for shoes or for Christmas presents; to have another beer or a dessert with your meal; a rose and a kiss for your sweetie or only a kiss.

The face of corporate austerity was everywhere and it was sneering at you. Hardships were unnecessary because the nation possessed the means to generate prosperity. Idle plants, mines, mills and shops dotted the country. Arable land was left unplanted and tons of food were destroyed or locked away to keep prices high. Good housing stock was bulldozed to make way for luxury apartments. The vast military machine dragged the economy down. The unnecessary struggle for the good life produced a cynical, self-absorbed age. This mean era followed hotly on the years of the flower children, Utopian dreams and communal spirit. Economic and political chilling of the protest era preserved the status quo by bringing forth the infamous 'me-decade.'

This was a breathtaking impoverishment. 'The greening of America' became a desert of lone jackals foraging at night. The economy demanded that we settle for less, accept inequality and authority. Conservative culture demanded that we do this on our own, privately. Meanwhile, dream and horror films boiled out of Hollywood, filling screens with ever more terrifying monsters, no end to star wars, and a string of 'go for it' flicks from *Rocky* to *Saturday Night Fever* to *Flashdance*. Distracting glitter accompanied an ominous fact of life: it was taking more and more to get you less and less. The new austerity produced this unhappy situation because it destroyed the very thing it needed to build consensus – the American Dream. The old order could no longer afford it. Rejecting reconstruction from the left, it imposed a reconstruction from the right. The fate of restoration depended on the acceptance of less in a nation held together by the pulsing desire for more.

Rest in peace, American Dream

The passing of the American Dream was fateful for all sectors but it especially damaged schooling. Education rested on its myth as the great upward equalizer. Student discipline and teacher authority depended in large measure on the chance to move up through school and on the economic stability of life outside school. Surrounded by a depressed job market, a decaying public sector, a shabby school building, and a bare curriculum, could students think education counted in this society? The enraging loss of the future was visible in every unpainted classroom, every overcrowded course. Public higher education was damaged also. Jokes spread on how many PhDs were driving taxis. Unless you graduated from the very best universities, you would lose in the job race. So much talk about 'the overeducated American' helped schooling slide down the ladder of respect, into a cynical exercise.[50]

Cynicism can be as politically unmanageable as open rebellion. The historic transition from protest culture in the 1960s to 'the culture of narcissism' in the 1970s only posed new and more widespread crises. The reversal of the 1960s arrived at the predicament of the 1980s through many mechanisms inside school and out. In three major waves of school reform, restoration policies revealed the importance of curriculum in culture war. Career education in the early 1970s, and the back-to-basics Literacy Crisis a few years later, both contributed to an alienation and decay which alarmed official commissions in 1983 as they launched a third reform effort. This epic search for order began in 1969 with a society in upheaval and a school system breeding dissent. Fifteen years later, neither education nor any other major institution was working to anyone's satisfaction. When the new restoration eventually retreats, culture war will open for another age of opposition whose success rests on learning from the culture wars of the past.

2 Settling for less, 1971-5:
the war for 'careerism'
career education depresses
activism and aspirations

Some people will have to do with less. . . . Yet it will be a
hard pill for many Americans to swallow – the idea of doing
with less so that big business can have more.

Business Week (1974)

We should view the future generations of learners in America
as coming to maturity at a time when society may not require
all their intellectual and developed capacities in the work
force.

Sidney P. Marland, Commissioner of Education 1970–3,
Career Education (1974)

The resistance to occupational programs by many students
who might profit from them has long disturbed community
college leaders.

Carnegie Commission on Higher Education (1971)

Because so many have been to college, a college education is
now a necessary but no longer sufficient condition for social
mobility. For some children of middle- or upper-class families,
college-going fails to keep them from *downward* social
mobility.

The Second Newman Report on Higher Education Policy
(1973)

A tale of two symphonies

At the moment 'career education' was invented in the early Nixon
Administration, the 1960s reached a crescendo. More than 500

campuses saw strikes and disruptions after the invasion of Cambodia in May 1970. Students were shot dead at Kent State and Jackson State by national guardsmen and by police. An army research center was blown up in August, in Madison, Wisconsin, killing a graduate student. Women were holding national demonstrations to mark the 50th anniversary of their voting rights. The militant student group SDS (Students for a Democratic Society) had dissolved into a terrorist underground while the Black Panther Party was being assaulted above-ground by police. In February 1971, over 10,000 protestors invaded Washington in response to Nixon's invasion of Laos, and were themselves illegally arrested. The sound of protest culture was growing louder.

Inheriting responsibility for changing the political tune was Commissioner-Designate of Education, Sidney P. Marland. He assumed federal command of the most radicalized part of American society, schooling. His crusade for careerism in the coming years confronted more than the wholesale dissent of the young. Marland found himself in the tough position of pushing an occupational idea rejected by students in the past.[1] Even more ironic, he had to extol the virtues of work while Health, Education and Welfare (HEW) issued *Work in America* (1973), a study revealing deep alienation on the job and weak links between occupational education and employment.[2] To make matters only more irrational, Marland promoted job-preparation in years of increasing unemployment. It was a time to see how much restoration could dance on the head of a pin.

Pin-heads and federal fathers

Marland's work on behalf of the new occupationalism won him the title of 'the father of career education.' As Commissioner from 1970–3, he was an upbeat leader well-suited for the awesome tasks before him. His enthusiastic style bathed an essentially unpopular idea in glowing promises. Recognition for his cheerleading contributions came from an immense career gathering in Houston in 1977, where he was wildly greeted. From the Nixon team, Marland moved to the Presidency of the College Board, where he played a key role in fathering the Literacy Crisis of

31

1975. His work offered some continuity in the first two phases of restoration reform.

Marland's skills helped the career phase prosper and the literacy war begin, but the themes were ideas whose times had come. With or without him, work and language were likely avenues for restoration. Job-training, wage-earning, the transition to adulthood, writing and reading, were powerful intersections of school and society. Historically, they were the vast social territories where authority had advanced its official culture in the past. Besides the suitability of the work ethic and of literacy for a reactionary era, which will be discussed in detail in the coming pages, Marland's success also depended on diverse national forces ready for a push against the 1960s, with him. Marland stood at the top of an immense, traditional education bureaucracy. The conservative school pyramid stretched across fifty states and over 16,000 school districts. In higher education, a system of 1,000 community colleges and 2,000 more elite campuses also housed an essentially conservative administrative corps, available for a counter-offensive against the changes of the 1960s. Marland's success was in focusing the political energy of this bureaucracy around a common program for careerism.

Marland knew how to orchestrate a national reform, capture press and professional attention, hegemonize debate with career issues, promote model programs in career-aggressive districts, and channel federal money to the new regime. Despite the relatively small federal contribution to local school budgets (about 8 per cent), Washington's aid can be highly targeted to have a high-profile impact on strapped district finances. The career offensive demonstrated once more that Washington can be a promoter of reform and a glueing center for a far-flung system. This central clout has been used for liberal programs born in the 1960s and then for conservative reversals born in the 1970s.

The need for a conservative reversal in education was pressing in late 1970, when a call came to Marland from the Nixon White House, even before he was confirmed as the new Commissioner of Education. According to Marland's tract and memoirs, *Career Education* (1974), the Nixon Administration wanted 'immediate attention to increasing the place of "vocational education" in the federal role,' with a 'concrete plan and a systematic design for a major administration initiative, with no increase in the budget.'[3]

The new Administration chose as its premier initiative the most expensive form of schooling while asking for no budget increase. Restoration school policy was off to a contradictory start, but this did not slow Marland. He caucused with his staff, devised the name 'career education,' and planned the new program 'to relate the occupational aspects of human development to all levels of learning and all relevant parts of academic instruction.'[4] All students, not only vocational enrollees, would study successively more work-oriented courses in career clusters beginning in the elementary grades. Some clusters would lead from high school into the job market, while others would point towards either community colleges or to the universities. Whatever the destination, all courses would expose students to occupational themes. The how-to of this new discipline was helped along by several books from Ken Hoyt, one of Marland's lieutenants.[5] A mere decade after the rushing spread of careerism, major school studies in 1983 would recommend the reduction of vocational themes to a bare minimum.[6] Apparently, the deep foundations laid by Marland and his associates were spacious enough to bury occupationalism along with the liberal arts, but that is getting ahead of the story.

The spread of career education in the early 1970s required some elaborate logistics. First, Marland needed a communications strategy to market the scheme as a new idea. Next, the program had to have a philosophy making it seem educationally sound, the best response to the current crisis. Third, the philosophy had to specify operational curricula. The theory had to be systematically laid out in guidebook style, detailed grade-by-grade, career-by-career in syllabus form. This would permit it to fit into the standard management of schooling. It would also pose it as a structured form of education familiar to the pedagogy of most classrooms. Management-oriented, mechanical curricula freed school districts from having to invest in their own curriculum design. A fourth element of logistics, after operational shape, was seed money. Enough funds had to be invested to spread word, develop pilot programs, print materials, hold conferences, so as to nudge some high-profile leaders and school systems into the plan. This would build momentum. Momentum from the right was key because of the powerful reforms from the 1960s, still alive in those transition years. Lastly, in regard to the liberal and left opposition, alternatives from below had to be de-funded and out-promoted so that no other curricular politics occupied as much cultural terrain. Official culture took its war on the egalitarian 1960s very seriously.

In the realm of communications strategy, the word 'vocationalism' had a soft profile in Marland's book and in the project evolution. This was a wise decision. Vocational education had a long and dismal history in the schools, so it could only weaken the program's appeal. I will briefly review the fate of vocationalism in the coming pages because that story helps locate the culture war of the 1970s in the century-long debates before it. While the word occupied small space in the new career drive, vocationalism itself was very much on Marland's mind. He was dismayed at the smallness of the vocational tracks in high school. The college-bound and general-education streams were huge. Vocational enrolments were perhaps 10 per cent of the high school class, no more. The result of this curricular structure was a double-trouble, according to Marland: an enormous number of students were being rushed on to higher education and an enormous number of students either dropped out of the general track and left high school, or stayed in general studies and graduated without any specific work training or discipline. The collegians were destined to become the infamous 'overeducated Americans' with too much of the wrong kind of education for the job market. The drop-outs and the general graduates from high school were undereducated and miseducated. The task was to cool out millions of collegians and to heat up millions of drop-outs. The depressed job market required curricular policy to set a floor of high school graduation and a ceiling of community college attendance for the vast majority of future workers. This essentially vocational adjustment of school outcomes avoided the downbeat language of 'vocational education.' It was engineered through the novel formulation of 'career education.' This disguise made it vocational and not-vocational at the same time.

While avoiding downbeat vocationalism in name, the career program drew on upbeat rhetoric of democracy and success. The egalitarian credentials of careerism lay in its proposal to orient every course and every grade into a single career focus. Careerism was not posed as the vocational side of the curriculum to which the losers were sent. Traditional tracks in 'academic' or 'general' or 'vocational' studies were to be replaced by democratic clusters of careers enrolling *all* students in the one best system at last. Some clusters would just happen to require university attendance, others community college, and still others no post-secondary education. Students in aerospace or medical clusters were likely to go farther in school and society than those in secretarial science or auto mechanics. In effect, the same channeling of students would occur, but in lower profile under new names. This political strategy to promote democracy in name if not in fact had been urged by James Bryant Conant in 1959, when he recommended the dissolution of formal names for different program tracks in high school.[7] The most scholastic students would still come from the higher economic strata and gather in the collegiate clusters. The appeal of the high-wage professions would attract students away from the cheap-labor clusters, as Marland himself observed in his favorite career school, Skyline High in Dallas, where the engineering and medical courses were over-enrolled while the lesser career-subjects were as ignored as the old vocational programs had been. Career education repeated the same politics as the community college movement before it: the promise of democracy and success with the delivery of unequal education and credentials for the social hierarchy. Students in the early decades of the two-year campuses avoided the low-wage tech tracks much like the students of Skyline High later on, because students know up from down.

The communications face of the career reform hid the invasion of schooling by the conservative work ethic. Soft disciplines in the humanities, arts and general studies, along with autonomous programs in experimental education, were undermined by the thrust towards courses most open to direct job-training. The broad critical learning possible in liberal arts, women's courses, minority programs, interdisciplinary studies, etc., represented the political problem of the 1960s which careerism in the 1970s helped to solve. Marland not only saw career education as an antidote to campus unrest, but he also gladly agreed to its vocational character, despite his 'career' tag. When one voc-ed advocate suggested that with career education vocationalism finally went 'big time,' Marland happily agreed.[8]

Vocationalism had always been working your way down the ladder of success, but now career education promised to help you climb up. Who would answer when the road did not lead to the American Dream? Devious stratagems can temporarily blunt the opposition in culture war, but they can also lead to even worse crises down the road, as was the case in the general school crisis declared in 1983.

Doctor of disguise

Any pedagogy extolling work-training tends to blame the victim. Instead of acknowledging chronic underemployment as a feature of private enterprise, Marland discussed youth discontent as rooted in their lack of job skills. Employment-training would open the door to jobs, and work would end youth alienation. Not only were students blamed for the shortage of jobs, but job-training was praised for being the new and spacious route to self-development.

Human development was lifted from its habitual home in the humanities and relocated in the most narrow form of schooling yet invented – occupationalism. The world was cleverly turning on its head in these dizzy transition years. Restoration careerism proposed to adjust students downwardly to the diminished life of the economy through a reform promising new avenues of self-development in the historically least-developing school subjects. The meteoric rise of careerism in the early 1970s was a marvellous dance of the bumblebees throwing up a dust cloud around the most provocative social issues of the 1960s – war, racism, sexism, inequality, dehumanizing education. The student demand for 'relevance,' one of the familiar battle-cries of the 1960s, was taken by Marland to mean making all courses relevant to work.

Work was treated as vacantly as any other of the issues from the protest era. No political problems belonging to the system were conceded here or elsewhere. Work had no political dimension. In the Marland tract, businessmen, politicians, consumers and workers were apparently all one happy family. Students needed only to be properly educated to take their place in this conflict-free enterprise. Career education did not recognize the long history of labor-management strife, that trade unions had emerged despite corporate-government interference.[9] Neither did it recognize that many jobs were unattractive, unrewarding, underpaid, unhealthy or unnecessary wastes of labor and resources. Of course, all these critical themes were ignored for the same reason the material of the protest age was bypassed – to prevent the social learning from which students become activist citizens who feel empowered to make history with their own hands from the bottom up. This quarantine of students from critical issues was a striking feature of career education. None of Marland's printed action plans included trade union members as resource people for school courses and the documents even wondered if unhappy workers should be exposed to students.[10] Like every pedagogy, it was never politically neutral.

Fool's gold

While schools and colleges joined the gold rush into careerism, an alternate perspective on work and education was published right under Marland's nose. This was the previously mentioned Health, Education and Welfare study called *Work in America* (1973).[11] It weakened some pillars supporting occupationalism. This report, coordinated by manpower specialist James O'Toole, found alienation and social pathology associated with work. Work was not the developmental and stabilizing experience Marland fantasized in *Career Education*. Further, O'Toole wrote about employers practicing 'credentialism,' or the arbitrary raising of credentials required for a job without raising the wages or the skill-level. They could do this because a vast oversupply of college-educated labor existed. The HEW report also found an ineffective link between occupational education and future employment. More than half of high school's vocational graduates took jobs unrelated to their training. The report declared, 'The relationship of the job to the field of training appears to have no significance in influencing the level of employment, wages, and earnings following graduation.'[12] No evidence could be found to show that vocational courses offered their graduates more help in employment or in wage rates than did the academic program. The conclusion proposed that a very expensive form of schooling had a low utility.[13] Some years later, a Carnegie study on vocationalism reached a similar conclusion and recommended eliminating vocational programs.[14] This anti-occupational theme was integrated in Ernest Boyer's Carnegie study, *High School*, in 1983.

Careerism served its political and economic functions in the early restoration, marshaling the conservative school forces for a Washington-led reversal of the 1960s and of high aspirations. However, it appeared expendable in the 1980s, with protest culture driven back and the crises still unsolved. One thing that made occupationalism expendable was its core weakness in the school-job linkage. Not only at the secondary level, this weakness spilled over into community colleges. In an early study of community colleges after their first decade of heyday expansion, Leland Medsker admitted in 1960 that 'In the rapidly developing age of automation the question of what constitutes the best preparation for employment has not been clearly answered.'[15] He confessed bewilderment in how to judge job-training at the two-year campus. Medsker raised the same issues of effectiveness which have dogged industrial education since the early debates: can an unplanned economy do manpower planning through schools? Can schools and colleges afford state-of-the-art equipment on which to train future workers? Does it make sense to reproduce the work world in the classroom? The irrationality of such an exercise leaves people overtrained and undertrained at the same time, thanks to the specialization of curricula which simply cannot change as fast as the job market.

Nevertheless, careerism swept through the community colleges in the 1970s, driving the humanities onto the ropes. Here, as before, the rush was on for fool's gold. Fred Pincus surveyed the data, up to 1980, relevant to the employment payoff for two-year occupational programs. He found that for community college graduates 'The economic benefits of vocational education are at best modest.'[16] Half of these program's graduates do not work in their fields of training. Pincus's extensive research concluded on careerism that 'Business and government leaders – those at the top of the heap – regard post-secondary vocational education as a means of solving the political problems created by the rising expectations of the working class.'[17] Pincus's assertions echoed the conclusions of two historians of vocationalism, Marvin Lazerson and Norton Grubb:

Career education is not directed at resolving social problems,

developing avenues of upward mobility, or making school
and work more satisfying experiences. It is aimed instead at
reducing expectations, limiting aspirations, and increasing
commitments to the existing social structure.[18]

If classroom occupationalism was an ineffective way to train labor,
it was at least one way to habituate students to the traditional
way of doing things. It's like playing house with dolls. Little girls
are not trained in how to be good mothers but they are trained
in the desire to be mothers. Curriculum rehearses students in their
dominated roles.

These flaws and anti-democratic realities were brushed aside by
Marland. He knew of the HEW report *Work in America*. He
referred to O'Toole as well as to another manpower expert, Eli
Ginzburg, who also doubted the employment benefits for a career
education campaign. Still, when culture war finds an idea whose
time has come, rhetoric leaps over the stubborn facts of life.
Marland revealed to us a vision of the future which made the
great career leap of faith so necessary:

> We should view the future generations of learners in America
> as coming to maturity at a time when society may not require
> all their intellectual and developed capacities in the work
> force. . . . It is not unlikely that by 1980 we will have table
> waiters at the Hilton who are M.A.s in French or nutrition or
> social science, happily engaged in intellectual, civic, and
> social pursuits, quite apart from their work lives.[19]

Millions of 'overeducated Americans' were facing a dreadfully
downbeat future. The most-schooled population on earth was
facing a transition to permanent underemployment. Curriculum
was called upon to manage consciousness for the passage into
cheap labor. Would graduates happily drive cabs? Would they
cheerfully use their French to translate menus for rich customers,
or use their nutrition science to advise them on a well-balanced
luncheon? How about using your master's in psychology to calm
down the eccentric chef or to counsel the unhappy couple arguing
at the corner table? If you were unfulfilled and underpaid at work,
you could always make it up by managing a Little League team.
When you get home from the game, you can pay your rent with
your degree and eat your civic pride.

Marland raced over these dilemmas in the same way Nixon lost seventeen minutes of the Watergate tapes. Too much reality made the rhetoric weak, so he preferred fantasy. One favorite fantasy was the restoration leap to the Golden Age. For Marland, that time was his boyhood in a small town. There, friendly tradesmen introduced him to a guild-like world of work. Oh happy time, when the dignity of labor came from stable self-employment and craft skills. The conservative road ahead is often an irrational path backwards.

Forward to yesterday

Career education's new name, promise of success, antidote to youth discontent, and systematic syllabi needed one more ingredient to enable an occupational offensive from the top down: money. This proved to be no problem. More than enough dollars were budgeted to mobilize a curricular reversal nationwide. Marland bragged how in 1971 he got the fifty state education chiefs to buy into the plan for a mere $9 million in discretionary funds. By the end of the second year, the amount of discretionary funds employed for career education added up to $100 million.[20] The winds of politics were shifting from left to right, aided by strong gusts from the new conservative center in Washington.

The Nixon Administration pursued broad policies of reversal in regard to the 1960s, especially around busing and integration, so the career initiative was not an isolated project of restoration. It did receive some priority funding, though. In 1972, a White House education bill was pushed through Congress authorizing $850 million for occupational programs at the community colleges alone for the coming three years, while vocational funds for public schools were budgeted at $416.9 million for fiscal 1972.[21] In constant dollars, the federal outlay for elementary and secondary vocationalism, including monies for career education there, increased from $532 million in 1968 to $723 million in 1972.[22] These huge outlays enabled the adoption of careerism in the grades of elementary school and in community colleges, as the vocational idea spilled out of its solitary single track in the high school.

The bandwagon drew in growing support as it organized a

conservative campaign. Among the organizations endorsing the career plan were the National Education Association, the National Association of Chief State School Officers, the American Vocational Association, the Association of Secondary School Principals, the American Association of Junior Colleges, the College Board and the National Institute of Education. Surveying this assembled force, Grubb and Lazerson found that by 1975

> Almost every state department of education has appointed career education coordinators; many states have passed or are considering career education mandates in their educational legislation, and have developed comprehensive career education development models. In 1974, 30 per cent of the country's 17,000 school districts had formally brought career education into their schools . . . publishers of educational materials are distributing increasing numbers of curriculum guides, testing materials, and books on the philosophy and implementation of career education.[23]

Such penetration of the national school system by the career idea demonstrated the organizing power of the federal government. It also showed how the education establishment had come through the protest era damaged but in shape for a concerted counter-offensive.

The occupational invasion was even more dramatic in the community colleges than in the lower grades. Both the job market and federal policies have a quicker impact at the post-secondary level than at the traditionally decentralized public school system. Thus, the job-market demand for business training over liberal arts and the federal push for careerism made dramatic gains for vocationalism at the two-year college level. In addition, the protest culture of the 1960s made a deeper impact on campus than in high school and below, so there was simply greater need for political reversal at the higher education setting. In their major study of the two-year network, Arthur Cohen and Florence Brawer wrote in *The American Community College* (1982) that

> Career education remained a subordinate function throughout the first fifty years of community college development until federal funding moved it to the fore. . . . On this surge of monies occupational education swept into the colleges in a

fashion dreamed of and pleaded for but never before realized by its advocates.[24]

Despite their voluminous research and deep insight, Cohen and Brawer did not connect this dramatic tilt to careerism with the political changes of the 1970s. Another observer of these trends did see the culture war involved in the curricular reversals. Joel Spring wrote about the politics of national education policy in *The Sorting Machine* (1975), including the Nixon-Marland response to the upheavals of the 1960s:

> The career education movement, like the new mathematics and science programs of the late 1950s, was an example of the power of the federal government to affect school curriculum around the country. . . . Marland believed career education was the answer to student rebellion, delinquency and unemployment. In his first annual report to Congress in 1971, he argued that disenchantment among youth existed because education did not lead to career opportunities. . . . Therefore, Marland believed, students and schools were in turmoil because the schools had never completely achieved the goal of sorting students for the labor market.[25]

In hoping to quell the unrest, Marland looked particularly to the community colleges, the Career Palaces of American higher education, for the strength of a work-ethic curriculum.[26] The dramatic tilt to liberalism and to liberal arts study in the 1960s was being matched by an equal tilt to work-training in the 1970s. A Utopian period with its head in the clouds was being replaced by a conservative one with its nose to the grindstone.

Tilt or wilt: order and curriculum

Perhaps the promotional force of careerism could cool the dissent shaking American education as the 1970s opened. The political equation here was complicated by an economic dilemma. Side by side with campus unrest there was an occupational crisis in the society at large. The baby-boom generation was graduating in untold numbers and was flooding a labor market unable to accept so many educated workers. Schools and colleges were already reeling from this critical mass of the young, and now it was the job market's turn. The 'overeducation' crisis was advancing even before Marland got his mandate for careerism from the White House in 1970. Harvard economist James Bright discussed in 1958 how automation lowered the skill requirements of the work-force.[27] His continuing research into this question led to an urgent warning in 1966:

> Excessive education and skill specification is a serious mistake and potential hazard to our economic and social system. We will hurt individuals, raise labor costs, improperly create disillusion, and destroy valid job standards that are not truly needed for a given task.[28]

The economy was moving in the exact opposite direction from the education system. Masses of students were being absorbed into higher education as automation kept reducing the skill levels required in the work-force. Lower craft as well as intellectual skills were required as numerical control grew even more sophisticated with computerization. This deskilling of the work-force was accompanied by a depopulation of the labor market, that is, a need for fewer workers to run the mechanizing economy. Thus, a chronic labor surplus required mass higher education as one means to absorb the underemployed, but this temporary arrangement was maturing into an overeducation crisis which exploded in the 1970s. Writing on the dangers, Ivar Berg observed in *Education and Jobs* (1971) that

> it is clear that there can be problems in countries that educate a stratum of the population whose occupational expectations are well beyond the opportunities the economy may provide in the short or even long run. . . . Increased education creates and partially reflects aspirations for jobs requiring greater skill and holding higher positions within the industrial hierarchy.[29]

Career education emerged as one mechanism to limit the consequences of mass college attendance.

The problem of containing aspirations in a college-educated generation had not eased by 1976 when Richard Freeman wrote his widely-read *The Overeducated American*. Freeman repeated Bright's and Berg's earlier concerns with a note of growing alarm:

The deterioration in job opportunities and occupational attainment for over a decade will create a sizeable group of dissatisfied educated workers whose position will be incommensurate with their training and aspirations. . . . Some of the highly educated in non-college jobs may resort to political protest and related modes of expressing dissent. . . . The extent to which those with dashed aspirations accept the new reality or seek to change it may turn out to be an important element in the political future. . . . The failure of many people to achieve their career goals . . . could lead to some political extremism.[30]

The overeducation crisis continued into the 1980s, when Russell Rumberger did another assessment of the changing skill needs of the economy.[31] A Department of Labor study in 1979 had also documented that worker dissatisfaction was rising.[32] Marland's career plan intended an elaborate downward adjustment of aspirations rather than a frontal dashing of hopes. Yet, the continuing fear of the 1960s and the continuing overeducation crisis of the 1980s meant that neither career education nor other restoration mechanisms had stabilized the political and economic situations. The student sabotage of depressant policies was recorded once again in that trampled terrain of culture war, the community college. Cohen and Brawer found that clever two-year college students confounded the career drive by using the expanding tech programs as *transfer* vehicles to four-year colleges.[33] By 1983, when a new official war on 'mediocrity' was launched, aspiring graduates were as big a problem as students who floated through or who dropped out from school. The career-depressant had enlarged tech enrolments at community colleges at the expense of lowering morale and learning quality. In the high schools, by the 1980s, one report after another found conditions ranging from pointlessness to stunning disorder.

Disorder in history

Historically, mainstream students have resisted downward adjustment through occupationalism. The mass expansion of high schools in the World War I era was one early instance of the popular rejection of vocationalism. Federal funding responded to business's calls for more industrial education in the public schools. The Smith-Hughes Act of 1917 was the vehicle to promote technical training in school at public expense, in an era of radical labor organizing. As masses of working students were taken into new secondary schools, they responded to the curriculum in a way that historian David Nasaw found stunningly unpredictable:

> What is most remarkable about this first generation of plain people to enter high school en masse is not their failure or drop-out rate, but rather the enthusiasm with which they entered the schools and selected for themselves precisely those courses the experts had decreed beyond their interest and capacity. They were not going to settle for anything less in the way of secondary education than the traditional academic program that their middle-class predecessors had enjoyed. . . . The more the educators – with the applause of the business community – moved to adjust the curriculum to their 'requirements,' the more they elected the traditional academic courses. High school to them meant Latin and algebra, not metal-working and sewing. . . . Both parents and children knew what they wanted – and that was to escape the workplaces the new programs were designed to prepare them for.[34]

The desire to escape cheap-labor channeling is an historic mainstream interest. It sabotaged the vocational intentions of the early high schools and then again in the formation of the community college movement forty years after. Low-quality training leading to lesser careers cannot possibly compete with the mass appeal of the learning, living and working styles of the elite.

Careerism is one way to define for the disadvantaged the kind of success they should expect. In addition to the wage-limiting effects of occupationalism there is political containment as well. In his massive study of education in upheaval in the 1960s, Charles Silberman observed in *Crisis in the Classroom* (1970) that the more vocationally oriented the student, the less inclined she or he was to rebellion.[35] The politically depressing effects of vocationalism have a history entwined with the wage-depressant features. Vocational education can be counted among the forces in this century which weakened the power of labor unions. The

45

original debates in the early decades of the twentieth century included a struggle over who would train apprentices, which had historically been a trade union function. The training of apprentices involved labor supply, which in turn affected wage rates and worker-discipline. After World War I, business displaced union-apprentice programs with more sophisticated internal training of its own and with a school curriculum in the nominally public sector. The immense public education system which grew in the decades after 1920 used public taxes for outright business training in its vocational programs, while absorbing a pro-business ideology into its academic offerings.

Working life has been so penetrated by commercial ideas that it is hard to see what an independent labor culture can be like. From consumerism to lotteries to foreign policy, authoritative elites take the lead in organizing public opinion. The vocational education saga dating back to 1917 played a role in the decline of labor autonomy. The extension of commercial culture and the rise of labor dependence has been noted in several discussions of vocationalism. Lazerson and Grubb presented the aggressive point of view taken by business in the vocational debates around the time of World War I: 'Existing apprenticeship programs and job entry were under the control of unions. Industrial education would, by providing an alternative method of training, weaken this aspect of union control. . . . The extent to which businessmen combined calls for vocationalism with hostility to unions influenced organized labor's attitude towards vocational training.'[36] In another study of this key period, Joel Spring found an 'hysterical anti-union bias in business's promotion of trade-school education.'[37] Spring wrote about business's interest in 'destroying union influence over trade training . . . because they felt that union control of the apprenticeship system was being used to maintain high wage levels by limiting the size of the skilled work-force.'[38] In her history of New York City schools, Diane Ravitch portrayed the school superintendent in this era as a man who 'feared that businessmen were trying to convert the schools into cheap labor-training programs.'[39] Nasaw also noted the vocational battle over training, wages and power:

The unions, having seized control of the last remnants of the apprenticeship system were, the employers charged,

46

manipulating it to keep the supply of workers down and wages up. If industrial training and certification for skilled and supervisory positions could be removed from the factory to the public high schools, then the unions would be unable to exercise any control on the size of the industrial workforce.[40]

Michael Katz concluded that 'industrial education has proved to be an ingenious way of providing universal secondary schooling without disturbing the shape of the social structure and without permitting excessive amounts of social mobility.'[41]

From the outset, then, occupationalism was a partisan battle between labor and management. Union resistance to the industrial program in schools managed to weaken the eventual shape of vocational education, as labor delegates took part in overseeing some aspects of the plan.[42] Still, vocationalism was then and now the vehicle of political offensives to depress wages and to weaken the opposition. Seventy years ago, labor-training left the union apprentice area and was absorbed in part by a vocational program of the schools. In the recent career drive, work-training for business moved out of its separate vocational track to invade the academic and general parts of the curriculum. This was the latest extension of business culture into the seemingly non-partisan activity called public education.

The spread of careerism from the top down and the resistance to it from the bottom up boil down to the questions of how much will labor cost and who will socialize whom. *Peer*-socialization builds solidarity at the grass roots. You owe your training to your peers or to a peer-organization. You will likely turn to each other for support in a strike, for information on domestic and foreign policy, for advice on which candidates to choose at election time. This is some of what an autonomous labor culture could offer its members. In contrast, socialization by the elite breeds *authority*-dependence. The bottom is divided against itself by the top. This process was understood by the more radical Chicago branch of the American Federation of Labor, which called Illinois' imminent industrial education scheme in 1913

> an effort on the part of large employers to turn the public schools into an agency for supplying them with an adequate supply of docile, well-trained and capable workers . . . aimed to bring Illinois a caste system of education.[43]

John Dewey also opposed the Illinois scheme 'as the greatest evil now threatening the interests of democracy in education.'[44] Dewey opposed the radical separation of vocational and academic study intended in the Illinois proposal. He went on to write that

> There is a danger that vocational education will be interpreted in theory and practice as trade education, as a means of securing technical efficiency in specialized future pursuits. . . . Education would then become an instrument of perpetuating unchanged the existing industrial order of society, instead of operating as a means for its transformation.[45]

The inegalitarian potential in occupational courses was apparent then – the same force against class-leveling which made careerism appropriate as the first major curricular counter to the egalitarian 1960s. Dewey offered instead a model for the democratic integration of academic and vocational studies:

> An education which acknowledges the full intellectual and social meaning of a vocation would include instruction in the historic background of present conditions; training in science to give intelligence and initiative in dealing with materials and agencies of production; and the study of economics, civics, and politics to bring the future worker in touch with the problems of the day and the various methods proposed for its improvement. Above all, it would train power of readaptation to changing conditions so that future workers would not become blindly subject to a fate imposed on them.[46]

The words 'blindly subject to a fate imposed on them' should echo loud in the silent mill towns of Ohio in the 1980s, where great industries rose and then disappeared, leaving thousands of families behind in depressed valleys. Highly-skilled workers wound up defenseless in front of employer plans. Skill without philosophy and without politics left them unable to see or stop the wrenching deindustrialization of the Northeast.

Making money, making history

Saint Dewey has taken his place in the laundered halls of American honor, but you have to look long and hard to find his ideas practiced in US classrooms. Dewey was an uncompromising egalitarian critic of official vocational schemes. He drew attention to the *class* bias built into the education system. Social inequality has sexist and racist dimensions as well.

Female students have traditionally been channeled into the women's programs – nursing, clerical, sales, teaching. Male students have had science, engineering, philosophy and industrial work as their preserves. This should hardly be news to anyone. We absorb it in school and daily life with the air we breathe. Schools introduce sex-typing early, sewing and cooking for one, manual arts for the other, science, math and leadership for one side, art, music and followership for the other side. Only recently, since the latest feminist wave from the 1960s, has sex segregation been challenged in work and in education. Progress has been made, but according to one report on women in education, the classroom climate remains a 'chilly' one.[47] More women are managing to enter the professions, but these high-level careers, as in the case of law, are facing a labor oversupply. They are not as glamorous or luxurious as they were in the heyday of the male monopoly. The wages of women in lesser occupations have also been slipping in relation to men's wages. These kind of jobs are the destinies of most women who work.

Besides evidence of sexual inequality in the job market and in education, there is also a long history of vocationalism being used against non-whites. Gunnar Myrdal in *An American Dilemma* (1944) wrote that occupational courses in the South 'usually meant training to do more efficiently the traditional menial "Negro job".'[48] Boys were trained for farming and girls for sewing and cooking even though the agricultural and domestic labor markets were oversupplied. As usual with occupationalism, much training was directed for jobs that did not exist. In the case of the South observed by Myrdal, curriculum served political and economic control of one race over another. The racist reasoning went opposite ways on the public idiocy of training blacks for work that was not available. On the one hand, it was argued that blacks were mentally inferior to whites and could not handle more than simple training. On the other hand, it was argued that they were fully capable of learning but it would make them unfit for menial jobs if they got too high an education. Myrdal observed that

Vocational education in the public schools of the South has also served as a means to keep Negroes from getting the general education given to whites, since it is felt – with good reason – that an academic education would make Negroes ambitious and dissatisfied with a low occupation, would 'ruin a good field hand.'[49]

It is hard to find examples in education history of people being kept in their place with liberal arts, so it made sense for Myrdal to remark on the occupational bias of segregated schooling. In the area of broad, general education, Myrdal added that 'There is a clear tendency to avoid civics and other social sciences in the Southern Negro public schools. They are not taught to any extent in the white schools, but a special effort is made to prevent Negroes from thinking about the duties and privileges of citizenship.'[50]

In the vocational courses of Northern schools, John Goodlad found distinct evidence of racial segregation. His eight-year study, *A Place Called School* (1983), directly addressed the unmistakable racism in career courses he visited:

Disproportionately large percentages of white students were found to be enrolled in vocational courses with more general content – home economics and Future Farmers of America agricultural classes – and in those oriented towards business skills – bookkeeping, marketing, etc. In contrast, disproportionately large percentages of Mexican-American students were enrolled in courses with content oriented toward specific preparation for low-level occupations – cosmetology, auto repair, industrial and institutional cooking and sewing, to name a few.[51]

Goodlad and his team of researchers observed over a thousand classrooms in a representative sample of US schools across the country. He asked 'is there equity among socioeconomic classes and whites, blacks and Mexican-Americans in regard to the circumstances and the outcomes of the [vocational] process?' His answer was 'no.'

At the collegiate level, career education in the 1970s was another strategy particularly aimed at keeping minorities in their place, according to Joel Spring's analysis of manpower policies since 1945.[52] Spring read careerism as the Nixon Administration's response to the disadvantaged, following minority demands for equality in the 1960s. This demand was contained by channeling minorities in disproportionate numbers into technical programs at open-door colleges. This renaissance of vocationalism under Nixon was also viewed by Frank Riessman as an attempt to 'dupe the poor,' especially minorities.[53] Riessman denounced the new careerism appearing after 1971 as a denial of liberal study to the minorities going to college. This would quarantine them from the most critical and aspiring curriculum. Such learning could make masses of people unhappy with their work as well as with the society as it is. Riessman saw vocationalism entering to head off these developments. He declared that in the case of non-whites:

> An attempt is being made to dupe the blacks and to persuade them that higher education is really a lot of abstract baloney that at best provides false credentials for the professionals . . . . Poor people may be persuaded that they are getting a union card via relevant, work-oriented courses and that they don't need any of that highfalutin college stuff. That would be a terrible pity and a gross deception.[54]

As a conservative counter-offensive rose against the liberal impact of open access, Riessman concluded that the open door to college could be important for further social change and 'efforts to restrict it and make it simply work and technician oriented would be highly retrogressive.'[55]

The community college movement from the 1950s had invented the open-door college, which began 'cooling-out' the upward rise of the non-traditional student.[56] In the restoration 1970s, the two-year campuses were called upon to restrict again mass access to liberal curricula. Marland's careerism vocationalized the community colleges in a hurry in the early restoration. This career direction had been recommended by a Carnegie study in 1970 and again by the Second Newman Report to Marland at HEW in 1973.[57] The great universities had been declared off-limits to the mass student in the 1950s. Now that minorities gained access to the open-door college, the liberal arts were being declared off-limits in the budget campuses.

Settling for less liberal arts

A cordon sanitaire was being drawn in the early 1970s between the technical and liberal consequences of education. Marland assured the victory of careerism over humanities by pushing through astronomical sums for vocationalism. The previously mentioned authorization of $850 million in 1972 for occupational programs at the community colleges alone was *three times* the entire allocation made for capital construction on two-year campuses.[58] While grossly imbalancing curriculum towards occupationalism, and while fortifying inequality in the mass and liberal curricula, Marland preached democracy in a rebuke to the elite academics:

> Let the academic preparation be balanced with the vocational or professional program. Let one student take strength from another. And for the future of education, let us end the divisive, snobbish, destructive distinctions in learning that do no service to the cause of knowledge and do no honor to the name of American enterprise.[59]

Following these sentiments, there was a decade-long imbalance which eventually led Reagan's Secretary of Education, T. H. Bell, to complain in 1983 how liberal learning must be supported on campus against the domination of narrow training.[60]

The liberal arts were simply out-of-sync with the needs of a depressant restoration. Social sciences and humanities boomed in the activist 1960s only to plummet in the conservative 1970s. The long divide between the academic and the occupational sat uneasily for a whole century in the school system. The weight of student aspiration kept occupationalism at bay until federal money and the economic crisis of the 1970s imposed the triumph of training over education. As the fear of unemployment drove students towards business and tech departments, the humanities shriveled in size and prestige.

The shrinking of liberal arts provided a political bonus to the conservative offensive as well as an economic cap on student aspirations. In the protest era, social science and liberal arts departments were often home to many radical students and professors. The ethical and social interests of these courses made such an arrangement possible. Liberal study was heir to the skeptical, speculative and rational traditions of Western thought. This permitted some space for critical intelligence and values-analysis. Science and tech programs offered far less critical exercise because Washington's Cold War with Moscow and its Trade War with Western allies made scientific study too valuable to the military and to business. The technical side of knowledge was more tightly integrated into the industrial and military apparatus than were the soft disciplines in the humanities. Cold War and Trade War had narrowed the scope of scientific inquiry while the liberal arts maintained some critical autonomy.

The capture of science for narrow class interests rather than for social needs came to Dewey's attention early in this century:

> the new science was for a long time to be worked in the interests of old ends of human exploitation . . . it put at the disposal of a class the means to secure their old ends of aggrandizement at the expense of another class. . . .
> Feudalism was doomed by the applications of the new science, for they transferred power from the landed nobility to the manufacturing centers. But capitalism rather than a social humanism took its place. Production and commerce were carried out as if the new science had no moral lesson but only technical lessons.[61]

Moral lessons fled science. They retreated to some parts of the humanities. The closeness of science to the power elite equaled its distance from the heart of ethics. Science has made business and the military powerful, so science education cannot include critical study of science in society. The very idea of business-dominated science or military-dominated research is anathema to the value-free pretensions of science. Many parts of the humanities would also like to be neutrally 'scientific.' Social sciences in particular have a strong bias towards the value-free myth. In this world of bogus neutrality, the philosophical roots of the humanities preserved some moral dimensions to its scrutiny.

The critical sincerity of some liberal arts programs opened them up to the stream of protest culture flowing in the 1960s. Only recently, environmental and anti-nuclear movements have forced an ethical dimension into parts of the science curriculum. Social issues now more frequently appear in tech or interdisciplinary science courses. In the 1960s, the tech side of the academy showed no cracks while the liberalists made many breaks with the system. In that era of mass enrollments and mass protest movements, this open corner of the humanities challenged the legitimacy of business, government, military and education elites. Many non-tenured faculty paid a price for challenging official ideology. Their firings made it clear that the university was no neutral Ivory Tower. Some knowledge was acceptable and other knowledge was outlawed. The liberal arts in the 1960s housed too much opposition thinking to survive in the reactionary 1970s.

With the shrinking of the liberal arts in the 1970s, some critical corners of university life were disabled. The legitimacy of the system suffered less attack as activist and ethical intelligence shrank. Business sent out a strong message of its intention to hire technical and professional graduates over liberal arts majors. The new restoration era imposed a long depression on the public sector, thus reducing the demand for public school teachers, a big source of liberal arts employment. Students in the 1970s got the illiberal message, feared for their futures, and began switching to tech and professional programs. One engineering dean was ecstatic about this mass migration:

> Higher education is undergoing what may be the most
> significant internal change in half a century. Professional
> fields such as engineering are becoming more important to this
> country's continued economic growth and quality of life. . . .
> It is not enough to report that some English majors are driving
> taxis or that things are tough for would-be kindergarten
> teachers. . . . What is really happening at America's
> universities is not some sort of general 'decline' but a major
> shift . . . toward career and professional education. The work
> ethic may even be returning.[62]

His celebration wonderfully combined careerism with discipline. Not only was the tech surge of the 1970s a return to political order, but according to this dean, it also meant the good life. Needless to say, unemployment and stagflation marked the declining quality of life in this period of career triumph.

Even if the promised horn of plenty never appeared from the tech revival, the 'soft' liberal arts and hard student activism both declined. One classicist observing the decline wrote why education in the new conservative age can no longer be liberal:

the liberal studies that eventually were worked out as studies worthy of free men were a program designed with the aspiration not to prepare dependent persons for performing their particular functions, but to empower autonomous participants to think critically about the full range of human activity and to judge soundly any and all efforts at action. . . . Where the participating citizen is in decline, there too liberal education will be in decline.[63]

This critical tradition of the liberal arts, available only to an elite until mass higher education in the 1960s, and then politically unacceptable in the 1970s, was brought up to date by Maxine Greene's challenge midway through the new restoration:

In the resurgent literature on liberal arts education, the primary emphasis (after the complaints about illiteracy have been uttered) is on keeping liberal studies alive, defending the traditional against vulgarization and attrition, enhancing the higher literacy, keeping the light from sputtering out. Very little is heard about students' idiosyncratic searches for meaning or about their youthful assessments of the way things are or ought to be. Very little is heard about renewal or about the possible connections between liberal education and a transformation of the common world.[64]

Greene's sharp intelligence focused earlier suggestions that traditional humanities had not served the mainstream well in the mass colleges.[65] Still, traditional liberal arts were too 'radical' for the restoration 1970s and were thus exiled to the curricular margins. In a fine ironic twist of history, the attack on liberal arts from the right provoked a reconstruction of liberal study from the center and the left as culture war moved from the 1970s into the 1980s.[66]

Swing low, sweet liberal arts

The swing to careerism thus had very little to do with improving the quality of life, with insuring economic recovery, with the superiority of professional over liberal education, or with rational manpower planning. Careerism from Nixon to Reagan was what it had always been – a confirmation of social inequality, a prevention against class-leveling, and a replacement of opposition intellect with business training. It has never been easy to fit each new generation into the arbitrary and unequal occupational hierarchy. The rebellious youth from the 1960s posed a special problem which made Marland's boss at HEW, Elliott Richardson, yell 'Christ!' when he learned how many millions of college graduates would be surplus by 1980.[67] Shifting curricular majors to careerism could be the finger in the dike. The new conservative regime in Washington was not the only observer of the career solution. From the left, Christopher Jencks wrote in 1972 about the threat of the school-jobs disconnection. If student occupational aspirations were not 'congruent' with actual opportunities, he wrote, 'the whole fabric of American society might begin to unravel.'[68]

This looming crisis was seen in the 1950s when elite policy-makers invented the community college movement for the masses. At that fateful moment, the decision was made to segregate non-traditional students onto lesser occupational campuses rather than absorb them into the first two years of existing liberal arts colleges. Cohen and Brawer argued in 1982 that community colleges were doomed to inequality once the choice was taken against having *all* freshmen and sophomores attend the *same* colleges.[69] One policy-prince of the Cold War, James Bryant Conant, explained in 1956 why the egalitarian road was not chosen and the occupational one triumphed:

> There would seem to be great advantages, therefore, in preparing now for the time, only a few years hence, when the flood of college students will be at hand. And those preparations, to my mind, should consist primarily in the establishment of many local two-year colleges. They should be planned to attract the large majority of the youths who now enter a four-year college or university with little intention of completing a four-year course of study. . . . If some such development does not occur, the pressure of applicants on the tax-supported universities will force a rapid and enormous increase in teaching staff. The quality of the faculty is bound to deteriorate and more than one promising center of research and professional education will become a training institution.[70]

As President of Harvard in the 1940s, Conant opposed the GI Bill, fearing a loss of academic quality from non-traditional students.[71] He recanted when the veterans proved themselves to be outstanding collegians. But, this recognition of the new students did little to convert Conant to egalitarianism. He pushed hard in the 1950s for the Cold War production of a scientific elite to win the arms race against Russia. This political priority required protecting elite research units. Therefore, the mass of Americans wanting higher education would have to settle for less, on inferior occupational campuses. Cohen and Brawer remarked sardonically that 'Community colleges certainly performed an essential service in the 1960s and 1970s when a mass of people demanded access. . . . How many universities would have been shattered if community colleges to which the petitioners could be shunted had not been available?'[72]

Lavish elite education and underfunded mass education are problems for a democracy. Everyone passes through a lot of schooling in this unequal arrangement, so the stench of class bias reaches every nose. As more unequal education gets distributed decade by decade, the democratic myths surrounding the undemocratic reality are forced to become more elaborate. The byzantine construction of career education can be read in this light, to argue for the democratic quality of yet another inegalitarian school scheme. At the moment Marland promoted careerism, Jencks completed his study *Inequality* (1972), where he estimated that twice as much is spent on education for rich children as on the poor.[73] He reported an even worse differential at the college level. State court decisions in the early 1970s ruled that equal amounts had to be spent on all children. That decision is still not fulfilled. In higher education, the vast funding differences are apparent as soon as you set foot on a budget campus or on an elite one. These gross inequalities have been marketed as a vast 'democratization' of higher learning.[74]

Tilting towards careerism and away from liberal arts retards both activism and aspirations. The ideological impact of career study is as important as its channeling of students towards low-wage jobs. The denial of humanities study interferes with critical learning. It lessens students' exposures to social issues and political values. This made careerism an ideal starting point in the early war against the 1960s.

Sidney Marland was the first among many handing out career shovels as the transition from protest to restoration began. Those shovels were good for digging a common grave for liberal arts, for rising expectations, and for dissent. If the career punch did not knock humanities and protest culture out of their crossing orbits, a second blow was waiting in the wings. Reports on declining Scholastic Aptitude Test (SAT) scores peppered the nation in the early 1970s. By 1975, Marland had become head of the College Board, the group sponsoring the SAT, in a year of its biggest dive. A 'Literacy Crisis' was ready to explode on the scene. This second culture war promised an even greater thrust than careerism, in the drive against equality and opposition.

3 Settling for less, 1975-82:
the war on 'illiteracy'
the literacy crisis and back-to-basics
promote authority

Nationwide, the statistics on literacy grow more appalling each
year. . . . Willy-nilly, the U.S. educational system is
spawning a generation of semi-literates.

Newsweek (1975)

More and more high school graduates show up . . . with barely
a speaking acquaintance with the English language and no
writing facility at all.

College Board report (1977)

Anyone who teaches English today knows that most students
can't write. Their writing skills have been in a steady,
downward spiral since the mid-sixties.

Donna Woolfolk Cross, *Word Abuse* (1979)

For the half-decade starting with the late 1960s, long-
established academic standards were abolished wholesale in
a spasm reminiscent of the Red Guards' destructive rampage
through China's classical cultural institutions.

Burton Yale Pines, *Back-to-Basics* (1982)

The decline in literacy is a fiction, if not a hoax. . . . Do those
who control our economic and educational systems really
want a totally literate workforce?

Richard Ohmann, *The Chronicle of Higher Education* (1976)

Reading and writing have no inherent disposition to produce
independent thinking. . . . Developmental literacy is usually
intended to make men harmless, obedient and productive.

Robert Pattison, *On Literacy* (1982)

Athena and Zeus

An explosion over literacy and basic skills slowly heated up in the early 1970s. SAT scores were declining year after year. This high-profile dilemma embarrassed the agency that sponsored the exam, the College Board (CB). In December 1973, the CB held a press conference on the decline but left the matter at that.[1] At the same time, countless thousands of non-elite students arrived on campuses to reap the rewards of open admissions. Faculty meetings and professional journals filled with debate on the problems of teaching 'the new learners.' *Newsweek* found 'back-to-basics in the schools' a lively theme for a feature story in late 1974.[2] Athena was about to burst from the brow of Zeus.

Zeus the thunderer at this juncture of history was played by the ubiquitous Sidney P. Marland, Nixon's former Commissioner of Education who was head of the CB in 1975. Marland had already promoted career education all around the country from grade schools to college, glamorizing work-training even as unemployment rose. Irrepressible Marland was an undaunted careerist even as HEW itself issued its study *Work in America* (1973), revealing deep alienation on the job and the weak link between occupational programs and employment. Now at the helm of the prestigious CB, Marland issued a press release in September 1975 on the latest SAT fall-off, the worst yet in the twelve-year downward spiral. His statement made the front pages of the *New York Times* and the *Washington Post*. Then, he rose to the seriousness of the moment by appointing a big-name panel 'to do all that we can to investigate and interpret this phenomenon to the public.'[3]

Concern about declining test scores had been mounting outside the CB. Some months before Marland acted, HEW had initiated one inquiry into eroding reading skills since 1965. A short while after that, the National Institute of Education (NIE) held a special conference on the declines. That meeting was of special significance first as a response to a growing crisis and second as a sign of the controversy to come. The NIE researchers who met in Washington in June 1975 could not reach consensus on what the test declines meant.[4] They did not view them as a 'general' collapse in literacy. Their report opened up a can of worms that would plague the CB for the next decade, because they raised doubts about exactly what the SAT measures and whether it accurately reflects student skills. The NIE report also listed those test scores which were rising along with those that declined, indicating a mixed picture rather than a uniform drop. Was the SAT itself suspect? Were rumors of a literacy collapse just a lot of hot air?

Here was a visible predicament involving the big gun of the testing world. Around since 1926, remodeled in the 1940s, the SAT was the premier gatekeeper to the best universities, whose degrees were the tickets-of-admission to the best jobs. More than a million students a year were taking the exam in the 1970s, and the unbroken string of declines stretched from 1963–75, when the very largest drops were recorded – ten points in the verbal section and eight in the math.[5] Something had to give. One key instrument of authority and hierarchy was at stake. Who would shoulder blame, the test-takers or the test-makers?

Sidney's second child

After Marland's press release, events moved quickly. Marland found himself once again in the right place at the right time with an idea whose moment had arrived. However, his labors were less needed now than they had been in the career phase of the restoration. The conservative tide had overtaken the 1960s by the time he reached the CB. A mounting conservative climate existed to use traditionalist themes like back-to-basics and anti-egalitarian notions like mass illiteracy.

The important role Marland played in this second campaign involved taking the initiative on an issue already under scrutiny. The appointment of a high-level official panel to study the problem sanctified the issue as a genuine crisis. The group that would eventually produce an important statement on the SAT decline was chaired by former Secretary of Labor, Willard Wirtz, a man especially interested in manpower planning. Among the twenty other members of the commission, there were such educational lions as Ralph Tyler, Harold Howe II and Benjamin Bloom. Tyler, in his seventies, was a grand old man of education. He had won renown originally for his important *Eight-Year Study* in the 1930s, which traced the life progress of graduates from non-traditional high school programs. Ironically, these experimental courses were the very kind of learning denounced in the Literacy Crisis. Tyler's panel-mate, Howe, was an educational figure also, a former Commissioner of Education himself. Benjamin Bloom was a well-known learning theorist from the University of Chicago. Columbia University's Teachers College was represented by Robert Thorndike, another recognized scholar. Such figures gave the commission visibility and credibility. With prestige, the Wirtz panel could fulfill Marland's hope to be the interpreter of the SAT crisis to the American people. Studies by lesser-known figures and by opposition critics would simply get less attention.

Funds for the Wirtz commission came from the College Board and from the Educational Testing Service (ETS). ETS is the producer of the SAT and other tests administered by the College Board. Both groups had an obvious political and commercial interest in the rescue of the SAT's reputation. Thus, their financing of the most important study of the problem was a questionable arrangement. Eventually, in 1977, the Wirtz group produced a document endorsing the SAT and decrying the decline in literacy among students. This helped ETS and the College Board pull their chestnuts from the fire as controversy mounted over the declines. But, then, a new controversy emerged on the report itself. The debate over the SAT's validity would simply not go away, spilling over into the crisis reports of 1983, which echoed calls for replacing the flagship of the testing fleet. But that is getting ahead of the story, because the Literacy Crisis bursting from the brow of Zeus in 1975 would not wait two years for Wirtz and Company to report.

Wirtz barely began to ponder the fate of more than a million SATs a year when the press made the Literacy Crisis into the new media darling. The big story in late 1975 belonged to *Newsweek*, just as it belonged there again in the 'excellence' crisis after 1982. With a sensational cover-story in December 1975, *Newsweek* made the SAT and the Literacy Crisis into household words. The cover pictured a schoolboy laboring with pencil in hand, under the bold headline of 'Why Johnny Can't Write.' The opening paragraph was a call to arms:

> If your children are attending college, the chances are that when they graduate they will be unable to write ordinary, expository English with any real degree of structure and

lucidity. If they are in high school and planning to attend college, the chances are less than even that they will be able to write English at the minimal college level when they get there. If they are not planning to attend college, their skills in writing English may not even qualify them for secretarial or clerical work. And if they are attending elementary school, they are almost certainly not being given the kind of required reading material, much less writing instruction, that might make it possible for them to eventually write comprehensible English. Willy-nilly, the U.S. educational system is spawning a generation of semi-literates.[6]

Newsweek threw caution to the winds. It set an alarmist tone which hung forever over claims of illiteracy. It also suggested that there is a traditional pedagogy which used to teach people how to write well. To give the problem substance, and to legitimize the solutions, the rhetoric employed suggestive half-statements, relative qualifications, appeals to authority, and skewed test-score readings. From this manipulative stew, it concluded absolutely that schools churned out morons. Look at the first paragraph again. You will find there such formulations as 'chances are,' 'real degree of structure,' 'minimal college level,' 'may not qualify them,' 'almost certainly,' and 'that might make it possible.' From these qualified semi-positions, the story leaps to the astounding absolute conclusion that a generation of 'semi-literates' is being spawned, much like schools of mindless fish. (If the noble salmon had a voice, it might object to such misrepresentation.) Such rhetoric is good copy to sell magazines and even good propaganda for the restoration cause. It aggressively promoted a traditionalist point of view through a fabrication of reality.

Still more fabrication of reality came from *Newsweek*'s selective reading of test scores to prove a drastic decline in literacy that threatened civilization itself. The story mentioned the SAT score decline and referred to the College Board's appointment of the Wirtz group. More attention was located on some results from the National Assessment of Educational Progress (NAEP). The NAEP would prove to be the leaky heart of the Literacy Crisis. Its extensive studies kept showing gains and stability in many areas during the 1970s. Set up in the late 1960s by the Education Commission of the States (ECS), NAEP began quadrennial achievement tests in ten subjects and four age groups (9, 13, 17, 26–35). From 1969 on through the years of the Literacy Crisis, NAEP measured these age cohorts every four years in art, career development, citizenship, literature, math, music, reading, science, social studies and writing. In terms of literacy, the national results showed slight improvements in reading comprehension and inferential skills as well as a rise in the percentage of good writers among 17-year-olds between 1971 and 1975.[7] In those years, the functional literacy of 17-year-olds increased from 88 per cent to 90 per cent, while 9-year-olds in 1973 wrote better than their age group did four years earlier. Instead of these improvements, *Newsweek* chose to highlight NAEP's findings of more incoherent sentences and paragraphs in the declining whole essays written by 13- and 17-year-olds. The full picture of ups and downs made reality far more complicated than the alarming distortion in *Newsweek*. A full view would have made it impossible to declare a Literacy Crisis. The aforementioned NIE conference was only one of several sources in this period which reached non-crisis conclusions. Other demurring voices will be examined in the coming pages along with those of the illiteracy camp. Partisan misreadings of the evidence reveal the culture war of this second phase of restoration. Without a Literacy Crisis there would have been no cause for launching a traditionalist crusade for the basics. Without back-to-basics, business culture, religious fundamentalism, and authoritarianism would not have regained such predominance in the restoration.

Traditional scholars became the final skew of *Newsweek*'s story. Among the alarmed luminaries was Jacques Barzun, previously referred to in Chapter 1 for his fear that school no longer taught 'the right words.' The literacy threat to civilization was endorsed by Marshall McLuhan, who claimed in the *Newsweek* pages that literary culture was 'through.' Karl Shapiro agreed that the United States was 'in the midst of a literary breakdown.' Then, the current head of the National Endowment for the Humanities, Ronald Berman, offered the most marvelous phrase on the 'regression toward the intellectually invertebrate' in American academics. S. I. Hayakawa was fitted into *Newsweek*'s call for a return to the language of authority, Standard English. As the conservative President of San Francisco State College in the late 1960s and early 1970s, during several bitter student and faculty strikes, Hayakawa became notorious for his combat against protest culture, including faculty firings. A picturesque segment on the evening news showed him ripping out the wires on a student sound truck, a good example of silencing the opposition. *Newsweek* simply described Hayakawa as a 'semanticist,' who said innocently enough that 'You just don't know anything unless you can write it.'

A year before the *Newsweek* story, the largest organization of English teachers, the National Council of Teachers of English (NCTE) had voted in its policy on 'Students' Rights to Their Own Language.'[8] This egalitarian document described Standard English as a privileged dialect, and as one dialect among many in a diverse culture. It is no secret that most people speak a form of English different from the language of teachers, of literature and of the elite. This simple recognition becomes a culture war when popular opposition sets everyday dialects as equal to elite speech. The 'right to your own language' is an egalitarian idea from the 1960s which *Newsweek* zeroed in on as a source of the Literacy Crisis. It specifically referred to the NCTE document and made clear, in its concluding paragraph, what the power struggle was all about in language:

> The point is that there have to be some fixed rules, however tedious, if the codes of human communication are to remain decipherable. If the written language is placed at the mercy of every new colloquialism and if every fresh dialect demands and gets equal sway, then we will soon find ourselves back in Babel. In America today, as in the never-never world Alice discovered on her trip through the looking-glass, there are too many people intent on being masters of their language and too few willing to be its servants.[9]

Language is part of the machinery that decides who will be masters and who will be servants. The dialect that dominates indicates the group that dominates. The nakedness of power politics here is unsuitable, however, for waging culture war, so the issue had to be hidden behind a 'neutral' screen of 'standards,' 'quality' and 'excellence.' Curriculum and civilization were defined in the Literacy Crisis as resting on the authority of elite language; that language was posed as a universal standard of culture rather than a class-specific form of expression. Everyday speech was a barbarian tongue unfit for civilized discourse in schools and colleges. The literacy camp thus surrounded itself with a neutral disguise in its claim to represent the general interests of civilization. In hiding the class-bound nature of correct usage, it could also disguise the partisan quality of its pedagogy. Back-to-basics could help restore order in language, school and society, but that order was in everybody's interest, not simply in favor of the elite, so the reasoning went.

If in late 1975 you favored Standard English and you worried about illiteracy and civilization, you had a good chance to make it into *Newsweek*. Only one lone English teacher was quoted there for her doubts on official versus everyday language. No opposition scholars equal to Barzun or to Hayakawa (such as Richard Ohmann, James Sledd or Basil Bernstein)[10] showed up in those pages. The sound and fury exploding over literacy signified that a conservative motherlode had been struck. A few years earlier, in the difficult transition from left to right, careerism was the big-money roller-coaster piloted by a super-showman lumbering in from Washington. Now, Marland and the federal center were less needed as conservative culture came into its own. The Literacy Crisis spread like prairie fire through the press, the profession, the spread-out school districts, the far-flung state legislatures. A rush to judgement was on around a truly glamorous issue. Who were the villains? What were the solutions?

An army of villains

Predictably enough, the 1960s were a key villain in this new restoration campaign. In his lengthy review of the test score decline, Christopher Jencks noted that blame was being laid at the feet of 'the innovations that took place during the 1960s,' with the intention of urging the schools to 'get back to the basics.'[11] *Newsweek* pushed the debate in this direction by declaring that

> The 1960s also brought a subtle shift of educational philosophy away from the teaching of expository writing. Many teachers began to emphasize 'creativity' in the English classroom and expanded their curriculums to allow students to work with contemporary media of communications such as film, videotape and photography.[12]

Continuing this theme, another Literacy campaigner, Donna Woolfolk Cross, said that 'Anyone who teaches English today knows that most students can't write. Their writing skills have been in a steady downward spiral since the mid-sixties.'[13] One university dean writing in *The Christian Science Monitor* saw the decline as a legacy of the 1960s, which brought lower quality education along with too much student choice in curriculum.[14]

The charge that the 1960s brought in permissive education – too little writing and reading, too many soft electives and too few required hard academic courses – was made in the Literacy Crisis period and then again in the 'excellence' flurry of the 1983 reform wave. Did innovation in the 1960s so thoroughly replace traditional curriculum, and did that innovation undermine the three Rs as well as academic rigor? Clearly, not all schools or colleges permitted experimentation during and after the 1960s, though many of them experienced serious political disruption. Among those places where innovative approaches were tried, not all experimental classes were spongy. Conversely, the paper rigor of traditional courses hardly transfers automatically into a learning rigor inside a student. The tendency of traditionalists is to assume that the familiar structures of a subject equal the structure of knowledge transferred to students. If education was such a simple transfer of skill and knowledge, schooling would not have had the continual crises famous in this century. Every side in the debate on pedagogy has a political interest in the outcome, so behind the charge of permissiveness is not so much a choice of rigor or fogginess but rather what ideology and social relations of learning will prevail in the classroom. This takes us back once again to the question of authority. The egalitarian experiments of the 1960s encouraged a break with the authoritarian form of teaching and the official canons of knowledge.

How far did this challenge succeed? It may be that the egalitarian surge of the 1960s was more successful in weakening authority than in establishing an alternate culture of learning *inside* schools. *Outside*, in residual movements and alternate projects, unofficial learning condensed into numerous informal units and networks. One extensive survey of innovation in the 1960s found resistance to change very severe in the English profession, for example. In *English in a Decade of Change* (1968), Michael Shugrue examined a broad body of literature, conferences, programs and proposals for reconstructing English education. He concluded that

> Throughout the 1960s, English teachers, their colleagues in other disciplines, and the principals and deans who administer our schools and colleges have accepted educational innovation with reluctance. . . . The English teacher in a large school district or a multiversity faces enormous difficulties if he tries to change the English curriculum.[15]

Shugrue was trying to find out if the post-Sputnik reforms and other proposals for active student learning had made a dent. He found most courses still dominated by teacher-talk and by literature. This result was confirmed in the 1966 Squire study of high school English classes, and by John Goodlad in field research in the late 1960s.[16] Perhaps more radical influences overwhelmed the classroom after 1968, in the heyday of the egalitarian years. Shugrue did look to the 1970s as a time when more innovation might take place. In that later decade, John Goodlad was in the field again for eight years, with a research team, completing the study of public schools mentioned in the previous chapter. From observations of over a thousand classrooms around the country, Goodlad confirmed again in 1983 that classrooms were still dominated by traditional pedagogy, teacher-talk and teacher-centered subject matter.[17] Jencks also investigated the charge that the 1960s watered down the curriculum. From his review of the test-score decline, in 1978, he found that 'secondary school students took *more* academic courses in 1970–1 than they had in 1960–1 or 1948–9.'[18] There was a small decline from 1970–3 in academic courses in high school. But these were the years of the career education offensive, when academic aspirations were being depressed in favor of occupationalism. The College Board report on the test-score decline also noted the occupational shift of these years.[19] Only in 1983, when the protest era was safely in the distant past, would some traditionalists admit that the career surge undermined the rigor of education.[20] In the Literacy Crisis phase, reversing the 1960s was still important enough to blame illiteracy on the egalitarian and experimental trends of the protest period, even without evidence to prove such a charge.

Careerism and the Literacy Crisis strengthened traditional curricula at the very moment of their greatest vulnerability. Opposition ideas were gaining popularity in education circles. The political scene was radicalizing faster than curriculum itself was changing, but over time, an egalitarian opposition might construct an imposing alternate curriculum. Campaigns for student power, for relevant courses, for non-graded and experimental classes, for minority programs, for free universities and free schools were springing up in countless places. Ivan Illich's idea of 'deschooling society' provoked widespread debate, but it was only one potent notion in a growing literature on radical alternatives.[21] This threatening trend had to be halted before it matured.

The restoration chilled the opposition by imposing the most austere depressants of the old curriculum – vocationalism and the three Rs. These were likely options for the restoration of authority through schooling. However, the very authoritarian nature of the new regimens only guaranteed student resistance. In effect, the new counter-offensives exchanged one kind of opposition for another. Occupational and basic skill programs created anti-intellectualism in the 1970s and 1980s. Such depressant education discouraged students from high investments in learning. While the student rebels of the 1960s had nascent ideas for alternative learning, the alienated students of the 1970s and the 1980s simply withdrew from schooling or else negatively sabotaged the classroom. The restoration created a new form of resistance as hard to cope with as the upheavals of the 1960s.

Blaming the 1960s and open admissions for 'the new illiteracy' is a standard conservative theme, but it also appealed to a left critic like Christopher Lasch. While some opposition scholars like Jencks and Richard Ohmann understood the depressant effects of back-to-basics, Lasch accused the democratization of education of eroding critical thought and intellectual standards without raising popular culture or equalizing wealth.[22] Besides agreeing with conservatives that excellence and equality were incompatible, he also indicted the age of protest culture. In *The Culture of Narcissism* (1979), Lasch wrote that

> the student movement embodied a militant anti-intellectualism of its own, which corrupted and eventually absorbed it. Demands for the abolition of grades, although defended on grounds of high pedagogical principle [reflected] a desire for less work and a wish to avoid judgement on its quality. The

demand for more 'relevant' courses often boiled down to a desire for an intellectually undemanding curriculum.[23]

Perhaps Lasch expected a youthful upheaval to mature overnight into a rigorous opposition curriculum. Impatient, he made the error of judging a formative period as a final one. The 1960s were a process of development, not a finished product. Lasch did not consider how the conservative reaction of the 1970s prevented the experiments from maturing. This is exactly what you would expect conservative culture to do in the realm of ideological warfare, but such a political dynamic escaped Lasch's notice, in a book otherwise filled with remarkable insights into those years. Further, it is easy to accept the conservative theme of 'the new illiteracy' if you look at education from only a professor's point of view. During and after the 1960s, the arenas of non-formal and self-organized learning offered educational experiences outside the classroom and off campus, without the structure of tests, lectures and term papers. Scholars trained in the traditional academy will find it hard to measure this kind of learning. Non-traditional scholars, such as Ronald Gross, see the value of self-organized education more easily.[24]

A left critic who held his ground against the Literacy Crisis was Richard Ohmann. He saw immediately the reactionary feelings against the 1960s in the debate on illiteracy. From the partisan flood of rhetoric, he extracted in 1976 a wonderful list of villains:

> structural linguistics, Webster's *Third*, less teaching of grammar, English teachers themselves who can't write, the fact that kids no longer read the bible, educationists' jargon, the 'new sentimentality,' the 'mono-syllabic speech habits of the young,' open admissions, the increase in mass education, the Free Speech Movement, Vietnam, Watergate, children's books, replacement of writings by telephone conversations, non-verbal parents, advertisements, popular songs, worship of the machine, the 'complexity and illogic of the language,' Herman Hesse, Abbie Hoffman, Zen Buddhism, the new primitiveness, the federal government. And always poor television.[25]

Ohmann suggested that when people set out to find the causes of an event that may or may not be real, you can expect some floundering. He thought there might have been a real decline in intelligence, especially among those declaring a decline in literacy. Ohmann matched wit with research, and from his full reading of test scores, he concluded that the Literacy Crisis was a fiction, if not a hoax. Goodlad later agreed that the facts regarding student achievement were 'obscured by inflamed rhetoric.'[26]

How could the facts not matter in an intellectual debate on education? This was a squalid moment in the teaching profession and in society. The restoration was cynically manufacturing reality around phantoms of illiteracy. Against the irrationality of make-believe, an opposition debate rose in a losing cause to stem the tide of the basics crusade.

A literate debate on illiteracy

Chasing phantoms is an irritating task, so the debate on literacy was heated on all sides. For starters, the Literacy Crisis was often 'proved' by the drop in SAT scores. Yet, the SAT *never* asked students to write an essay. It has always been a multiple-choice exam whose verbal section tests students on definitions, analogies, syllogisms, sentence completions and reading comprehension. After 1973, the SAT was shortened by 30 minutes to allow time for a new Test of Standard Written English (TSWE). TSWE does not ask students to write either. It is a multiple-choice exam in standard usage, not a composition exercise. Once a year, the College Board offers a version of its English Composition Achievement Test (ECAT) which asks students to write for 20 minutes. This absence of writing samples is easy enough to explain; it is simply cheaper and easier to machine-score multiple-choice exams than it is to evaluate written essays. The question is, then, how do results from a non-writing exam translate into evidence for a decline in literacy? In the study commissioned by the College Board, Wirtz admitted that 'We can't prove that learning how to write is related to a decline in scores on a test that requires no writing.'[27] Wirtz then asserted that careful reading and writing had apparently gone out of style, citing NAEP studies of eleventh-graders where in a six-week period about half wrote three or fewer papers. Still, was this less than these students had written in the past? Was this related in any way to the SAT score decline? Was something *new* being measured that proved a literacy decline?

A second embarrassment in the rescue of the SAT was the confusion of 'aptitude' and 'achievement' tests. The SAT touted itself as an aptitude exam for which cramming did not help because it measured innate ability to do well in college. Then, in the Literacy Crisis phase, the SAT was dragged out to prove a decline in student achievement. The dropping scores were read as a drop in student literacy skills. The College Board only made the confusion worse by finally selling cram books to help students raise their SAT scores. The threat to the SAT's authority was recognized by Jencks and Crouse, who wrote that 'Claiming more for one's products than they can accomplish is a sure recipe for losing credibility.'[28] They asserted that 'College applicants have never had either equal opportunities or equal incentives to master anything. A "pure" measure of aptitude for higher education is therefore unattainable.'[29] They recommended replacing the SAT with achievement tests in the very areas the SAT actually tested students now. This same theme of replacing the SAT was echoed again in an even more powerful setting when Ernest Boyer issued his 1983 Carnegie study, *High School*.[30] Carnegie had founded ETS in 1948, along with the American Council on Education and the College Board. Now, Boyer was proposing to replace the SAT with a more comprehensive Student Achievement and Advisement Test (*SAAT*!!). This deterioration in the SAT position, where over a million students each year were vying for tickets of admission to the best universities, led the President of ETS in 1983 to denounce the ceaseless media use of the SAT to prove the decline in achievement.[31] However, the prestige and visibility of the SAT made it the daughter of the regiment instead of the prince of exams. Some eight years after the sensational *Newsweek* story, the new computer-produced daily *USA Today* used the SAT again, in a cover-story on the educational crisis of 1983.[32]

Here, then, was one instance of how an exercise in order produced only more disorder. Out of the twelve-year drop in SAT scores, the College Board commissioned Wirtz to judge the SAT's validity, even as a succession of austere curricular reforms swept the nation's schools – back-to-basics, minimum competency tests, remediation, etc. Happily enough, in 1977, Wirtz reported that the SAT was still a reliable indicator of future success in college, with a predictive validity of .42.[33] High school grades did slightly better as predictors, with a value of .50. The problem was that the SAT kept slipping after 1977, making headlines that kept the Literacy Crisis debate boiling. The slide hit bottom in 1981 and edged up a year later. The years of the greatest drops were 1972–5, when careerism aggressively entered schooling. Wirtz noted the occupational shift of those years and mentioned that career students do less well on the SAT than liberal arts majors. Yet, the panel had nothing to say about this strident direction in school policy. The study, after all, was commissioned by 'the father of career education' himself. More from the political investments of the Wirtz report can be found in its silence on class size and cuts in school budgets. These factors were dismissed in favor of safer causes of decline: more electives and fewer traditional courses, less homework, too much television, unstable family life, and the political disruptions of the prior decade.

Even though causes seemed to be everywhere and nowhere at the same time, Wirtz did gather all the pieces into a clear endorsement of the Literacy Crisis theme. The 'Introduction' claimed that 'More and more high school graduates show up in college classrooms, employers' offices, or at other common checkpoints with barely a speaking acquaintance with the English language and no writing facility at all.'[34] This was an unbecoming example of party-line politics, as if the report had to gather dissonant threads into a simplistic, conservative thesis. For sure, the report's own findings and often enlightened support of experimental and critical-reasoning curricula did not point in the direction of the illiteracy camp. The grandest irony is in the evidence it gathered, which justified *no* declaration of a collapse in literacy. Wirtz repeated what the NIE conference had found two years earlier – some test scores were rising, some stable and some declining. Six of the College Board's own achievement tests showed increases in this period. So did the Law School Admissions Test and the Medical College Admissions Test. The Preliminary Scholastic Aptitude Test for high school juniors was stable in the early 1970s and only then began a delayed decline. Wirtz awkwardly acknowledged that NAEP scores 'show results differing considerably' from other standardized test declines. Basic literacy, reading performance and writing mechanics, especially among blacks, showed either increases or slight declines through NAEP. To ice the cake, the Wirtz study also admitted that 'There are no reliable comprehensive measures yet of the comparative competence of today's youth with yesterday's.'[35] Once again, the evidence did not support the Literacy Crisis alarm about the collapse of civilization. Still, the SAT was in decline, and some other tests as well. Why?

Wirtz's most valuable contribution was presenting two phases in the long score decline.[36] The first phase, up to 1970, was referred to as the 'demographic decline,' because from two-thirds to three-quarters of the total SAT drop was attributed to changes in the test-taking group. More people from non-traditional, non-scholastic backgrounds were simply going on to college in greater numbers. The SAT was testing a larger population than the elite cohorts of the past. Traditional academics had never served the mainstream students well, but now these students had collegiate aspirations en masse, so the most academic of all exams entered their lives. The second phase of the decline, in the estimation of the Wirtz group, was designated as a 'cognitive' fall-off, because after 1970 the composition of the college-going population stabilized and only 20–30 per cent of the decline could be attributed to the non-traditional students taking the SAT. Open access to college had allowed the SAT to measure the scholastic development of a larger sample of students. This suggested that the scores did not represent a decline in literacy but rather an increase in accuracy. A previously invisible group was now part of the college-bound, SAT population. Calling this event a Literacy Crisis suited those who disliked open admissions. Aside from anti-egalitarianism, the score decline was bad publicity for the College Board and for the school system. The national debate on the test declines made visible just how poor a job traditional schooling does, with its twelve years and billions of dollars in the lower grades. The irrational answer to the failure of traditional education turned out to be even more traditionalism, in the form of basics and tougher academics. This was a way of explaining away the crisis by blaming the students for failing to learn the important things school tries to teach. I will return to this transfer of blame to the student in a later discussion of the politics of the basics crusade.

The period of 'cognitive decline' after 1970 still needed some reasonable explanation beyond television, unstable families and too many electives, but the 'demographic decline' was noticed by Richard Ohmann a year before Wirtz issued his report. Without the benefit of a research staff and two years' study time, Ohmann concluded that

> there were fewer drop-outs from high school: i.e., more students taking the standard tests from the part of the population that used to leave school before senior year. . . . Young women are less excluded from education now than ten years ago: many who would not have had a go at college then are doing so now. Presumably this new group is less well prepared than the women who used to choose higher education. If so, the 'decline in literacy' translates partly into an *increase* in equality and social justice.[37]

It was left to the opposition to celebrate the SAT decline as an index of rising social justice.

Justice, or just us?

Opposition to Wirtz, the Literacy Crisis and the back-to-basics camp came from a number of places in the teaching profession. One dissenting professor claimed that Wirtz reappeared just long enough to create more confusion and to guarantee ETS a big market for its SAT.[38] Another critic, Stephen Judy, then editor of the NCTE high school journal, was incensed at Wirtz's hypocrisy, first cautioning us against jumping to conclusions on the score decline and then baldly declaring that students can barely speak or write.[39] Judy heard verbal richness in student speech if they allow you to hear them and if you have the ability to listen. He was right to focus on student silence as a sign of alienation. Teacherly impatience with students' refusal to read, write or speak defines silence as illiteracy rather than as resistance, a performance strike. The way school imposes silence on students was described by John Dewey at the turn of the century:

> when there are no vital interests appealed to in the school, when language is used simply for the repetition of lessons, it is not surprising that one of the chief difficulties of school work has come to be instruction in the mother tongue. Since the

language taught is unnatural, not growing out of the real desire
to communicate vital impressions and convictions, the
freedom of children in its use gradually disappears, until finally
the high school teacher has to invent all kinds of devices to
assist in getting any spontaneous and full use of speech.[40]

The theory of imposed silence was updated for the 1970s by Paulo
Freire. His counter-alienation methods for breaking 'the culture
of silence' helped sustain opposition ideology during the Literacy
Crisis.[41] Freire understood that reading, writing and speaking were
not neutral acts of learning but were rather political moments of
alienation or animation, disempowerment or empowerment. For
Wirtz and the Literacy Crisis faction to recognize alienation as
key to student performance, they would have to accept the
partisan nature of schooling. They could not admit such a culture
war over curriculum, because their legitimacy rested on their
claims to a neutral standard of excellence.

Another critic of the Wirtz standard broke through the myths
of student silence by doing what the commission failed to do
– ask students what they think. Anthony Wolk struck on the
wonderfully novel idea of consulting students on their own diminished performance in the SAT.[42] Their answers supported the
notion of a performance strike rather than a collapse of literacy
or achievement. To them, SATs simply mattered less than they
used to, so they saw less reason for investing major efforts in
them. Getting into college was easier now. Further, the returns
on college investment were diminishing thanks to the economic
crisis. When students exercized themselves on tests that had more
tangible meaning to their plans, like law or medical school exams,
they showed what they could do. Even the NAEP, by focusing
on specific skills and knowledge, was able to record stable and
rising achievements, unlike the unfocused SAT, which was
guarding college gates already flung open, and which could not
open job-gates slammed shut.

From another angle on the test-score decline, Leo Munday
surveyed statewide rather than national test results. From seven
long-term instruments, he found evidence of decline.[43] However,
Munday saw the declines in such states as Iowa and California as
long up and down cycles dating back to the 1940s. The decline
was not a collapse and he predicted an upswing. Of course,

Munday was observing achievement tests, not aptitude ones. None had the prestige of the SAT and none pretended to make life-judgements on innate capacity to do high-level work. Another critic who favored achievement over aptitude tests, Anne Hulbert, noted that the great debate on illiteracy had led ETS to admit that the SAT measured *learned* skills.[44] She wrote that 'The reign of aptitude tests had regrettably only reflected inequality of conditions in our schools, and perhaps even indirectly reinforced the dismal disparities by implying they're innate and inevitable.'[45] The voice of egalitarianism was sustaining itself in a distinctly anti-egalitarian time.

More dissent came from the NCTE in the rebuttal of illiteracy by Edmund Farrell, an NCTE officer who served as consultant to the Wirtz group and as Chair of the College Board's own English Committee. Farrell declared in 1977 that 'the present uses of standardized tests are adversely affecting students, misleading lay people, and having a pernicious effect upon the English profession.'[46] These were strong words from an insider who broke ranks to tell it all. Farrell said that the best way to get strong universal literacy was to see that all schoolkids had well-educated, affluent parents. He referred here to the Coleman and the Jencks studies on inequality which concluded that family income was the primary determinant of school achievement.[47] Farrell turned the tables on the Literacy Crisis by blaming the system for social inequality rather than blaming students for illiteracy. This was an echo from the 1960s challenging the new wave of the 1970s. Farrell concluded his acidic attack on ETS and the College Board with humanistic questions also reminiscent of the 1960s: 'What kind of citizens do we want? What will they need to know and be able to do? What feelings or attitudes should they have towards others who will share the planet? What can the schools do now to help students anticipate and control change in their lifetimes?'[48] These questions were almost identical to ones raised by Charles Silberman in *Crisis in the Classroom* (1970).[49]

The heated debate on literacy and the SAT produced charges that the 34,000-member National Association of Secondary School Principals (NASSP) engineered a study of the score declines to prove the value of traditional courses over electives.[50] This influential and orthodox group was accused of selecting certain high schools so that the results would show that the more traditional the curriculum, the less susceptibility to decline. This charge was printed in the prestigious *Phi Delta Kappan* in 1979, which included a weak rejoinder from the deputy director of NASSP.

Despite the dissent, back-to-basics programs and galloping new regimes of standard testing were sweeping the nation in 1977. The largest teachers union, the National Education Association, came out against the crusade for standardized testing, but the steam-roller moved on. Less than a year after Marland appointed the Wirtz commission and a year before it reported, in 1976, some twenty-nine states had already moved toward competency-based skill programs, with minimum achievement goals tested from grade to grade. Eventually, two-thirds of the states adopted such a plan.[51] The basics spread like a plague.

The remedy is the disease

A good working definition of back-to-basics was offered by Ben Brodinsky in the hottest days of the basics crusade. In a 1977 issue of the *Phi Delta Kappan*, Brodinsky called back-to-basics 'today's media event.'[52] He also dubbed it 'nostalgia's child' for its Golden Age pedagogy. Brodinsky offered a dozen items characterizing the back-to-basics thrust:

1. Most of the school day will be devoted to reading, writing and arithmetic. Phonics is the method to teach reading rather than whole-word or phrase methods.
2. In high school, the basic subjects are English, science, math and history. Textbooks should not display non-traditional values in sex, religion or politics, nor promote criticism of the nation or the family.
3. Pedagogy is teacher-centered with stern discipline.
4. Frequent drills, homework every day, testing, and class recitation on required material.
5. Traditional letter or number-grading, issued often.
6. Corporal punishment permitted. Dress codes should be enforced, including student hair styles.
7. Academic criteria for promotion; no social promotion.
8. No 'frills' such as 'clay modeling' and 'sex education.'
9. Fewer electives, increase required courses.

10 Eliminate experimental and innovative courses, and
   methods in value-clarification.
11 Eliminate social service courses such as drug education,
   driver training, etc.
12 Return patriotism and respect for religion to schools.[53]

This was the most conservative and comprehensive formulation
of the basics movement. Brodinsky surveyed a diverse national
campaign where only parts of the total agenda were implemented
from one district to the next. Even though the whole program
rarely appeared in one place, he saw the restoration of authority
growing from the fever of testing and the rush of basics programs.
Brodinsky quoted one educator who saw back-to-basics producing
'a generation of minimal mediocrity,' a prophetic preview of a
key theme launching the alarms of 1983.

The rush to the basics made no sense to Jencks either. Given
that the NAEP recorded student gains in basic literacy and student
weakness in higher-order composition and analysis, what could
the basics do but make the strength stronger and the weakness
weaker? Jencks's long review of the test-score decline argued for
a maximal pedagogy to stimulate critical thinking.[54] Ohmann, too,
had pointed to critical literacy as the skill needed.[55] The whole
picture of fraud and irrationality made sense, however, in the
kingdom of culture war. Here we had no evidence for a Literacy
Crisis followed by a curricular remedy for strengthening skills that
were already strong. This idiocy baffled Jencks far more than it
surprised Ohmann, because Jencks shared more of the criticisms
of the 1960s than did Ohmann. However, even if Jencks was
unenthusiastic about the protest era, he was also unimpressed by
the claims of the Literacy Crisis. To him, the noble SAT had
become a dinosaur, with its linguistic antiquities so out of tune
with the discourse of the new age of mass higher education. Jencks
also disputed the language-leveling claims of the illiteracy camp
because he found that rural Iowa recorded score declines even
though it lacked the urban street language which supposedly
corrupted written English in the 1960s. He also found that children
from single-parent and working-mother homes did as well as those
from two-parent households, so the absorption of women into the
work-force could not be blamed for the declines. Targeting other
villains dear to hearts of the Literacy Crisis, Jencks found no

evidence that students were reading watered down texts. Further, if television was a great menace, why did the declines not start in the 1950s, when TV became a mass experience? And why did the declines mostly affect older students if kids of all ages were moronized by TV? There were simply no answers to such research questions which could have proven the negative influence of television. Jencks merely observed about the SAT decline that

> It probably means that high school students are not spending as much time and energy learning the things the SAT measures. . . . On its face, a test of this kind is not a very suitable device for assessing how well schools are doing their job, since it measures a great many things they do not and should not teach.[56]

Jencks's analysis points to a performance strike by students and a Legitimacy Crisis of the authorities as reasons to explain the cognitive declines mostly apparent after 1970. He agreed with Wirtz on social turbulence weakening school and teacher authority. To Jencks, the protest period discredited the old order without building a new one in its place. He explained the resulting drift in school with a colonial metaphor:

> Teachers are in many respects colonial administrators whose primary problem is simply the maintenance of public order in an alien land. When the natives become restless, they are inclined to try bread and circuses. . . . They stopped bugging students who did not want to work. In return, these students were expected not to organize open revolt against the school's nominal authority. . . . There was also a failure of nerve among those in authority. Teachers and administrators were less certain they had a right to make decisions for or about the young. Teachers were more sensitive to student opinion and more worried if students were bored.[57]

It does not flatter Jencks or the students for him to designate them as natives. But, this is the way Jencks saw the sorry dilemma of the Legitimacy Crisis, a power vacuum. The vacant detente between students and the authorities moved Lasch to the same condescending irritation:

> Under cover of enlightened ideologies, teachers (like parents)

have followed the line of least resistance, hoping to pacify
their students and to sweeten the time they have to spend in
school by making the experience as painless as possible.
Hoping to avoid confrontations and quarrels, they leave
students without guidance, meanwhile treating them as if
they were incapable of serious exertion.[58]

This Legitimacy Crisis, though unnamed and unresolved, also
drew the attention of Ernest Boyer in his important study of high
schools during the 1983 reform wave. Boyer wrote that

there is a kind of unwritten, unspoken contract between the
teachers and the students: Keep off my back and I'll keep
off yours. . . . 'Beaten down' by some of the students and
unsupported by the parents, many teachers have entered into
a . . . corrupting contract that promises a light work load in
exchange for cooperation in the classroom. Both the teacher
and the student get what they want. Order in the classroom
is preserved, and students neither have to work too hard nor
are too distracted from their own preoccupations.[59]

Another key participant in the 1983 reforms, Theodore Sizer,
noted that 'The agreement between teacher and students to
exhibit a facade of orderly purposefulness is a Conspiracy for the
Least, the least hassle for anyone.'[60] After his tour of schools
in the new crisis phase, Sizer wrote of the power struggle that
students

run schools. Their apparent acquiescence to what their elders
want them to do is always provisional. . . . However much
we adults may want them to be eagerly receptive and respectful
of our agenda for their schooling, the choice to be that or
something else – neutral, hostile, inattentive – was
unequivocally theirs. If we want our well-intentioned plans
to succeed, we'll have to inspire the adolescents to join in
them.[61]

Sizer and Boyer wrote in the third reform wave, when inspiration
of students became important again. Phase three, discussed in the
next chapter, turned to the promise of success through academics
and computers. The powerful company of Jencks, Lasch, Boyer
and Sizer, through two phases of restoration reform, noticed the

Legitimacy Crisis but missed the depressant politics of careerism and basics both. Sizer called for inspiring students and Jencks called for high intellectual rigor, but the problem of the 1970s was the 1960s, and curriculum was organized to deflect student aspirations and activism. Jencks knew that the Vietnam era and the boring curriculum of school had undermined authority. He criticized teachers for their spongy relativism and weakness of will. It was up to them to rescue education from its vacancy by imposing a thinking seriousness on students.[62] He ended up supporting the restoration drive for minimal competence while insisting that teachers must reassert the authority of maximum learning. This proved to be a peculiar kettle of fish. On the one hand, Jencks ignored how the conservative age needed minimums to restore order after the protest period. On the other hand, he assumed that maximum learning will be politically acceptable in an age of tyrannizing basics. Lastly, he did not define an alternate standard of rigor which could make learning oppose the elitism of the old order. Jencks's critique failed in the same way he said the 1960s failed, in not defining an opposition pedagogy to carry forward the building of new intelligence.

Now, this is no simple task, so if you are going to flounder, it might as well be on a Gibraltar rather than a sandbar. The terms of culture war help spell out why a new standard of intellect called for by Jencks and by Lasch could not emerge in this period. On the one hand, education devoted to mass excellence is on a collision course with the established order. An unequal society needs an unequal distribution of thinking skills. Higher education for masses of students has been a threat to political stability because it encourages economic and political demands. In the face of a deepening school malaise, it is simple enough to blame the Legitimacy Crisis on spongy teachers and illiterate students, but the origins are in the restoration need to lower critical thinking, opposition politics, and material expectations.

Education from the 1960s threatened to distribute too much power to the bottom – the power of egalitarian politics, the power of critical learning, and the power of credentials to demand higher wages. The emptiness of any single classroom simply represents the reversal of these emerging powers in education. Society and its schools do not benignly allow opposition ideology or egalitarian trends to flourish. A hierarchical order with an elite perched at the top cannot allow critical education to reach the bottom, unless it is prepared to cope with political and economic eruptions like the 1960s. None of the observers of the Legitimacy Crisis, including left critics like Jencks and Lasch, understood how restoration school policy had to prevent the trends from the 1960s from maturing.

While the economic and ideological threats from the 1960s were deflected, students did not lose their power to sabotage the system. Sizer understood this best in his picture of students' controlling what adults can do in the schools. Woe to the teachers caught between the nominal authorities above and sabotaging students below. Order is demanded by the top and freedom by the bottom. Teachers must choose between institutional or student-centered allegiance. If teachers build opposition, they risk their jobs. If they impose schoolish regimens, students make their jobs impossible to live with. This stalemate is the 'stupefaction' Lasch saw school producing. The official reports of 1983 named it 'mediocrity' and issued a call for 'excellence.' The truth is that students are not stupefied or mediocre. They are refusing to perform under these oppressive conditions, even though by now they do not know how the current conditions came to us. It is easy enough for their elders to miss the dynamic of culture war also. The restoration fought the 1960s to the current reversal. The authorities are not able to motivate students with their curricula and students are not able to replace the official courses of study. This is a degenerate condition for which conservative culture seeks authoritarian answers that only reproduce the crisis.

The price of the future

The politics of culture war fit into the troubling cognitive decline after 1970, but so did the long economic crisis. Wirtz mentioned the job shortage and Jencks referred to it also, but neither dealt in sufficient detail with the impossible loss of the American Dream. The overeducation/underemployment problem is an open sore that will not heal in the near future. The earlier promises of career education have not been kept. The basics crusade sent another large depressant message. Students read reality with more care than they read the SAT or textbooks. Working hard in school simply does not pay off, especially at the secondary or community college levels. The long reality of underemployment and the recent threat of nuclear war have put their futures in doubt. In response, they refuse scholastic discipline and work discipline in the present.

The end of a future worth working for is an inconsolable loss. One economist who discussed the depressant effect of the job crisis on test scores was Henry Levin. He wrote that students

> simply sensed that the traditional imperatives for doing well
> in school were no longer binding. Stimulated by anti-war
> dissent in the late sixties, students began to reject the authority
> of the secondary school. With the economic downturn of the
> seventies and the easing of college admissions, the trend
> accelerated. Students put less effort into their schoolwork
> and shifted away from traditional subjects required as college
> preparation.[63]

Levin doubted that back-to-basics could discipline students into higher performance:

> As long as job prospects are poor and college admissions easy,
> how likely is it that the schools will succeed in getting students
> once again to embrace rote learning, respond to strict grading
> policies, and take hard courses that don't interest them? In
> my view, this type of reform is not likely to succeed with the
> vast majority of youth because it is based on empty promises.
> Improvements on basic skills will not increase the number of
> productive jobs in the economy or the challenge of existing
> ones.[64]

A low-performance economy with a minimal basics school system cannot expect high-performance from students and teachers. Levin zeroed in on a primary cause of the performance strike. The economic crisis as a villain of 'illiteracy' would be an embarrassing topic for official Literacy Crisis supporters like Wirtz, but even left critics like Lasch and Jencks overlooked its significance.

Levin confirmed Freeman's earlier estimate (in *The Overeducated American*) that the jobs crisis would be here for a long time. If education could not get you a good job, then at least school should be intrinsically exciting, Levin thought. However, if school officials announced the end of the school-success link and invited students to learn in school for their own immediate joy, they would only undermine their legitimacy even more. Here we would have the school system itself announcing that it is a dead-end. In fact, it and the American Dream are dead together. There is no future of prosperity after this long road of school discipline, so make each school day memorable for itself. Of course, Levin wanted to rescue the life of the mind from the pits of economic disaster. But it could not work. Self-growth is the poor sister in a long-term school philosophy emphasizing work-training and civic responsibility first. School has to present itself as a mobility machine and as a nation-builder, a place for work credentials and a place for melting us all into one country. Of course, it has not influenced the rate of mobility despite its claims as a great upward equalizer,[65] and it has yet to create a racially integrated and sexually equal society. The ship of state was sinking from such great expectations of the school system, but to admit in the 1970s that education cannot deliver success was the same as admitting that the American System cannot provide the good life. This would only confirm the students' sense of school's pointlessness. It would also encourage thoughts on society's pointlessness.

Education as a rewarding personal experience was limited to the realm of adult and continuing programs. For mass education, the restoration needed an exercise in austerity, not pleasure. Levin's connection of economic crisis to back-to-basics and to the test-score decline was another impossibility for the conservative camp. To pose the economy as a cause of decline would be to blame the system. The restoration's task was to rehabilitate the system by blaming students and teachers for personal failures. As blaming-the-victim maneuvers, the Literacy Crisis and the basics crusade had considerable strengths to offer the conservative cause. Before discussing the strengths of the literacy phase, as a balance to the limits and the opposition, there is one unusual hypothesis on the test-score decline which has received virtually no attention. Did atmospheric testing of atomic weapons in the Cold War 1940s and 1950s cause student cognitive declines in the 1960s and 1970s?

No nukes!

Initial studies by Ernest J. Sternglass and Steven Bell suggested in 1979 and 1983 that atmospheric blasts influenced SAT declines after 1963. By correlating annual fall-out levels with annual SAT scores, they predicted in 1979 that declining scores would level off in 1982.[66] Sternglass, a radiological physicist, and Bell, an educational psychologist, matched SAT scores with nuclear tests and found the steepest drops in scores occurred seventeen to eighteen years after the largest above-ground detonations. They wrote that

> The initial finding that suggested our hypothesis was the fact that the sharpest decline in SAT scores ever recorded in a single year occurred in 1975, 18 years after the largest test series in Nevada, when extremely large quantities of radioactive iodine-131 were found in commercially available pasteurized milk. This short-lived fission product (with a half-life of eight days) is known to concentrate strongly in the fetal and infant thyroid. . . . This fallout acts on the thyroid of the developing fetus in the mother's womb and during infancy, when the thyroid is known to control the development of cognitive functions.[67]

The graphs they produced showed mirror reflections between the kiloton yield of any test year and the depth of the SAT decline eighteen years later. According to this measurement, the higher the atomic yield in any annual test series, the greater the SAT drop in eighteen years. This new hypothesis led them to say about the more familiar villains of the test-score decline that

> such society-wide factors as television viewing, the Vietnam War, the effect of child-spacing, the gradual change in the number and mix of students taking the tests, or poorer performance of US schools could not account for the highly localized fluctuations of SAT scores – changes that were strongest in the western states, particularly Utah, known for a high level of scholastic achievement among its predominantly Mormon population.[68]

Mormon Utah was no stronghold of protest in the 1960s and no center of educational experimentation. That traditional, religious, family-oriented state recorded the largest SAT declines. This runs counter to all the villains touted by the Literacy Crisis for the collapse of test scores. Without protest culture, without alternate education, without urban ghettoes, without family breakdown, why should students from a conservative state lead the way in declining SAT scores? It is important to recall the feverish, Cold War atomic testing of the 1950s, where a series of especially dirty blasts peppered Utah with fall-out. Cancer rates in this area were suspiciously high in the decades after the tests. In addition, the disastrous filming of *The Conqueror* took place here in the 1950s, and some forty-six members of a 220-person crew eventually developed cancer, fatal in the cases of stars John Wayne, Susan Hayward and Dick Powell. Were Sternglass and Bell on the track of the most sinister villain of them all?

Their research opened up an unexplored area of the test-score decline but it left some important questions unanswered. If cognitive growth in infants and fetuses was generally affected during the worst years of atmospheric testing, then we would expect all instruments to show score declines eighteen years later. Sternglass and Bell focused on the most visible and controversial exam, the SAT. It not only showed the worst drops eighteen years after the worst blasts, but it also *stopped* declining eighteen years after the 1963 nuclear test ban treaty between the US and the USSR, which ended atmospheric tests. This suggestive correlation will have to be applied to other cognitive instruments, including ones that showed increases in the 1970s. The Iowa achievement tests showed an extended pattern of decline in the 1970s, with twelfth-graders showing tell-tale fall-offs in the key years cited by Sternglass and Bell.[69] However, the NAEP recorded cognitive gains in some skills during these years. Can the NAEP be broken down into regional scores to prove the 'Utah model' of declines in the areas of worst exposure to radiation? This same regionalization will have to be applied to the other large national testing sequence, the American College Testing Program (ACT). ACT is taken by about a million high school seniors each year. National composite scores from 1970–82 on ACT reflect steep declines in the eighteen-year cycles following the biggest atmospheric test years of 1953, 1955 and 1957.[70] The gross score needs micro-analysis to determine if a state-by-state breakdown similar to Utah's SAT scores can verify the nuclear factor. Until nuclear exposure can be demonstrated in other batteries of test results, it will remain a promising villain-in-waiting.

The promise of American life

Despite the limits, frauds, contradictions and oppositions, the Literacy Crisis and its back-to-basics aftermath were powerful offensives. They even had distinct advantages over the earlier careerism, in reversing the 1960s. Illiteracy and basics related to curriculum and to employment in simpler ways than Marland's byzantine structures for career education. Occupationalism did have clout in lowering students' goals and in displacing critical studies, but it also possessed a grand flaw dogging its fate. It promised success and turned you into cheap labor. Even worse, after you played by the rules, you could not count on a job in your field of training. The sneering turmoil of the job market hung like an albatross around the neck of careerism. Occupationalism kept the failures of the economy visible while providing training that was at once accessible and unreliable. In contrast, back-to-basics and minimum competency testing kept the failures of students and teachers highly visible, while making *no* claims on the employment future. Basic skill programs displayed the failure at the bottom in the classroom while hiding the failure at the top in the economy. This made the literacy initiative a strong means of rehabilitating the system.

The system came under a lot of negative scrutiny in the 1960s and the business crisis of the 1970s threatened to expose it only more. How could unemployment and the declining standard of living be explained away? Students were standing with diplomas in hand in front of taxi garages and McDonald's wondering what cabs and burgers had to do with degrees in teaching or architecture. The Literacy Crisis was a second bypass of the failure of business and government to provide jobs. It became no longer enough to go after job-skills, because now there was a whole new world of skill you were missing – literacy! Until you read, wrote, spoke, added, subtracted and divided like cultured citizens, you could not expect decent employment.

Consider how the definition of 'success' moved down one giant notch from the career phase. Instead of moving on from career education to a career, success now meant moving from the remedial program to the regular school or college curriculum. Testing and remediation erected an internal gate within education. All students were tested and the arbitrary passing scales recorded gigantic failure rates. Remedial programs expanded like gold-rush towns in the late 1970s. Success in this new ballgame was permission to go on from extra-dull classes to simply dull ones. Boring school became ultra-boring, so students and teachers withdrew even further from performance, and had their withdrawal defined as their 'mediocrity' by the official observers of 1983.

Think of what the new world of illiteracy meant day to day. If you were slow in passing the new skill tests, or if frustration with the enlarged testing bureaucracy irritated you enough to make you drop out, who could you blame but yourself? Your own weakness with language and math was the root of your failure. Skill-tests measured your deficiencies in ever more precise numbers, in reading, writing and math. Three more anxiety-producing subjects would be hard to find. Each could be quantified to the nth degree. From the measurable minutiae, the authorities determined the standard of success. Fortunately for this restoration offensive, the computer revolution arrived just in time to keep track of the new ocean of test scores.

Thus, phase two of 'settling for less' was a monumental addition to conservative culture. Instead of education being the high-profile preliminary to work, the basics were now the preliminary to career *study*. Your task was not to think of a job at the end of the school rainbow, but simply to get to the job-*training* under the rainbow. Careerism still ruled the waves, but it was now supported against its subterranean weakness by a second front in literacy.

This curricular restoration of authority called for a rather perverse indictment of the individual. The protest period had brought together too many people who learned they had a right to criticize generally the whole system. Reversing this trend, careerism first, but then the Literacy Crisis even more so, identified the *isolated self* as the locus of fault and the target of correction. The logistics of illiteracy took this reversal far. Batteries of tests were taken individually. Test results were passed out individually by mail or anonymously by number on a public score sheet. In the 1960s, masses of people confronted the system together. Now, the system was confronting you, alone.

This disempowerment needed the collaboration of teachers to succeed. With many important exceptions, teachers on the whole implemented the literacy offensive. They were vigorously marshaled as test-givers, test-scorers, bad-news messengers, and remedial instructors. This made the control of teaching by the authorities more secure against the experimental threats of the 1960s. Teachers found less room to test alternate pedagogy because the official pressure to teach to the tests was formidable. Those teachers inclined to join students in protest politics found their new testing roles compromising to their solidarity with students. Teacher-support often stabilized the immature student politics of the 1960s, so the loss of any teacher-mentors was damaging. Teachers no less than students suddenly found themselves on the defensive in the face of so much punitive surveillance from the authorities. Their competency was being intensely probed in a society where business and government had to hide their own dismal incompetence.

Hide and seek

The Literacy Crisis, back-to-basics and minimum competency testing were a conservative culture of 'accountability.' They forced the bottom to be accountable to the top. The protest period had been an age of egalitarian accountability, when the bottom forced the top to answer for its wars, its racial and sexual inequalities, its pollution of the earth, etc. As Shugrue, Silberman and Goodlad found,[71] most English classes never left the basics, so they were ready to enforce authoritarian accountability. There were cracks in this facade, though.

As you go up the grades, you generally find more freedom for English teachers. The professional teacher prefers autonomy rather than standardized pedagogy and tests. In college especially, but to a large degree in high school and below, English teachers want freedom to run their own classes. They often feel that teaching the basics is as boring as studying the basics. Perhaps it is even beneath them, given their collegiate training in literature. Besides, many prefer humanistic over rote methods of instruction. Writing classes are susceptible to self-exploration, multi-media methods, value-based inquiry and interdisciplinary study. The liberal tendency in English was observed by Kitzhaber in his 1963 study of freshman composition:

> The effects of an English course cannot be isolated from the effects of a myriad of other influences which lie entirely outside the English teacher's control. . . . No one should expect a particular device or method or kind of subject matter in the English course to transform what must always be a slow and difficult process. . . . Moreover, the teaching of composition is an art, not a science, and can be approached in many ways with apparently equal success.[72]

That good teaching is an art rather than a science has broad support among educators. Such an ecumenical idea is incompatible with the dogma of rote basics and mechanical competency testing. English teachers had long exposure to literature as well as to authority in grammar, to writing as inquiry and as self-discovery as well as to the discipline of composing. Thus, the Literacy Crisis faced an unreliable, humanistic group. This opposition minority developed a wealth of creative and critical alternatives to minimal basics.[73] This heroic sideshow will be featured shortly as the antidote to the powerful thrust for the basics.

The old circus of the basics

English teachers were among the first called upon to help make some unhappy history in the restoration. Their profession was needed by business and government to ease students into a permanently diminished future. Schooling had to do more than keep people in their places. In a low-growth economy with long-term high unemployment, school had to lower the perception of what your place in society should be. The basics had played this role before and now could downwardly adjust people again.

One historical window from which to witness the depressant mystique of the basics was offered by David Tyack in a study of American education. He recorded a reconstruction-era exchange between a white genteel Southerner and a Northern schoolmarm teaching newly-freed slaves. The Southerner wrote about his fear of liberal study and his preference for the basics:

The impression among the white residents of Charlottesville is that your instruction of the colored people who attend your school contemplates something more than the communication of the ordinary knowledge implied to teaching them to read, write, cypher, etc. The idea prevails that you come among us not as an ordinary schoolteacher, but as a political missionary; that you communicate to the colored people ideas of social equality with the whites. With your first object we sympathize; the second were regard as mischievous, and as only tending to disturb the good feelings between the races.[74]

His curriculum of choice was the simple three Rs, because they posed the least empowerment of students. A supervised scribble through rote basics is the most likely curriculum to support the status quo. In the radical reconstruction days, the schoolteacher wrote back her determination to continue offering broad liberal study, an egalitarian ideal overthrown after 1877.

Nearly a century later, the depressant basics saga was retold in the new community college movement. Burton Clark's discussion of downward adjustment in higher education centered on the use of literacy classes and testing. He wrote in 1960 that

In one junior college the initial move in a cooling-out process is pre-entrance testing: low scores on achievement tests lead poorly qualified students into remedial classes. Assignment to remedial work casts doubt and slows the student's movement into bona fide transfer courses. The remedial courses are, in effect, a subcollege. The student's achievement scores are made part of a counseling folder that will become increasingly significant to him. An objective record of ability and performance begins to accumulate.[75]

Clark concluded that remedial depression was an important and even legitimate function of the mass college, but one that could not be openly acknowledged to students. He asked, 'Is the junior college to advertise that one of its major tasks is to remove from higher education those students who should not be there according to the standards of other colleges?'[76] The final part of his question revealed the class bias of seemingly neutral 'standards.' Elite universities and colleges have set the standards for mainstream campuses. For these budget units, literacy testing and remediation joined the pillar of careerism in erecting a lesser house of higher education.

Basics under every bed

The basics in education have a long history of supporting authority, so it was no surprise that schools, districts, colleges and state education departments tripped over each other in the race to set up competency programs in the 1970s. You did not count in education unless you could wring your hands over student illiteracy, tabulate an impressive amount of failure, denounce the levelers who brought us to the brink of savagery, and impose martial plans to remedy the problem. The discipline-appeal of the basics was remarkably durable. Some seven years after *Newsweek* made illiteracy into a media star, the front page of the UCLA alumni news in 1982 featured a story on 'UCLA vs. the Literacy Crisis.'[77] The article lamented the lack of basic skills in freshmen as if this was a new discovery. Apparently, nearly a decade of skills-programs were not solving the literacy problem. The issue was still so grave in 1982 that UCLA opened a multi-million dollar, computer-assisted literacy program. High-tech was being phased into low-pedagogy. This was more bad news for teaching as a profession and for the humanities. Budgets and teaching time were drained from liberal arts and from experimental courses to support the hardware, software and staffing needs of the war on illiteracy.

The politics of that war had been rehearsed in the Cold War 1950s. In that decade, according to Joel Spring, the scrubbing of left-wing ideas in society meshed with the rise of Golden Age basics in school:

> it was argued that all teaching in the curriculum not related to the teaching of basic disciplines should be eliminated, as a means of combating communism and socialism. This argument created the feeling that teaching these basic skills was linked to the promotion of American ideals and Americanism. An emphasis on basic skills would return the schools to their original state, before the invasion of un-American ideas.[78]

The protest 1960s followed, with major disruptions of schools and colleges, including UCLA, when its star basketball center, Bill Walton, was arrested in anti-war demonstrations. In the conservative reaction of the 1970s, Gene Maeroff saw strident patriotism built into the back-to-basics crusade:

> Singing the national anthem every morning does not help a child learn to read better; wearing a dress instead of jeans does not help a child improve in long division. What the schools need more than ever is a curriculum that prepares students for the fullness of life. The argument is not whether reading, writing, and mathematics ought to be emphasized. They should. All too often, however, back-to-basics is a crude exercise for denuding the curriculum of depth, a subterfuge to save money . . . it is an approach to learning, but perilously close to a rigidity that builds strong backs and weak minds.[79]

Maeroff noted the authoritarian effects of the basics, but he observed as well something about the new campaign which Brodinsky also noticed – the basics were cheap curriculum. Low-cost basics made students and teachers settle for less at the very moment they were in schools running on austerity budgets.

The depressant basics theme spread out to many corners of life. After a spectacular debut in education, the theme distributed itself through the social lattice. Several supermarket chains began marketing house brands under such labels as 'Basics,' 'No Frills,' and 'No Name.' The Grand Union 'Basics' label was attached to a chocolate-flavored syrup whose two main ingredients were corn syrup and water. In addition, major airlines began offering 'No Frills' discount fares. Laker Airlines soared for a while on such promotion but it was up to People Express to make the basics into a travel success. General Motors began advertising the attention it gives to basic detail in its cars. As late as 1983, one of the fanciest housewares stores in New York plastered its windows with the single giant word 'BASICS.' In December of that year, in yet another expensive advocacy epistle on the opinion-editorial pages of the *New York Times*, Mobil Oil argued that liberal social programs remained 'a basic problem' we would have to cut back farther if we were to 'get back to reality.' The business crisis of the 1970s and 1980s made such cuts necessary, and a new generation of politicians emerged speaking of 'an era of limits.' The diminished vocabulary even appeared in this time in popular books like E. F. Schumacher's *Small is Beautiful* and Francis Lappé's *Diet for a Small Planet*. The sails of the 1960s were being drawn in rapidly.

The basics motif tilted discussion towards the theme of economic exhaustion. Big dreams and big demands were made out-of-sync with the new recession. It appeared that blind fate rather than economic policy or corporate investment made the basics necessary. Local governments promoted blind fate by accepting the depression in public programs without a whimper. Municipalities began selective cuts, protecting what were named 'the basic services': police, fire, sanitation. In one of the more dramatically bankrupt cities, New York, cutting back to the basics did not include cutting off subsidies to banking and real estate interests. Executives making hundreds of thousands of dollars a year met to decide how much the average New Yorker would have to give up after the fiscal crisis of 1976.

The basics idea spread the 'settle for less' policy throughout society. One of the more curious forms of the basics theme came out of a large construction conference in 1981. The *New York Times* reported on the 'Home of the Future: Size Will Shrink But Not the Price: Builders at Gathering See Return to the House of the 50s.' This report summed up the ironic conquests of a disabled restoration. Its language referred to the housing crisis in words appropriate to the Literacy Crisis:

> More than 40,000 of the nation's home builders gathered here [Las Vegas] this weekend amid their industry's worst slump in almost a decade, and they sent a message to Americans: Think small.
>
> Like the American automobile, they said, the American dream house is shrinking. But, they said, be prepared to pay more for less.
>
> The house of the future, they said, is likely to be the house of the past – much like the modest no-frills homes mass-produced by American builders in the years after World War II.
>
> 'We have to go back-to-basics, to the kind of house you built in the 50s,' said Thomas Garofalo, a builder in Waterbury, Conn.[80]

Less than three years later, this 'settling for less' and 'paying more for less' in housing was confirmed in a 1983 *Wall Street Journal* front-page story, 'The "Affordable Home" is Tiny and Not Really Cheap.'[81]

To adjust people to the injustice of 'settling for less' and 'paying more for less,' the basics motif in school and society bathed daily life from ankle to earlobe. The classroom, the workplace, the job market, all became stations for diminished expectations. Austerity eased itself in through the claims of illiteracy in students and the spectacle of economic exhaustion in society at large. The collapse in literacy, however, was as manufactured as the economic 'cold bath'[82] thrown on society as a political coolant in the early Nixon years. With the depression of aspirations and activism, and with the demand to produce more and pay more for less, student-teacher-worker alienation grew. The performance strike in the classroom and on the job reflected not mass mediocrity but rather popular resistance to austerity. The political mystique of the 1960s and the economic mystique of the American Dream made the programs of authority bitter.

From dream-house to out-house

Phase two of 'settling for less' advanced in school and society through two powerful ideas whose time had come – the Literacy Crisis and back-to-basics. They helped explain away the economic crisis and the test-score crisis by blaming students for illiteracy. This blame 'proved' the inadequacy of most students and the superiority of some, thus justifying inequality in school results and in social status. Making inequality legitimate again after the strong egalitarianism of the 1960s also helped restore the authorities who sat at the top of the social hierarchy.

Testing and remediation in the basics not only produced scores justifying inequality, but they also threw up more obstacles to getting a good job through education. As students scrambled through one ingenious testing category to another, their progress towards credentials slowed. The 'father of career education,' Sidney Marland, who saw the dangerous overeducation crisis coming, and the prophet of 'the overeducated American,' Richard Freeman, could breathe sighs of relief for all the Literacy Crisis did to make the road to graduation slower. In the logic of official manpower planning through curriculum, the underemployment crisis would be named an overeducation crisis, and then overeducation would be solved by manufacturing 'underachievement' through illiteracy.

The economic system would be rescued not by the creation of *more good jobs* that deserved higher wages, but rather by the creation of *fewer job seekers* with credentials suitable for the limited number of high-paying jobs. For this culture war through literacy, correct usage and Standard English were important weapons. Far from being neutral standards of excellence, they were absorbed in a campaign to defend an irrational system against exposure. The politics of curriculum pointed to the fake problem of language to distract from the real problem of an unequal and unworkable economy. Ideology is one thing, and angelic neutrality is another. So, official policy continued to ignore evidence of student strength in basic skills,[83] because the illiteracy theme was too important for the conservative reversal of the 1960s.

Angelic complaints from traditionalists that language was collapsing were accompanied by more direct means to produce lower aspirations. At the same time that the Literacy Crisis became a household word, open admission to college was being restricted by entry exams, by higher tuition, and by raised gates between community and senior colleges. Complex maneuvers were needed to win the restoration culture war. Literacy and correct usage were rushed in to support a system falling quickly into ideological ruin.

Life among the ruins

Even though back-to-basics advocates ignored student achievement in the basics and then carried the day with minimum competency programs, many opposition voices developed humanistic alternatives to literacy. One widely-read alternative was Peter Elbow's *Writing Without Teachers* (1973). He popularized the 'teacherless classroom' as a self-directed learning method. Elbow was part of a pedagogical undercurrent in the 1970s towards a creative composing process in the classroom. Another scholar who broke with mechanical literacy techniques was Mina Shaughnessy.

Her influential work in the City University of New York led to a widely-discussed guide for the basic writing teacher, *Errors and Expectations* (1977). Shaughnessy had one leg in traditionalism and one in experimentalism. Her description of the writing dilemma of open admissions classrooms captured this duality:

> Not surprisingly, the essays these students wrote during their first weeks of class stunned the teachers who read them. Nothing it seemed, short of a miracle, was going to turn such students into writers. . . . Here were teachers trained to analyze the belletristic achievements of the centuries, marooned in basic writing classrooms with adult student writers who appeared by college standards to be illiterate.[84]

Five years later, she remarked, these same teachers underwent many changes in attitudes and methods. However, many others did *not* change, supporting the eventual counter-attack against open admissions.

Shaughnessy was one writing teacher who tried to situate instruction in the actual language habits of her students. From this sympathetic and inside view of what student 'errors' meant, she proposed teaching correct usage based on the origins and kinds of writing mistakes actually made. This exerted a pull against mechanical grammar classes, but Shaughnessy did not begin with the highly-developed student voice and did not investigate the question of critical literacy, or writing for what? Still, she acknowledged the potentials of her students and the limits of what she and other teachers know about the learning process:

> Without a better understanding than we now have of the spoken language of the young men and women who are classified as basic writers and of the differences between written and spoken language, we cannot determine with accuracy what the students already know but cannot put into practice because of their stiffness or hesitancy with the medium of writing. . . . Lacking a model, we cannot say with certainty just what progress in writing ought to look like for the Basic Writing student and more particularly how the elimination of error is related to their overall improvement.[85]

A basics alternative, more inserted into the Literacy Crisis debate, was offered by Stephen Judy in *The ABCs of Literacy*

(1980). Judy made his opposition to the back-to-basics camp evident from the beginning. He accused official basics advocates of ignoring the fact 'that heavy stress on skills instruction historically has *never* done a particularly good job of creating a literate society; nor is there significant evidence to suggest that there has been a wholesale abandonment of skill work and drill in the schools.'[86] Judy saw in the illiteracy camp a contempt and repugnance for the students declared illiterate. 'Every outcry of "back-to-basics",' he wrote, 'has followed on the heels of major expansion of the educational system.'[87] He took a celebratory attitude to open admissions similar to Shaughnessy's, that the expansion of education should be congratulated and met on its own terms.

Judy proposed literacy as *an act of knowing* rather than as a mechanical command of correct usage. For a writing pedagogy to stimulate literacy as discovery of meaning, it had to follow some priorities, according to Judy:

- People should learn to read and write by reading and writing, not by piecemeal drills in writing mechanics or reading mechanics.
- The literacy class must be informed by what students know, what they can do, and how they already use language.
- These classes must be constructed for each classroom situation by the teacher, not from the outside by standard tests or syllabi.
- Literacy study should be interdisciplinary and taught across the curriculum.
- Community members should be brought in as resources and students should do field projects out of school, in the community [a non-traditional, non-scholastic 'paideia', according to Judy, where learning, experience and community intersect].
- Teachers should write with their students.
- Student talk is important as a skill for oral inquiry.
- Teach students to be their own editors, and their own peer-evaluators.
- Encourage collaborative learning projects.
- Use magazines and paperbacks over textbooks.
- Publish student work constantly to create a student literature.[88]

These were some of the suggestions Judy made for a humanistic literacy program. He thought optimistically that if classes were made smaller or if schools could be closed for a year so that all parties could talk things over, the dilemma of the Literacy Crisis and back-to-basics could be solved.

Two years after Judy's intervention in the Literacy Crisis, Herb Kohl offered an even more political alternative for basics pedagogy. In *Basic Skills* (1982), Kohl began from the premise that education should stir students to democracy, critical thinking and independence. He challenged the conservative myth of the Golden Age which underlay the debate on literacy: 'One thing that almost everyone expressed was a desire that the public schools return to their former excellence, that we find a way to go back to the basics. I pushed people on their ideas about this Golden Age of Education, and people acknowledged that if it existed, they hadn't been part of it.'[89]

Like Judy, Kohl did not examine the economics of austerity behind curricular austerity. Instead, Kohl wrote a wonderfully imaginative account of a 'teaching family' whose fate was enveloped in the past two centuries of public education. Further, Kohl exposed authority in the new basics upsurge: 'The need to drill students in so-called basic skills is used to mask the more desperate attempt to control students' behavior. . . . Because the system is rigid and hierarchical, creativity in teaching has been replaced by ingenuity in categorization.'[90] As an alternative, Kohl proposed six basics:

– Ability to use language well, centered on the study of Standard English as well as on the ways rules get made and changed.
– Ability to think through problems and to test solutions, the powers of critical thought and of experimentalism.
– Ability to use science and tools to accomplish projects, from the tool of the hammer to the tool of the computer.
– Ability to use imagination in the making and appreciation of art, which is an essential, not a 'frill.'
– Ability to understand how people function in groups and in history, in studying political change, economic development, work, and cultural differences.

- Ability to continue learning on your own, to teach others, and to learn from others outside school.

Like Judy, Kohl emphasized opening pedagogy to the power of the students' voices. Further, he focused on the value of printing presses for students in schools, through which they could constantly print up and distribute their own literature. He also advocated such student-generated projects as a self-help medical clinic in school and environmental field-studies outside school.

Kohl's 'open classroom' model for the basics still absorbed Standard English as the primary language vehicle. This preference was not shared by Robert Pattison in his history of usage, *On Literacy* (1982).[91] Pattison proposed teaching correct usage as a second language to everyday speech. He agreed with Judy that Standard English was a sorting device stacked against non-elite students. If it was studied as a foreign tongue, it would be brought down from its political pedestal, while the rich idiom of conversation would be elevated to critical discourse. In such an egalitarian framework, students would not be penalized for their own idioms. They would learn the standard forms for access to traditional classics and for social survival, in terms of getting jobs and legal needs. He denied universal claims of excellence for correct usage, describing it as the language of the triumphant middle classes. To back up his claims, he offered a close reading of correct form in various societies since ancient Greece.

In his survey of the temporal and political nature of correct usage, Pattison saw literacy standards linked to the ruling powers of an era, who defined acceptable forms of language. He denied that literacy equals mere reading and writing skills, that literate individuals are more civilized than the unlettered, that literacy spurs economic growth, and that literacy promotes democracy. Literacy education is entirely compatible with authoritarian rule, he asserted:

> The teaching of correct written form has for the state the
> collateral advantage that, besides creating a generally
> intelligible medium of communication free of ambiguity, it
> inspires in the learner respect for authority. The ideal
> bureaucrat or soldier will not only spell well but will
> acknowledge the competence of a dictionary. His training
> has not only the practical application of good spelling, but the

101

more formidable result of instilling in him a sense of
regularity and obedience.[92]

Pattison understood the historical and affective consequences of
correct usage in ways that eluded Shaughnessy and Judy. His
second-language approach to Standard English was an egalitarian
gesture. The formal usage coming down from the pedestal was to
link up with the slang rising up from the gutter. This Utopian
vision insisted on literacy as 'consciousness of the problems posed
by language . . . a potent form of consciousness. . . . It remakes
our lives.' The problem is, what would everyday language become
once it is self-conscious and empowered? Similarly, how would
traditional knowledge change once empowered learners critically
examine the classics? Pattison tended to view the two idioms –
correct usage versus the language of rock culture – as static entities
which would not be themselves transformed by *the passionate
awakening of the mind*, as Pattison described genuine literacy. I
will return to this question of literacy and empowerment in the
last chapter, on opposition alternatives.

Using the power of rock, rocking the power of usage

The activist education scene of the 1960s was testing the power
of unofficial literacy. The empowering potential of unsupervised
learning is education's promise. Uncomfortable with the drift of
politics, the authorities countered in the 1970s with strategies for
containment, one of which was based in a sanctioned form of
literacy. The language-testing offensive turned the tables on
students, who were forced to shift to the defensive in the 1970s.
Still, the clock could not be turned back to the Golden Age before
the 1960s. Back-to-basics and minimal curricula produced a standoff between resisting students and illegitimate authorities.

This student-school stalemate between boredom and anger on
one side, and authority on the other, grew so severe that a new
'mediocrity' crisis was declared in 1983. A third phase of official
reform burst on the scene. The alarms about the decline of
education were so grave, that only the Sputnik furor after 1957
equaled the concern. A great debate was launched, in search of

academic 'excellence.' The restoration had not yet found order and consensus.

4 Settling for less, 1982-4:
the war for 'excellence' and against 'mediocrity'
authority and inequality disguised as
excellence and high-tech

It is possible that our entire public education system is nearing collapse.

> John Goodlad, *A Place Called School* (1983)

The rhetoric of toughness is so predominant today. There isn't the idealism and compassion that has been behind significant school reform in the past.

> Theodore Sizer, quoted in *Time* (1983)

National interests must be served. But where in all of this are the students? Where is the recognition that education is to enrich the living individual?

> Ernest L. Boyer, *High School* (1983)

Our national defense, our social stability and well-being and our national prosperity will depend on our ability to improve education and training.

> *Action for Excellence* (1983)

From the bottom to the top of the system, professional social reformers abound. They are more interested in equality than in excellence. . . . The war for the public school will be fought at the local level, where parents and back-to-basics educators find themselves in alliance with a conservative White House.

> Peter Brimelow, *Fortune* (1983)

Annus mirabilus

Our once unchallenged preeminence in commerce, industry, science and technological innovation is being overtaken by

104

competitors throughout the world. . . . If an unfriendly foreign
power had attempted to impose on America the mediocre
educational performance that exists today, we might well have
viewed it as an act of war. . . . We have even squandered
the gains in student achievement made in the wake of the
Sputnik challenge. . . . We have, in effect, been committing
an act of unthinking, unilateral educational disarmament.

A Nation at Risk (1983)[1]

With this lament and memorable call to arms, the National
Commission on Excellence in Education (NCEE) launched a
thousand ships in 1983. Chaired by David P. Gardner, former
Army intelligence officer[2] and President-Elect of the University
of California, the NCEE made 1983 a hinge of history. In the
year of wonder in education, a score of other major studies came
hot on the heels of the Gardner report while over a hundred
commissions set up shop to work on school reform.[3] From the
highest levels, alarms spread on the state of public education.

Education made it to the headlines and to the evening news
again. The media brought the bad news into every living room
and put the school crisis on the front-pages. For fifteen years,
the country had been hearing too much bad news – Vietnam,
Watergate, Abscam, oil shocks, interest rates, joblessness,
inflation, CIA meddling, acid rain, Love Canal, Three Mile
Island, nuclear-plant cost overruns, Beirut. Suddenly, in 1983, the
worst news of all came from the classroom. What went wrong?

The NCEE warned that a 'rising tide of mediocrity' was
drowning education and thus threatening our future as a nation.
The new generation of students and their teachers were do-little
underachievers. This deep performance strike, here named
'mediocrity,' was an intolerable malaise. So much official finger-
pointing, hand-wringing and agenda-making meant that something
big was in the air. A meridian of some kind had been crossed.
The Reagan Administration, vulnerable for its cuts in school aid,
for weakening affirmative action, for desiring to close the federal
Office of Education, for supporting school prayer and tax-credits
for private schools, took the offensive by declaring an education
crisis. The debut of *A Nation at Risk* was moved from a journalists'
conference to the White House, to give the new campaign a fast

start in that fateful Spring of 1983. Could the massive stir from above generate public support below?

Public confidence in all institutions was in as bad a malaise as the school system itself. The bad news and hard times of the 1970s reduced public support for the traditional leaders and institutions of American life, to all-time lows according to the study by Lipset and Schneider.[4] In 1981, Kenneth Keniston wrote that 'The majority of Americans now believe that government serves the interests of big business rather than of all the people, that birth and connections matter more than effort and ability in getting ahead.'[5] Rising doubts about the fairness of the system did more than disable the conservative drive for consensus. The spread of disaffection had a broad social pathology. Vandalism, alcoholism, drug-taking, and more crime and violence in daily life were some signs of a disintegrating society. Other signs closer to the 1983 reports involved the declining performance and productivity in school and on the job. These everyday forms of resistance are where people vote on the system. That vote showed deteriorating confidence in the state of affairs. This is the political and affective crisis underlying the school alarms of 1983. By that year, high-placed policy-makers faced tides of popular alienation. To recognize it for what it was – mass alienation – they would have had to investigate official policy instead of students and teachers.

The crooked path to excellence was paved with a lower standard of living. School budget cuts, depressant reforms in curriculum, and wage-freezes for teachers and other workers helped the tide of discontent gather. By themselves, career education and back-to-basics were a ten-year culture war on the 'frills.' The quality of your education can be considered as part of your standard of living. As the mass of students got less and less through the 1970s, they quite naturally gave less and less. Students not only reacted to the degraded conditions for learning, but they also responded rationally to the lower payoff on educational investment. They knew about the 'overeducation' crisis. It meant taking jobs beneath your credentials and your hopes, so why work harder for degrees or set sights high? 'Overeducation' balanced precariously with official claims of 'illiteracy' until the commissions after 1983 remodeled the crisis in terms of general teacher-student under-achievement. The voice of authority was speaking loudly again, even though it had taken a beating in the 1960s and even in the 1970s. Who would listen to it now?

Suspect authorities reinterpreted the disorder their own policies had produced. To capture initiative for yet another wave of reform, policy-makers chose big formulations and sweeping alarms. Single-issue campaigns for careerism and the basics were obsolete by 1983. These one-dimensional reforms were displaced by a general program for excellence, which is a key word in the lexicon of traditionalism. The new culture war around excellence and mediocrity used global rhetoric on economic recovery, world trade, and national security. The comprehensive overhaul of curriculum proposed extensive new requirements and new testing of students, as well as new management regimens for teachers. For students, the basics were redefined in an elaborate package amounting to 'ultra-careerism' and 'ultra-basics.' As will be explained shortly, the new school road to the job market was spelled out in baroque detail. Business forces moved even more aggressively into curriculum and the schools, in an education analogue to the economic restructuring taking place under supply-side austerity.[6] In school and in society, the official program of the 1980s called for transferring resources to the elite, to the private sector from the public, to high-tech development at the expense of other sectors, to a new arms race as the leading factor of economic recovery, and to weakening union organization in the centralizing of more control by management. In effect, curriculum after 1983 shaped itself around a larger 'social contract' being written by the commissions for the rest of us. The authors of this new overhaul came to the education panels from the most elite research universities and from the most important corporations.[7]

Phase three, then, intended more than merely reversing the 1960s. By 1983, the 1960s were already history, good material for nostalgia. Further, the single-issue reversal strategies of the 1970s had merely produced a stalemate in education. If the success and failure of careerism and back-to-basics were the *de*activation of students, the task for the 1983 reforms was to *re*activate them in directions needed by business and government. The appeal to excellence and to nationalism meant to provoke fires of sanctioned achievement. But could another round of austerity accomplish this? Could even more disempowerment of the bottom inspire performance by teachers and students? How could a comprehensive plan make its way through two giant teacher unions, fifty state school departments, 16,000 local districts, 80,000 individual schools, and over 40 million students and teachers? If the reform failed, the standoff could degenerate into a worse malaise or even into a new era of protest. The stakes grew higher with each episode of reform.

1983 and after was the most risky and complex episode of all. It more than summed up the culture war of the first two phases. The total agenda of 1983 put the whole system up for scrutiny and reform. This official gamble stimulated debate on how all of education and society arrived at such an impasse. Ironically, the system itself reached a point where it encouraged critical looks at the system. In unraveling this moment, this chapter will survey the rhetoric of alarm, the offical agendas for reform, and the surface themes from which the overhaul emerged. Then, 'subter-ranean' issues will be examined, from between the lines, in regard to racism, the arms race, anti-unionism, and the sources of econ-omic decline. Lastly, these pages will discuss the prospects for success and failure of the third wave.

A four-alarm fire

After the NCEE declared in *A Nation at Risk* that 'History is not kind to idlers. . . . America's place in the world will either be forfeited or secured,' *Newsweek* rushed a sensational cover-story to press on this 'scathing' look at education. *Newsweek* suggested a state of siege – 'Can the schools be saved?'[8] The paragraphs told us that 'The writing on the blackboard in Washington last week was bleak. . . . The sum of this report is that one of the fondest assumptions of American life – progress from one gener-ation to the next – has been nearly shattered.'[9] The loss of the American Dream was blamed on bad schools. This suggested that the NCEE was getting its message across, that educational mediocrity was disarming and depleting the nation. The beauty of this explanation for the economic crisis was that school was the solution as well as the problem: education for recovery.

The loss and recovery of the good life was only one herring dumped at the schoolhouse door. A second explanation of the school-economic crisis was suggested by the cover photograph itself. Under the large words 'Saving Our Schools' there is a picture of a high school classroom. At the center of the photo, a pink-shirted white girl raises her hand in a crowded class. She is nearly surrounded by minority students all wearing blue shirts. They are also raising their hands. There is a sleazy suggestion here of what needed saving from what. The racial dimension of 'excellence' was the least noble feature of the 1983 agenda, and it will be discussed in some detail in the later part of this section.

To build perception of 'mediocrity,' the NCEE turned to the SAT as one key index of several showing decline in achievement. The NCEE presentation of the SAT repeated earlier distortions. In a now familiar litany, the NCEE pointed to the long SAT decline from 1963–80, but it chose to ignore some key facts. The SAT *began* declining in the heyday of the post-Sputnik reforms. The SAT *stopped* declining the year before the NCEE reported. In 1982, black SAT scores *were rising faster* than white scores. This complicated picture of reality conveniently disappeared in each restoration episode. Such facts in 1983 unfortunately contradicted some of the NCEE's claims, namely, that schools squandered gains made in the wake of Sputnik and the continuing decline still puts the country at risk. The NCEE was also mute on the positive NAEP scores from the 1970s, choosing instead to quote selective results which indicated a literacy crisis. The manipulated picture of mediocrity in *A Nation at Risk* claimed that US students scored below high-schoolers of other countries, that some 23 million American adults and some 13 per cent of 17-year-olds were functionally illiterate, that gifted students scored below potential, and that science and math study was drastically down.[10] But was functional illiteracy better or worse now than ten or twenty years ago? Could you compare US high schools to other Western school systems which sent on a more elite fraction to secondary study than we do here?[11] Science and math study was declining, but so were liberal arts in this period, thanks to the defunding of school budgets, the career imbalance of curriculum, and the poor job market for graduates in these subjects. The NCEE avoided locating the math-science dropoff in the context of economic decline under the restoration. *A Nation at Risk* played off patriotic and Golden Age sentiments when it pointed out that 'Americans like to think of this Nation as the preeminent country for generating the great ideas and material benefits for all mankind. The citizen is dismayed at a steady 15-year decline in industrial productivity, as one great American industry after another falls to world competition.'[12] The villain of decline is 'productivity,' which pointed the finger at mediocre performances in school and on the job, by students, teachers and workers. An unproductive population has brought us to such a fix. School was complicit because of easy grading, easy admission to college, too little homework, watery textbooks, too little writing and reading, poor teaching and weak incentives for excellence among teachers.

A month after the NCEE bombshell, the Twentieth Century Fund issued its crisis report, *Making the Grade*. Its commission of high academics was badly divided on what federal policy had done wrong in the past twenty years, but the report still insisted that 'There are few problems more critical than those facing the nation's public schools. . . . By almost every measure – the commitment and competency of teachers, student test scores, truancy and drop-out rates, crimes of violence – the performance of our schools falls far short of expectations.'[13] The majority of the Fund's panel accused federal policy of tilting too much to 'equality' since the 1960s, thus slighting 'quality' in education.

The major alarm in the next month, June 1983, was *Action for Excellence: A Comprehensive Plan to Improve Our Nation's Schools*. It was second only to *A Nation at Risk* in stylistic grandeur and political impact. Published by the governor's group called the Education Commission of the States (ECS), this document was sometimes referred to as 'the Hunt report,' after Governor James B. Hunt of North Carolina, who chaired the ECS Task Force on Education for Economic Growth which produced the study. Hunt had a crowd of executives from fourteen major corporations joining the governors and the one union official on the task force. The report said

> There are few national efforts that can legitimately be called
> crucial to our national survival. Improving education in
> America – improving it sufficiently and improving it now – is
> such an effort. . . . The stakes are high. If we fail, our children
> will experience a growing sense of loss and failure: a sense of
> falling behind that will reflect the reality of falling behind.[14]

Hunt carried forward at the states' level what the NCEE launched from the federal center. Washington and ECS became two national leaders of the new phase. The malaise in schooling, economics and public opinion made tandem offensives necessary. *Action for Excellence* characterized the leadership crisis this way:

> Our greatest overall educational deficiency in the United States, however, may be one that is impossible to assess through achievement tests, and impossible to measure by the usual yardsticks for gauging the adequacy of our public commitment to education. *This deficiency is our absence of clear, compelling, and widely agreed-upon goals for improving educational performance.*[15]

Hunt's devotion to ending the performance strike made him the best-known figure in the third phase, while California's chief of schools and Tennessee's Governor followed second.[16]

The alarms continued after Hunt, as 'in search of excellence' became a best-selling theme in school and society.[17] The next major statement belonged to the National Science Board (NSB). In September 1983 its special commission on pre-college education issued a dramatic study on *Educating Americans for the 21st Century*. In stylistic passion equal to the others before, the NSB document warned that

> The nation that dramatically and boldly led the world into the age of technology is failing to provide its own children with the intellectual tools needed for the 21st century. . . . Already the quality of our manufactured products, the viability of our trade, our leadership in research and development, our standards of living, are strongly challenged. Our children could be stragglers in a world of technology. We must not let this happen; America must not become an industrial dinosaur. We must not provide our children a 1960s education for a 21st century world.[18]

The NSB rose to the math-science crisis by offering precisely costed-out plans for reviving tech in school. The sums overwhelmed the paltry education program of the Reagan Administration. Where Reagan set aside $50 million for science programs in 1983, the NSB called for *$1.5 billion in the first year alone*. The next decade would require joint federal-state financing of some $5 billion more, for curriculum development, pilot projects for selective programs, teacher training, special student scholarships, and computer hardware subsidies for school purchases.

Besides announcing the costly teeth of the third phase, *Educating Americans for the 21st Century* also named the 1960s as the age of obsolete, mediocre curriculum. Other reports implicitly criticized the 1960s as originating too much student choice in courses. The Twentieth Century Fund joined the NCEE and ECS claims that federal monies had tilted too far to programs for the disadvantaged, thanks to the 1960s. The NSB's war on mediocrity also supported the earlier NCEE charge that students had become mathematical and scientific 'illiterates.' This new formulation of illiteracy in the third phase advanced beyond the claims of the earlier Literacy Crisis. Only the Three Rs collapsed in 1975. In 1983, illiteracy meant all of math, science, technology, writing, academic information and higher-order reasoning. The official appraisal of student skills curved downward dramatically in 1983 in a spiral that might match the dive of the economy. In the restoration world of chicken and egg, the school dive caused the prosperity dive. The NSB defined the cognitive-economic relationship like this:

> Alarming numbers of young Americans are ill-equipped to work in, contribute to, profit from and enjoy our increasingly technological society. Far too many emerge from the nation's elementary and secondary schools with an inadequate grounding in mathematics, science, and technology. This situation must not continue. . . . We must return to the basics, but the 'basics' of the 21st century are not only reading, writing and arithmetic. They include communication, and higher problem-solving skills, and scientific and technological literacy.[19]

The NCEE had begun the reinvention of the 'basics' in 1983, which the NSB here took up enthusiastically. The required 'basics' grew higher as the economic crisis grew worse. The amount of academic work now considered a minimum for the job market was arbitrarily and unilaterally extended.

The 'new basics' represented 'ultra-careerism' and 'ultra-literacy.' This was a sophisticated leap beyond the single-reforms of the 1970s.[20] Students after 1983 could not expect good employment from simple career-training or from simple mastery of the

112

'old basics.' Phase three presented career education and basic skills as merely the road to cheap labor. The Hunt report spelled this out as the difference between 'basic jobs' and 'learning to learn jobs.'[21] To get over the hump to 'learning to learn jobs' and then on to 'professional jobs,' you had to devote yourself to what the NCEE called 'the new basics.'[22]

'The new basics' were math, science, computers, higher-order reasoning, and new-old academic study in English, social studies and foreign language. The vocabulary of 'basics' drew on the cultural capital of phase two because back-to-basics was still a powerful theme in the ongoing austerity. But phase three intended to overcome the depressant effects of minimal skill programs, with a Catch-22 breakout. The Catch-22 in the reinvention of the basics kept adding new layers of requirements for success. Once, career-clusters and basic literacy were the hoops to jump through; 1983 added an immense academic layer to these demands. Satisfying the minimums was not enough to gain good employment. New maximums adjusted the formula for success to the heightened performance desired from students. The American Dream was dangled before students' eyes again in 1983 but it was put in the distant future. In reality, it was in our distant pasts. The farther away 'the good life,' the greater the required curriculum to get there. A long economic crisis set the model for a lengthening of the basics.

The NSB put 'the good life' in the twenty-first century. The new social contract through curriculum set the payoff to students far enough into the future to make it easy on the authorities. The official consensus forming itself around extended basics, new long-term academic requirements, and a distant Dream, was helped along by a key report from the College Board (CB). The CB report called *Academic Preparation for College* appeared in the very heat of the alarms. While the NSB spoke of math, science and technology as the new basics, and the NCEE report *A Nation at Risk* spoke of the 'five new basics,' the CB went several better by inventing *six* 'Basic Academic Competencies' and *six* 'Basic Academic Subjects.'[23] Computer competency was added separately to make it come out as a baker's dozen agenda. This small, articulate document, sometimes referred to as 'the green book' because of its cover, precisely defined the cognitive outcomes for 'the new basics.' The redefined demands for basic *competencies* were in reading, writing, speaking and listening, math, reasoning and studying. The academics newly defined as part of the basics called for exacting goals in English, the arts, math, science, social science and foreign language. The words 'competencies' and 'subjects' coveniently distinguished non-college and college-bound tracks for the high school. Yet, the CB declared that leaders of business and industry thought academic training good even for those students going directly to work after high school. This suggested that academics were to be the universal menu. Twelve years earlier, career education had been declared the curriculum for all. Then, all students were tested for minimal basic skills. Now, the academic programs which had traditionally served only an elite and which had been decidedly shelved in the first two campaigns against the 1960s were brought out for all.

This decisive turn away from simple occupationalism and minimum proficiency was pronounced in phase three, from *The Paideia Proposal* of 1982 to Theodore Sizer's crisis report of 1984, *Horace's Compromise*.[24] It informed the major policy statements from the NCEE, the ECS, the NSB, the CB, as well as the demurring studies from a liberal undercurrent, in the Boyer and Goodlad reports.[25] On the one hand, the third phase reformers faced the monumental problem of activating students and teachers out of their performance strikes. So a minimal, depressant third wave would only make the school malaise deeper. This required curricular pyrotechnics, high ideals. What else did they have on hand except high-tech and academics to meet this need? On the other hand, the recognition that depressant careerism and depressant minimum basics had chilled things too far was conditioned by the ongoing economic crisis. The still-exhausted, still-stagnant economy of early 1983 made it imperative to blur the troubling link between education and employment. A long road through academics for all students was one way of delivering more school now, promising more prosperity in the future, without requiring anything from the economy in the present. A weak job market amounted to a moving target which the pistol of education kept missing. Less direct aiming and less shooting meant more credibility to school and society both. Long-term academics as 'the new basics' extended the curricular path to a general terrain called future employment without having to specify exactly what your job might be later on. The new social contract thus required students to work harder now for an unspecified future. This released society from having to meet any specific student expectations. Thus, phase three's 'new basics' reinvented 'settling for less': demand high-performance from students now, promise a big payoff in the future, deliver little now.

The wizards of excellence

As a consensus emerged at the top, the alarms kept appearing. In a Carnegie study on *The Condition of Teaching*, Emily Feistritzer wrote that

> All the data about who currently is going into the teaching profession are grim. Not only are far fewer persons choosing teaching as a career, but the academic caliber of those who are is decreasing. The reasons for the decline in quantity and quality of those electing to become classroom teachers are not hard to understand: low pay, poor working conditions, little opportunity for upward mobility within the profession, and lack of status in society. . . . Over half the teachers in a 1981 survey said they either certainly or probably would not become a teacher again. This is a shocking increase in the number of dissatisfied teachers.[26]

Her report provided a mountain of data supporting the teacher performance strike. The research Feistritzer assembled was in support of the main Carnegie contribution to the third phase, Ernest L. Boyer's *High School*. Boyer noted that 'After years of shameful neglect, educators and politicians have taken the pulse of the public schools and found it faint.'[27] Another major report repeated the alarms but broke with the stylistic grandeur and the traditional remedies – John Goodlad's *A Place Called School*. Goodlad declared that 'American schools are in trouble. In fact, the problems of schooling are of such crippling proportions that many schools may not survive.'[28] Goodlad was a progressive stalwart who looked more closely inside the classroom than any other researcher. His deviant and largely ignored point of view will be discussed later on. As a final note to the major alarms, there was John Brademas's end-year report on graduate education which sounded a 'warning to all who care about America's future: our graduate enterprise is troubled; so is our national capacity to face and master change, to chart and define the future, and to enjoy the rich blessings of democracy secure in the knowledge that others will not create the future for us.'[29] Brademas echoed the Business-Higher Education Forum's claim that 'We stand at the hinge of history,'[30] requiring the kinds of sacrifices a nation makes in wartime. If education did not help restore American competitiveness in the world, democracy could be lost along with prosperity, the Forum warned.

The warnings and alarms set the stage for a remarkable convergence of opinion at the top. The authorities developed a consensus which focused mainly on high school and which had no room for progressives like John Goodlad. The consensual agenda was the new social contract through curriculum which reorganized teachers as well as students in public education. The key items of consensus could be summarized in the following outline:

1 *Raise academic requirements* – Minimum competencies have been set too low. Expect more writing and reading from students. Reduce student choice in curriculum, so that *all* students study academics in high school. Replace electives with required math and science study. Collapse general and vocational courses into one core academic track.

2 *Computer education* must enter the curriculum as a part of basic literacy. This can be part of requiring more math and science.

3 *Higher-order reasoning* should increase students' problem-solving abilities as well as their capacity to adjust to changing work demands.

4 *More time on learning tasks* – Lengthen the school year to 200 or 220 days. Lengthen the school day from 6.5 to 8 hours. Free teachers from non-instructional tasks like hall monitoring so that they can teach more. Assign more homework each night and require more textbook study. Spend more time on Standard English and correct usage.

5 *Stricter discipline* – Separate unruly students from mainstream classes and expel the violent ones. Parents should cooperate in encouraging respect for teachers.

116

Segregate problem-students into special academies. Make conduct rules clear and enforce them firmly.

6 *Make it harder to enter college* – Open admissions discourages students from high performance. Send an academic message to high schools by raising admissions standards to college. Colleges should require study in the new academic basics, including foreign language, for admission.

7 *Merit pay and master teachers* – The salary scales for teachers are too gradual. Recognition of excellence in teaching requires more steeply graded salary differences. Establish meritocratic ranks in the teaching profession to provide incentives. Merit pay would give teaching a performance-based career ladder. Where necessary, enforce differential pay schemes to offer higher salaries for math and science teachers. The shortage in such teachers can be remedied by paying them more. At the top of the career ladder, set up the title of 'Master Teacher,' who would have special curriculum development responsibilities as well as augmented pay and prestige.

8 *Teacher quality* – To attract high-achievers into teaching, raise entry-level salaries and provide forgiven loans and scholarships to those from the top 25 per cent of a class who major in education. Teacher education should be more in subject matter and less in education courses. This will make teachers more competent transmitters of a content area. New teachers should take competency exams in literacy and in their area of licensing. Current teachers should take in-service seminars. Promote a crash program to meet the acute undersupply of math, science and engineering teachers.

9 *Selective investment in quality* – Federal and state funds should be targeted at programs committed to increasing student performance, especially in academics, technology, computers, math and science. Washington should tilt its aid towards 'quality.' Business should work closer with schools, providing equipment, facilities and trained staff. Pilot programs in academic excellence should serve as models for all schools.

This consensual agenda became a project from the political center of the restoration rather than from its right wing. Centrists tended to be federally-oriented, nationally-acting from the top down, corporation advocates, constitutionally secular, and globally attuned to commerce and diplomacy. The 'new right' of the restoration tended to be nationally organized from local units up, religiously fundamental, suspicious of Washington, with a biblical social agenda for legislating good and evil. The 1983 agenda avoided issues dear to the new right, such as school prayer, creation science, and tax credits for private schools. The centrists were also mute on ultra-conservative campaigns to stop busing and sex education. The 'new basics' emphasized secular academics but the official plans ignored the disease of censorship spreading from the right. Secular humanists who had been right-wing targets for ten years could draw only cold comfort from the new agenda, while conservative censors would not be chilled. The consensual program also insisted on the importance of Washington, thus denying the conservative demand for the abolition of the Department of Education. The depressant tilt to simple careerism and minimal basics was adjusted to the centrist 'new basics,' a less right-wing program of 'academics for all.' At the same time, the centrist third wave shared some common ground with the earlier ascendant right of the restoration: mandating traditional subjects with no electives allowed, weakening teacher unions with merit pay, strengthening authority with strict discipline, more testing and homework, rolling back open admissions, the primacy of training students for business demands, customizing curriculum to the job market, promoting Standard English over bilingualism and a common-culture/core curriculum emphasizing the American Heritage.

The road to centrist academics passed through a number of compelling influences besides the protest 1960s and the ultra-conservative 1970s. In the late 1970s traditional humanists began their own rebound from the minimal curricula of the early restoration. Liberal arts were fading even faster than student movements as some efforts to restore the humanities took wing. *The Paideia Proposal* (1982) was the most widely-discussed of these efforts, but there were a number of non-traditional, left-of-center conferences which also took up the cause of the declining humanities.[31] Among the other themes influencing phase three were

Trade War and Cold War, as the US position declined in both.
Still other themes were the growth of high-tech and the role of
computers in the new arms race of the 1980s. Further, the stagnant
economy pushed the consensual agenda forward in a number of
ways. One had to do with sophisticated anti-union strategies to
adjust current labor to a permanently diminished economy.
Another involved adjusting future labor (students) to long-term
uncertainty in the job market. Two arms stretched out from this
fertile mulch, one reaching back for traditional academics and the
other ahead for computers.

The Paideia panacea

The Paideia Proposal came out of a Paideia Group organized by
Mortimer Adler, one of the grand old traditionalists of American
education. Adler was then Director of the Institute for Philosophical Research and Chairman of the *Encyclopedia Britannica*.
Since his youthful days at the University of Chicago in the 1920s
and 1930s, with Robert M. Hutchins, Adler had been the premier
promoter of the great books approach to learning. In his eighties
by the third wave of the current restoration, Adler assembled an
influential group for the renewal of academics: Jacques Barzun,
quoted in the Literacy Crisis of 1975; Ernest Boyer, then leading
the Carnegie study from which he would write *High School* (1983);
Theodore Sizer, former Dean of the Graduate School of
Education at Harvard and author of a third-wave crisis report
also, *Horace's Compromise* (1984); James O'Toole, manpower
expert and author of the important study *Work in America* (1973)
which contradicted some of the key claims of career education;
and Adele Simmons, President of Hampshire College.

Adler translated Paideia to mean 'the general learning that
should be the possession of all human beings.'[32] From this starting
point, he gave the most scholastic definition of what that general
learning should be, an extended and guided study of great works
and the classics. There was nothing inevitable about Paideia
becoming an academic curriculum. During the protest era, Charles
Silberman used the word Paideia several times in his *Crisis in
the Classroom*, defining it as social education which prepares an
informed and activist citizenry through all the experiential

119

agencies of the community.[33] Adler-paideiacs fit the conservative tenor of the time, where curriculum turned to the authority of the classics for fixed values, for the restoration of an officially-sanctioned common culture. That official culture had broken down in the 1960s, as Christopher Jencks said, when agreement ended over what to teach and what to learn.[34] Restoring an authoritative common culture ('the right words' according to Barzun) was tantamount to restoring authority itself. Through this politics of curriculum, Adler's notion of Paideia became a stalking horse for the 1983 consensus on 'the new basics.' The Paideia program offered a structured academic pedagogy which influenced the 'core curriculum' plans of 1983.

Through two small books on Paideia, Adler provided enough diagrams, definitions, course names and methods to make an academic resurgence credible. The plans proposed a non-vocational, one-track, general education for all students with no electives permitted. This common curriculum had a required core in language, literature, fine arts, math, science, history, geography and social studies. Three-fifths of class time would be didactic lectures by the teacher. The remainder would be divided between socratic seminars on required reading and coaching sessions on literacy, numeracy, speech skills and problem-solving. Given Adler's massive promotion of classics, fixed authority, lectures and pre-programmed syllabi, it was illegitimate for him to dedicate *The Paideia Proposal* to John Dewey, who denounced the pedagogy of the talking teacher and the vice of externally imposed ends.[35] But, legitimate or not, it was clever politics, because Adler wanted to propose the new academic regime as the fulfilment of democracy through education. Dewey, Adler's lifelong antagonist, was suddenly embraced as the inspiration for Paideia, for Dewey was the American patron saint of democratic learning goals.

Dewey would also roll over in his grave if he read Adler's claim that 'We are a classless society.'[36] Dewey observed in *Democracy and Education* (1916) that

One would not expect a ruling class living at ease to have the same philosophy of life as those who were having a hard struggle for existence. . . . The great majority of workers have no insight into the social aims of their pursuits and no direct personal interest in them. The results actually achieved are not the ends of *their* actions, but only of their employers.[37]

Dewey stuck to defining non-participation as a form of slavery, insofar as a slave is someone who has to carry out the intentions of a superior authority (*Experience and Education*, 1938).[38] Paideia did not permit students any co-participation in deciding curriculum. Adler still insisted that it was the fulfilment of democratic promise because it would finally educate the masses to the knowledge required for being a citizen. If he needed some insight into the undemocratic reality of school and society in 1983, he could have turned to one of his own Paideia members, Theodore Sizer, who wrote in *Horace's Compromise* (1984) that

> Among schools there was one important difference, which
> followed from a single variable only: the social class of the
> student body. If the school principally served poor adolescents,
> its character, if not its structure, varied from sister schools
> for the more affluent. It got so I could say with some
> justification to school principals, Tell me about the income
> of your students' families and I'll describe to you your school.[39]

Sizer was amazed to find 'class' such an important part of inequality in schools. He was also surprised to find *the subject of class* absent from the curriculum. This structured silence in curriculum makes sense only in light of education's role in a class-based society – simultaneously creating inequality while denying its existence, promising democracy while imposing authority, socializing students into accepting arbitrary limits while provoking student resistance to those limits. Sizer would have to leave his establishment perspective behind to understand why 'class' is so important and so ignored in the function of education. That conflict underlies the actual *dysfunction* of schooling insofar as students choose to sabotage the schizoid experience offered them. The conspiracy of silence around 'class' was continued through *The Paideia Proposal* and through the official curricula offered in the third-phase reports.

Myths like 'the classless society in America,' like 'democracy depends on education,' like 'the lecture and the textbook are the best transmitters of learning,' abound in the Paideia program. Perhaps the grandest mystification was that educational excellence was the road to economic recovery. The third phase's war for excellence and against mediocrity could have taken its charge from Adler's declaration that school reform was synonymous with prosperity:

> Trained intelligence, in followers as well as leaders, holds the key to the solution of the problems we face. Achieving peace, prosperity and plenty could put this country on the edge of becoming an earthly paradise but only a much better educational system than now exists can carry us across the threshold.[40]

Adler's grandstanding made Paideia in 1982 the crucible for the great official eruption of 1983. Paideia brought together the individuals and influenced the ideology needed for the traditionalist surge of phase three.[41] However, the war for excellence and against student mediocrity only hid the failure of the economic system to cope with two other battles: Cold War and Trade War.

Sputnik marries Toyota: a new monster romance

The ghost of Sputnik appeared in many official reports and media stories of the third phase. The years after Sputnik was launched in October 1957 were the last time a national furor over education reform was unloaded from above. In 1983, it often seemed that the costs of renovating schools and colleges, of hiring new teachers and paying them more, of financing the changeover to computers, of developing new curriculum, were far beyond what the fiscal crisis and the weak national consensus would allow. In the strapped and divisive days of the 1980s, one university chancellor wailed, 'Sputnik II – where are you when we need you?'[42]

Even before Sputnik began circling the globe, the Cold War was used by official reports in defining the crisis needs of education. In its 1955 *Annual Report*, the Educational Testing Service noted the serious shortage of science teachers and scientists, as well as the small number of high school students who chose to study math and science. It posed the global context of the school crisis in Cold War terms:

> Even more serious than the problem of the shortages as such

is the very rapid rate at which the Communists may be gaining on us in technological fields. Far behind us in the supply of skilled manpower ten years ago, they are now graduating 50,000 trained scientists and engineers annually, in contrast with our 20,000. At this rate, it will take only a few years for their scientific manpower to outnumber ours. And it is certainly food for thought that the Library of Congress received 1119 monographs on scientific subjects from Russia in 1954, and only 843 from the United States![43]

Among the interferences to scientific dominance in US schools, ETS cited teacher shortages and resistance of the best students to math-science courses. But it also accused progressive educators of interfering with the use of filmed instruction – that is, teaching technology through technology, in pre-packaged modules that bypassed teacher invention and student-centered methods. This official desire to use centrally-prepared technology to replace teachers and to technify curriculum was a handsome preview to the computer invasion of the classroom after 1983. Film lost out in the Sputnik crisis, taking a back-seat to new curricula and textbooks prepared centrally by government-sponsored experts.

In the Sputnik days of the Cold War, it was easier to build a national consensus around education reform. The East-West confrontation stood out starkly in a world still recovering from World War II. Anti-communist hysteria had been whipped up in the US for years before the Soviets finally threw 184 pounds of technology into space. Washington panicked the nation again about the Red Menace. The crisis was explained away as a failure of education to produce the scientists and engineers needed for US domination of Moscow. The panic in official circles was real enough, because so much machinery had been thrown into creating obsessive fear of communism, only to have the dreaded enemy leap ahead of the very private enterprise system that was supposed to be superior. Boyer wrote of those days, 'Our confidence was shaken. Our very survival seemed threatened.' By the 1970s and 1980s, the Red Menace had become elusive. No one enemy or event summarized the threats from Moscow or made clear the need for national unity. Boyer mused on the transition from Sputnik to the 1980s:

A quarter of a century ago, it seemed relatively easy to isolate our challenge and respond. Today, with dozens of crises crowding our universe, we see not a single gleaming speck, but a dark, foreboding cloud. The world has become a more crowded, more interconnected, more volatile and unstable place.[44]

The single speck was Sputnik's nightly passage over a humiliated Washington. The lost simplicity of the Cold War could also be read on the gleaming cover of *Life* magazine in its special 1958 issue on the 'Crisis in Education.' The cover showed side-by-side faces of a grim Moscow schoolboy and a happy-go-lucky Chicago high-schooler. While the Russians were deadly serious, in the US in 1958

> The schools are in terrible shape. What has long been an ignored national problem, Sputnik has made a recognized crisis. . . . Most teachers are grossly underpaid (some are not worth what they get). A great many who know their jobs well . . . have to work without help, understanding or proper tools. . . . In their eagerness to be all things to all children, schools have gone wild with elective courses. . . . The nation's stupid children get far better care than the bright. The geniuses of the next decades are even now being allowed to slip back into mediocrity. . . . There is no general agreement on what the schools should teach. . . . Most appalling, the standards of education are shockingly low.[45]

The rhetoric of alarm in 1958 was very similar to the language of 1983, but this is a common feature of the long, repetitive and never-resolved crises of education. Even if the language and villains were similar, the simple East-West red-baiting of the 1950s was pushed aside in the 1980s by the tangle of Trade War.

At a Carnegie Conference in New York in February 1983, 'Education and Economic Progress,' the historic transition from Cold War to Trade War was noted:

> In 1957, Sputnik and national defense issues drew forth massive public interest and support. In the 1960s, the Great Society and social justice became the incentive for reform and support. Today, the needs of the economy are paramount. The economic challenge from Japan and other countries is the modern Sputnik, a powerful lever for the reform and support

of education. Indeed, the conference concluded that the present economic challenge is more profound than Sputnik and as fundamental as the change from an agrarian to an industrial economy after the Civil War.[46]

The NCEE shortly agreed, beginning the reform rush with *A Nation at Risk*:

The risk is not only that the Japanese make automobiles more efficiently. . . . It is not just that the South Koreans recently built the world's most efficient steel mill, or that American machine tools, once the pride of the world, are being displaced by German products. It is also that these developments signify a redistribution of trained capability throughout the globe.[47]

Trade War also dominated the influential ECS document, *Action for Excellence*, even though it mentioned national defense more than other reports. The Red Menace had passed as the goose that laid the golden eggs for education. That goose now spoke Japanese and German, and was laying Toyotas and Nikons instead. The Business-Higher Education Forum acknowledged the primacy of Trade War over Cold War by putting economics first and national security after, in its own crisis report for 1983:

Unless the United States improves its ability to compete, unless we develop a comprehensive, coherent, long-term approach, and unless we address our problems from a broad perspective, we fear that domestic economic revitalization will remain an elusive goal. . . . Unless we rebuild the American economy and strengthen our education system, it will be increasingly difficult – if not impossible – to maintain a just society, a high standard of living for all Americans and a strong national defense.[48]

Gone was the simple Golden Age when the world was divided between them and us. The rise of competitive allies had become the bigger headache for Washington.

Aspirin for Japan-fever

The soft profile of the Cold War and the high profile of the Trade War were also conditioned by the lingering effects of Vietnam.

125

Hints of foreign conflict brought marches to the streets and fears of 'another Vietnam.' The long CIA operation against Nicaragua in the early 1980s indicated how Washington's military hands had become tied since Vietnam. The prospect of military intervention was a political liability in the years after Vietnam, when even the military warned against using American troops for combat without consensus at home.

This post-Vietnam pacifism made anti-communist saber-rattling hard for official reformers. Cold War and national defense were simply not available, as they were in the days of Sputnik, to shake money free for education. On the other hand, everyone saw Toyotas and Datsuns around them, so it was easier to provoke two kinds of nationalist feeling. One was anger at the Asians out-competing US industries. This sentiment led to some ugly incidents, including the bludgeoning to death of a Chinese mistaken for a Japanese in Detroit by a laid-off auto worker who was acquitted in court. A second sentiment was gung-ho admiration for the Japanese way of working and educating. A traditional, authoritarian, far-away society was held up as a model.

Numerous glowing reports on Japanese schools appeared, connecting disciplined classrooms with productive workplaces.[49] The education-economy link was made also in *Time*'s cover-story on the 1983 crisis. *Time* declared that 'State officials equate better schools with healthier economies.'[50] *Fortune* also ran a cover-story on the new school debacle, suggesting that 'schools were the main cause of the decline in America's industrial might.'[51] The example of Japan proved this thesis because Japan was prospering and Japan had disciplined schools. Boyer demurred from this worship of foreign models and from the glib linkage of education to economic advances: 'Today, the push for excellence is linked to economic recovery and to jobs. We're being told that better schools will move the nation forward in the high-tech race.'[52] These passive, doubting lines stand out in an otherwise stylish and assured report.

Did education cause the recession? Could schooling lead the recovery? Was Trade War resting on geometry classes in high school? The unlikely thesis of education for economic growth depended on school reform becoming a new force for production. Taken at face value, such a pronouncement missed the utterly dependent position of education vis à vis political and economic

trends in society at large. Further, the dull routines of school and
the hit or miss connection of education to jobs make it hard to
see the classroom as the wedge of economic growth. This line of
reasoning read history backwards to create some melodrama,
some great stakes and grand hopes for school reform. Such dramas
and hopes, in the absence of a Red Menace, could stir public
interest in paying for changes in education. As a manufactured
strategy, it had little to say about the real relation of education
to economics, but a lot to say about the politics of culture war.
In terms of economics, the following paragraphs outline an opposition appreciation of the economic crisis.

The 1983 reports ignored an awesome economic reality: capital
now had wings. Money flew electronically around the world, in
search of excellence, defined as the best areas for profits. Those
areas tended to have cheap labor and expensive dictators. The
multi-national corporations and finance banks thus did not belong
to one country any more. People and governments retained
national identities while economic power became meta-national.
These forces were above the authority exercized by any nation-
state. A great deal of local and national business activity remained
under the international umbrella, but the key decisions being
made at the top were done so on global terms. In this new age,
posing school as a devil of decline, and personal hard work as an
angel of recovery, only mystified the real power and real roots of
the crisis.

The finance apparatus made decisions to chill the US economy
in the early 1970s.[53] That chill helped depress the activism and
aspirations threatening authority. It cooled the protest culture of
the 1960s and the wage expectations of labor. At the same time,
multi-national corporations evacuated the unionized Northeast
and headed for cheap-labor areas in the South, the West and
abroad. Further damaging the economy, the huge military budget
burdened the declining industrial base. Japan and Germany did
not have to support giant war machines and their economies
benefited from civilian investments instead. The military sector of
the economy yields less employment dollar-for-dollar than does
non-defense spending. This reduced the consumer buying-power
of the work-force, thus depressing the two-thirds of business
activity generated by non-military production. In other areas of
conservative economic policy, cuts in public sector budgets, low

levels of social investment in roads, bridges, transport, housing and services, also accelerated the decline. Unwise public and private investment in nuclear power was another piece of the austerity puzzle. The refusal of US industries to modernize their plants allowed industrial units abroad to become more productive, a poor management decision which workers were not allowed to participate in. Lastly, conservative austerity in the 1970s lowered worker morale and raised resistance, thus depressing the human factor in productivity. Besides declining wages, increasing living costs, deteriorating public services and rising unemployment, there was also computerization of labor which replaced high-skill, high-wage jobs with lower-skill, lower-wage ones. This vast tapestry of forces produced a decline that dragged schooling down with it. Students and teachers experienced two austerities, in their degraded schools and in their after-school lives. Their classrooms did not start and cannot stop the national fall from moneyed grace.

This view of what happened to school and the economy since 1970 never made it into the official reports, for good reason. It would, of course, pose corporate policy-making as antithetical to quality mass education, to the good life, and to democracy. From another angle on the myth of education for economic growth, it is possible to see the few outcomes business really needs from schooling. One is a limited supply of highly-trained personnel. A second is an oversupply of middle- and lower-range labor. A third is high-level research and development in a handful of major universities. A fourth is a curriculum which adjusts students to the labor market, as well as to the domestic and foreign priorities of the corporations. A fifth outcome is education as a business activity itself, an open market for business goods and services. If the 1983 crisis was observed from these five outcomes, the official eruption makes more sense. Business leaders complained that the highest-achieving students were not achieving as much. The performance strike was eating into their supply of reliable top employees. The increases in achievement by blacks at the bottom of the social ladder was an egalitarian advance which could not possibly help the corporate need for executive material. The schools continued to churn out more middle- and lower-range labor than the job market could absorb, but these new young workers lacked the work discipline business wanted. The student-teacher performance strike at the bottom did not injure the research function of major universities, but the economic crisis hurt this corporate resource in two ways. On the one hand, graduate school became more costly and less available to large numbers of even talented students. At the same time, the job market for scientific graduates slumped after 1972, thus discouraging students from the long haul of doctoral work. In addition, the cost of maintaining high-level research facilities strained university budgets. This decline of the graduate enterprise, detailed in the Brademas report,[54] cut into what the campus could offer to the corporations. One answer, implemented at the University of Michigan,[55] was to finance a massive high-tech renovation of the research facilities by drastically cutting budgets in the soft disciplines, like education, arts and environmental study.

In terms of curriculum which adjusted students to corporate policy, the 1970s showed mixed results. As protest culture declined from the 1960s, students shifted en masse to career study and to a middle-of-the-road politics. Yet, campus activism on the left simmered near the surface and steadily increased. By 1984, anti-nuclear and anti-intervention actions were permanent fixtures in the college scene. *U.S. News and World Report* warned about the new youthful activists that 'No great national issue threatens them directly, as the draft did during the Vietnam era. Yet few doubt that this generation of young people, as skeptical and career-minded as they are, would hesitate to rise up if the "right" issue came along.'[56] If students were too susceptible to causes, too undisciplined and low-achieving to be go-getting employees, there was also a problem with education as a market for business. Budget-gutted schools and colleges were simply worse customers in the new depression. One answer to this was the bonus of pushing computer literacy as a new required basic. The 80,000 public schools and the 3,000 colleges in higher education would be rushing to buy hardware and software. Government-subsidized purchases of computer equipment would guarantee a hot new market for high-tech corporations.

The myth of 'education for economic growth,' then, disguised 'education for high-tech corporate growth.' Whether or not this would trickle-down to a general recovery remained to be seen, but we were promised paradise again and again. The sophisticated business strategy in phase three twisted public education towards the area of high tech *without* proposing a single-element reform. The package was comprehensive, not one-dimensional as in the career or in the literacy phases. Called 'excellence in education,' the broad overhaul was the education version of 'profit-led' growth. Because high-tech was the most profitable sector of the economy, corporate planning skewed development in that direction, in school and in society. Such a skew had to be presented as in the *general* interest, if popular consent were to be won. So, the reforms called for 'the new basics,' general academics for all, career education and literacy skills. High-tech was the dominant factor in a broadly-constructed rearrangement.

Inside such a total plan, selective over-investments could easily be made in math, science and engineering, from above, by administrative fiat. Similarly, math, science and technology teachers could easily be paid more than humanities faculties, thanks to a nominally non-discriminatory 'merit pay' scheme controlled by management. Nothing in the plans guaranteed equal resource-allocation. This anti-democratic feature, which will be discussed in greater detail below, was buried in the comprehensive machinery proposed in the third phase. The simple promise emerging from the agendas was that a high-tech tide would float all academic ships. All traditional subjects had a stake in the renewal, a tide of 'excellence' which would reverse the tide of 'mediocrity.' This imagery repeated the legend spreading in society-at-large, that high-tech growth would float all household ships. The promise of a general recovery with computers made high-tech a formidable cultural weapon. Even a critical sage like John Goodlad was ecstatic about the educational potential of the microcomputer.[57] His enthusiasm was shared by George Leonard, author of *Education and Ecstasy* (1968). Leonard criticized third-phase reforms as a business-as-usual hoax, but he offered an alternative in a computer-centered high school.[58] The high-tech wave was washing over all of us. It was so big that we could not escape it and could not see it at the same time. It was becoming a blind faith which only more critical scrutiny could save us from.

Gimme that high-tech religion!

Business values rode into curriculum once again on a new wave of computers. In 1982, Adler's Paideia Program recommended the use of calculators in first-grade math, leading to computer programming in later grades.[59] The NCEE joined the high-tech faithful in declaring that 'Learning is the indispensable investment in the "information age" we are entering . . . the demand for highly skilled workers in new fields is accelerating rapidly . . . new jobs demand greater sophistication and preparation.'[60] It recommended a half-year of computer science as a 'new basic' in high school. The Hunt report agreed that computer literacy be one of the new required basics. Another branch of this church, the Twentieth Century Fund, told us that

> the exigencies of our fast-changing technological world call for
> many more skilled young people than ever before in our
> history, which means increased demand on our schools . . .
> the skills that were once possessed by only a few must now
> be held by the many if the United States is to remain
> competitive in an advancing technological world.[61]

The College Board and the National Science Board repeated the chapter and verse by including computer education in their academic requirements.[62]

By itself, the computer can be misrepresented as a neutral technology. Isolated from its origins and from its uses, the microprocessor could be discussed as simply a vast new tool for information and communication. If the politics of curriculum are not examined, computer education may be disguised as a non-partisan study of the latest human invention. When you do not examine economics, employment or equality, it is simple to pose computers as both the new basics and as the new road to a career. This construes the curricular role of business in a helpful light, because the arrival of hardware, software and computer courses simply means the promise of learning now and jobs later. The most sensible and forward-looking of all the 1983 observers, John Goodlad, eloquently insisted that computer education is needed:

> Our world is being transformed by the extraordinary capability
> of this most versatile of man-made tools. . . . How can we,
> as a people, continue to be almost completely unconcerned
> about this inexcusable omission of one of the most important
> inventions of all time, the basis of a social revolution capable
> of molding the destiny of every human being?[63]

Goodlad denounced the absence of adequate high-tech education in the thousand schools he studied. He did not suggest how computer literacy could be absorbed into learning so that it promoted education and democracy over training and obedience. This omission stood out in a report advocating student-centered teaching.

Another forward-looking critic, George Leonard, envisioned a student-controlled, computer-based high school curriculum.[64] User-friendly terminals would do the basic cognitive instruction in a mastery-learning model. Leonard, who referred to Goodlad's report on the deadly boredom of school, saw students working individually at microcomputers until they mastered the material. This basic information would be accompanied by group seminars, inspiring lectures from gifted teachers, and collaborative projects. Among the unanswered questions here is the dilemma of who will program and define the basic instruction for computer-learning. Will this material be a digital form of the remote, laundered information or skills now offered in textbooks and skill-drills? Leonard assumed that 'basic information' and 'basic skills' could be neutral and cognitively broken down into programmable units suitable for machine-teaching. The struggle over the core curriculum and the American Heritage in the restoration indicates that the subject of any course is a political issue. Not only are information and skill politically defined by the course of study, but could a computer train critical thought if there was no human voice for debate? Computer-assisted instruction bypasses the exchange of human voices. Even if the digital module presents problem-solving exercises, the terms of the exercise are still pre-programmed before the learner gets to the keyboard. Further, Leonard assumed that all schools will have enough computers to allow ample hands-on time to students, and that all students will have computers at home to work on, so that access to the new technology and language was equal. This would require income and funding changes left out of Leonard's and Goodlad's critiques. Those questions reveal the inequality hidden behind high-tech and will be examined shortly.

Among the participants in the heat of the 1983 reports, Boyer alone demurred from the high-tech religion. He asked some pointed questions: 'Is the software as good as the equipment? What educational purposes will be served? Which students will use the equipment, when and why? Are teachers able to fit the technology and the software into the curriculum?'[65] Boyer thought high-tech should be a subject in the curriculum for study, so that students investigated computers in a liberal studies format. Still, he thought that if terminals could be provided for all students, the possibilities might be endless. He did not consider that future technology might be so user-friendly, or even voice-activated, as to make training needs minimal. A year after Boyer wrote, some official reservations on high-tech entered late and in low-profile in the Dupont report, *High-Schools and the Changing Workplace*.

Kids learn computers fast and will be slowed down in a program supervised by adults. Teachers are likely to have trouble keeping up with their students, if students are permitted freedom to interact with the technology in their own ways. One long-term advocate of education for student freedom, Herb Kohl, thought through the curricular issue of high-tech in critical ways that eluded Boyer, Goodlad and Leonard. In his important contribution to the literacy debate, *Basic Skills* (1982), Kohl subsumed computers into a participatory basic skill to understand scientific and technical ideas and to use tools. His suggested curriculum on computing and computing devices, from the abacus to the microprocessor, called for

> a study of miniaturization and its role in developing the power
> of computers, as well as a study in the use of base-two
> number systems, an introduction to data processing, to BASIC
> and other computer languages, to the limits of computer-
> stored information; the social history of IBM, as well as the
> effect of computers on working-class people.[66]

Kohl's inclusion of the effect of computers on working people raised a question of inequality missing in the official and demurring reports. To what degree is the computer overhaul of school and society a cheap labor, anti-union, pro-arms race strategy? Kohl opened these issues to study without pursuing them deeply in his own book. The other heralds of computers do not even take them on. It is easy enough to see that wealthier students are *already* ahead in the high-tech race for the twenty-first century. They have home computers to practice on no matter what hardware their better schools manage to buy. Students from poorer districts not only get less spent on them in every way at school,

133

but also have less spent on them at home. Their less-funded schools will have fewer computers for them to learn on. Their lower-paid parents will not be able to supply them with home microprocessors. They will join their more affluent peers at the video arcades, practicing to fire the new laser weapons being readied for them by the military. The richer kids with more arcade quarters can also practice at home the job skills which will give them a leg up on business's new demands for computer literacy. In an unequal society, the tools are simply not distributed equally. What is happening with computers is a replay of what is happening around Standard English in the area of basic literacy. The language and power of the dominant strata is passed on to the children who grow up in those families. If computer literacy is the new coin of the realm, richer kids will learn it and use it before others. Lower-class culture passes on its deficits to the new generation, whether in speaking, reading, writing, computers, or the psychology of domination. The group that inherits street slang, pencils and typewriters in the age of correct usage and the microchip will discover itself not developed for the best jobs waiting in the twenty-first century. There is simply no democratic way to include computers in curriculum until students and teachers first critically study the impact of high-tech on society, and then all homes and all classrooms are provided equal hardware and software.

Chips on your shoulder

The absence of democracy in the computer-school linkage is matched by the false promises of jobs down the education-employment road. One voice deflating the grandiose hopes for computer jobs was a self-made, high-tech millionaire who went on to become a Republican Congressman from California's Silicon Valley, Ed Zschau. It was reported in 1983 that Zschau

> has been disabusing his colleagues in Washington of the notion that the electronics industry is an economic cure-all. . . . The electronics tycoon arrived just when it had become fashionable to talk of high-technology industries as an all-purpose tonic for the nation's economic malaise and flagging productivity.

Zschau said people got carried away with these visions of the electronics industry, which currently employs roughly two million Americans. . . . Similar notes of caution have been sounded lately by some of the 'Atari Democrats' who months ago were trumpeting the virtues of high technology.[67]

This will be a hard message to get across given the propaganda barrage of the high-tech corporations. Their profits in a stagnant economy and their trendy new products legitimize all sorts of unreasonable, glamorous promises. Some support for Zschau's cooling-out on the high-tech glamor came from research by Henry Levin and Russell Rumberger at Stanford. By examining federal job statistics in the 1980s, they found that future employment would continue to favor jobs requiring little or no training beyond high school. This contradicted the official claims that a new world of jobs was opening up, demanding higher skills and hence justifying 'the new basics' and its higher demands on students and teachers. Disputing the myth of higher-skill labor from high-tech, Levin and Rumberger wrote that

Although employment in high-technology occupations will increase quickly in percentage terms over this decade, the contribution of these jobs to total employment will be quite small. Machines will be able to perform more complex mental tasks as more advanced software is developed. But the use of sophisticated equipment will not necessarily require workers with more sophisticated skills. In fact, past technological advances suggest the opposite. . . . Computers are far more sophisticated today than they were 10 or 20 years ago. But, programming and using computers are considerably less demanding today, and many computer-related jobs require virtually no knowledge of computers.[68]

The demands for computer curricula to meet the high-skill needs of the new job market are mostly high-tech propaganda. It is a false promise which may gain work and school discipline while adjusting people to less. The trendy, glamorous world of high-tech was useful for giving a cosmetic facelift to the largely bad news of the nation's jobworld. Through the smoke-screens and disguises of the computer boosters, the reality is that high-tech promises a multitude of lower-paying, lower-skilled and less union-protected jobs, in relatively modest numbers, instead of the flood of high-skill, academically-demanding occupations they say are waiting just around the bend in the twenty-first century.

Computers can easily reduce the brainpower and the manpower needed to do the work of the economy. They will also fail to affect many jobs that will continue into the next century without high-tech applications. One crisis that matured in the mid-1970s was an 'overeducation' dilemma which still harasses corporate, school and government policy-makers. Vastly distributed education in the US has been producing more brainpower and more upwardly mobile manpower at the very moment when high-tech is reducing the need for brains and for hands in the industrial sector. The robot is fast becoming the worker-of-choice for management, but it will still take some time before high school and college can convert their human charges into the androids desired by General Motors. The real job-short, deskilled future awaiting the 25 million students now in high school and college was suggested in Levin's and Rumberger's research:

> the five occupations expected to produce the most new jobs
> are all in low skilled areas: janitors, nurses' aides, sales
> clerks, cashiers, and waiters and waitresses. These five jobs
> alone will account for 13 per cent of employment growth
> between 1978 and 1990. . . . While jobs for computer systems
> analysts will increase by over 100 per cent between 1978 and
> 1990, only 200,000 new jobs will be created. In contrast, there
> will be over 600,000 new jobs for janitors and sextons . . .
> about 150,000 new jobs for computer programmers are
> expected to emerge during this 12 year period, a level of
> growth vastly outpaced by the 800,000 new jobs expected for
> fast food workers and kitchen helpers.[69]

The federal Bureau of Labor Statistics (BLS) offered even more insight into the promise of high-tech. It estimated that high-tech accounted for only 3.2 per cent of all employment in 1982 and will account for only 6 per cent of all new jobs by 1995.[70] The updated figures for 1995 supported Levin's and Rumberger's earlier research. Some of that reality appeared in the one third-phase crisis report to criticize seriously the high-tech religion.

High Schools and the Changing Workplace: The Employers' View, appeared in May 1984. Even though this report was chaired by Richard Heckert from Du Pont, it was in touch with the reality of high-tech, perhaps because Henry Levin was on the panel that produced it. Echoing Levin's earlier claims, *High Schools and the Changing Workplace* declared that

> Schools alone cannot cure the ills of the national economy; however, a well-educated workforce is important to the cure. . . . High-technology industries will grow rapidly, but will not become major sources of employment because they start from so small a base. . . . Today, with the age of the small computer upon us, hundreds of thousands of Americans still work – and for the foreseeable future will continue to work – as pencil-and-paper bookkeepers. . . . Just as the automobile revolution did not make us a nation of automotive engineers or automotive mechanics, the computer revolution need not transform us into computer programmers and technicians. . . . Many people assume that advanced technology requires higher skills; in reality, it often requires different, and sometimes lesser, skills. Just as the word processor's keyboard resembles the typewriter's, so the skills needed to operate both of them overlap. . . . In some occupations, advanced technology will reduce the demands for skills from some workers. New diagnostic tools used in the health services, for example. . . . The shift from mechanical repair to computer repair requires new knowledge, but the simplicity of product design and the power of the new technology to assist in diagnosis may make computer repair less demanding than traditional repair.[71]

Even though this report focused on the needs of the high school graduate *not* going on to college (the majority), it still concluded that an academic program was appropriate for all students. Its unorthodox evaluation of high-tech did not extend to its call for core competencies and work discipline identical to the other official reports.

The meager job prospects from high-tech also worried William Serrin, frequent labor reporter for the *New York Times*. In one of several articles on this theme, he wrote 'As new computer-based technologies are installed to improve productivity and reduce labor costs, there is growing concern about whether the nation will create the number of jobs it needs, in regions where they are most needed and at wage levels to which many people have been accustomed.'[72] Other reports noted the ease with which high-tech plants can be moved to avoid union organization and to exploit cheap labor more fully, especially that of women.[73] The use of machines to lower wage costs, increase productivity and increase management power was hardly news in 1983. The Luddites had notions of this some two centuries ago. In 1932, progressive educator George Counts wrote that 'automatic machinery increasingly displaces men and threatens society with a growing contingent of the permanently unemployed.'[74] The deskilling and disemployment impacts of technology were also discussed extensively in Harry Braverman's *Labor and Monopoly Capital* (1974).

Thus, in the business-oriented computer craze, there is a depressant reality behind the glamor. Perhaps, the microprocessors pouring into classrooms may yet be taken over for democratic and humane purposes by students and teachers, who refuse to settle for less. In the early gold rush, the third-phase computer curriculum is tilting interest towards high-tech, similar to the way careerism first, and then basic skills, dominated schooling when they erupted earlier. Each adjusted students downward, but none had the trendy appeal of high-tech. The school-business link now being forged around computers not only falsely promises good jobs, but it also draws on the playful excitement of new technology.

The forged future: toying with success

High-tech in the 1980s was the third major restoration idea whose time had come, but like other key technological inventions of earlier eras, it was a multi-dimensional experience. Like radio, TV and the internal combustion engine, the microcomputer is a factor of production, a means of extending business culture, a weapon in domestic culture war, an element in the arms race, and a vehicle for developing training curricula. Not least of all, each major invention has also been part of 'play.' Radio and TV fill the leisure time of the day while packaging safe news and aggressive advertisements. In addition, they offer establishment politicians a communications monopoly through a powerful medium. The automobile was another complex economic development. It not only gave the oil corporations a giant hold on everyday life but it also permitted such social policy as suburbanization. Cars also became a leisure-time sport for men as well as a status symbol, a fast transport to other leisure places, and a private place for backseat sex.

High-tech in the 1980s made its appearance in daily life on the side of play. Video home recorders and games gave domestic entertainment a new dimension. The telephone answering machine added an extra to social life. The advances in stereo technology offered maximum sound at home, in the street via 'ghetto blasters,' or privately, through plug-in miniaturized 'walk-mans.' The new computer age also created the video arcade as a spectacular kids' hideaway-fantasyland. Add to this the minutely-covered space shuttle flights, which stirred imagination, and you have a formidable appeal for trusting high-tech.

The excitement of play and the appeal of new jobs from a growing industry made computers in the early 1980s too powerful to resist. The heyday expansion of high-tech also owed a debt to the Carter-Reagan arms buildup. This helped create a spot shortage of labor in the tech industries. To cope with its labor needs, high-tech began a brain-drain of math, science and engineering teachers out of education into the civilian and military sectors of the economy. Pay and working conditions were better there than in the depressed schools and public colleges. The short-term labor need was estimated by the Business-Higher Education Forum at 40,000 engineers a year.[75] The brain-drain of educators was one way to solve this shortage and the tilting of curriculum to math and science was another. Education schools were pressured to produce more math, science and engineering graduates while public schools forced more math and science requirements on students. This would solve the long-term labor problem for high-tech. Curriculum for *25 million* students in high school and college was tilted after 1983 to supply 40,000 engineers plus the 350,000 computer workers cited by the BLS. Relative to the size of the student body involved, high-tech's labor problem was tiny. Relative to the clout of high-tech industries, this labor need resulted in a national campaign for math-science school reform.

Eventually, the labor shortage will mature into a labor over-supply. The surplus of computer workers is inevitable, thanks to the 'cobweb' effect referred to by Freeman in *The Overeducated American*.[76] A great rush now to computer programs will graduate far more labor five years later than the tech market can employ. By 1984, the 'shakeout' phase in high-tech was already underway, as several mid-sized companies went under, and IBM squared off with Apple and others in a drive to grab more of the market. The inevitable surplus of high-tech workers will depress wages in this field. The schools will then have collaborated in a process of lowering salaries and increasing corporate profits.

Education will churn out an oversupply of tech labor at public expense by pointing all of curriculum in that direction. Liberal studies can face the crisis in several ways. They can accept stiffer official requirements for academic courses and play ball with the austerity. Liberal arts will then rebound from the margins for the wrong reasons – to use academics as an effective sorting of elite from lesser students. If critical study of the new requirements and the new high-tech is avoided, this will be a bargain with the devil. Dr Faust had some experience with such an attractive deal. Without a Red Menace to trickle-down money to the depressed humanities, liberalists may argue that they have no choice but to go with the arms race/high-tech/Trade War bandwagon.

Letter-quality equality versus dot-matrix excellence: the crisis of white mediocrity

The shotgun wedding of high-tech to high culture, computer literacy to the traditional academics of the past, was an attempt to merge the Space Age with the Golden Age, the 1990s with the 1950s. Even those critics who applauded the computer as an educational tool – Goodlad, Leonard, Kohl – denounced 'the new basics' as business as usual, unlikely to make a dent in the learning needs of students. Theodore Sizer put it this way:

> The Outside Influentials will decide that the 'solution' to their
> sense of the Current High School Crisis is to change the
> curricular labels once again, to urge more in mathematics and
> science, and to puff up the autocratic tendencies in each
> school principal. . . . They will find another panacea this time,
> probably the computer. And of course, it won't make much
> difference.[77]

140

Sizer complained that toughness had overwhelmed compassion in the reform burst of 1983, and he had good reason to worry. Media stories highlighted get-tough and computer-based education plans, applauding such principals as ex-sergeant Joe Clark in East Patterson High School (New Jersey) who walked the hallways with a bullhorn during class change. Uneasy with the drift into curricular computerism, Ernest Boyer asked, 'Where is the recognition that education is to enrich the living individual? Where is the love of learning and where is the commitment to achieve equality and opportunity for all?'[78] Boyer, like other sensitive liberal critics, missed the corporate thrust towards work-discipline and the arms race built into the third-phase agenda, but he was correct to identify the problem of equality versus quality, equity versus excellence. After all, when Reagan's Secretary of Education, T. H. Bell, first appointed the NCEE in August 1981, Bell complained that school had been focusing too much 'on bringing the bottom up.'[79]

The NCEE wisely softened this tone when it issued *A Nation at Risk* eighteen months later:

> We do not believe that a public commitment to excellence and educational reform must be made at the expense of a strong public commitment to the equitable treatment of our diverse population. The twin goals of equity and high-quality schooling have profound and practical meaning for our economy and society, and we cannot permit one to yield to the other in either principle or in practice. . . . Our goal must be to develop the talents of all to their fullest.[80]

The NCEE warned that aspirations and performance would be damaged if the new reforms attacked equality. There was a danger here that the trumpets of excellence would clue the great mass of non-academic students into expecting failure. For decades, school and society had produced excellence and quality for only an elite fraction at the top, so how could these concepts now be used to motivate the giant bottom? A year before the NCEE reported, Mortimer Adler in *The Paideia Proposal* warned about the connection between low performance and low prospects for the future:

> Hopelessness about the future is bound to affect motivation

in school. Why do the hard work that good basic schooling would demand if, after doing it, no opportunity exists to work for a decent living? This bleak prospect makes for the drop-out, or, what is just as bad, turns the energetic into the delinquent. While still in school, they regard themselves as prisoners serving time.[81]

The official reformers from the best universities and from the largest corporations could thus not hope to stir mass action unless they promised everyone prosperity and equality. This led to the second shotgun wedding of the third phase, following the one between traditional academics and high-tech. Matrimony number two was the forced union between equality and quality. The College Board protested in its influential little green book that 'Concern for educational quality must not lead to actions that limit aspirations and opportunities of disadvantaged and minority youth or that would reverse the progress that has already been made. Rather, concern for educational quality must be expressed in a commitment to quality for all students.'[82] The Board then promptly offered an academic program neatly divided into collegiate and non-college 'basics' suitable for tracking high school students into two very different destinies. The defensive insistence on marrying quality to equality can be found in such other key third-phase reports as the Twentieth Century Fund's *Making the Grade* and Governor Hunt's *Action for Excellence*. Their language is almost identical to the protestations of the NCEE and the College Board. Meanwhile, the Fund insisted that federal funds should now tilt towards gifted students, while Hunt set up his elite 'model' North Carolina School for Science and Math, for 400 *gifted* juniors and seniors, funded at *thrice* the per capita amount accorded high schools for the rest of the students.[83]

The hidden agenda to invest in the best while promising equality to the rest had inequity written all over it. The inequality was imposed on the basis of class, sex and race. In the newly-valorized basics – computers, Standard English, collegiate academics – students from the wealthier homes were bound to succeed over those from less-rich families. In the new imposition of math and science, men were bound to dominate women. Girl students did better in verbal and written courses, while boys excelled more in math and tech. The war-oriented reforms of 1983 naturally tended to reward males, the potential soldiers for the looming conflicts. By tilting curriculum to the crash preparation of math, science and engineering graduates, the official agendas gave men an advantage, thus cooling the egalitarian impact of feminism in education.[84] If richer students and male students were given advantages over poorer ones and female students, perhaps the largest inequality was imposed on minorities. There is reason to read the 1983 agenda as *a crisis in white mediocrity* and as an elite reaction against minority advances.

The racial interests of the third phase were embarrassingly revealed in the *Newsweek* cover mentioned earlier. The very white teenage girl is at the center of the photo, surrounded by dark-faced students. She wears a pink shirt which nicely sets off the paleness of her skin, as she eagerly raises her hand in class. All the other students surrounding her are dressed in dark blue, which accentuates the shaded hues of their faces, as they too raise their hands. Could this racist iconography be an accident? It came from a classroom in North Carolina, Governor Hunt's home state.

Twenty years of integration, busing and federal compensatory programs for the disadvantaged had begun the slow desegregation of the nation's schools. As will be discussed shortly, these efforts had also produced rising black achievement scores and lower black drop-out rates in a period when these figures for white high school students were worsening. What kind of program could restore racial separation in the schools? The old-fashioned George-Wallace-in-the-doorway approach had been erased by mass protests. The new agenda based on Standard English, computers and college academics, with a nationalist crusade to win the Trade War and Cold War, could once again segregate elite, white students from the minorities. This separation would draw on the seemingly neutral ideas of high-tech excellence, merit, aptitude and achievement.[85] What was needed was a tough meritocratic program, tough school administrators who could militarize discipline, and a selective injection of funds wherever 'quality' raised its fair head. Should students or teachers balk at the arrangement, tough school principals or supervisors will loudly let them know where the door is.

The NCEE signaled this direction by insisting that school get out of the social reform business. It said that curriculum was 'routinely called upon to provide solutions to personal, social and political problems that the home and other institutions either will not or cannot resolve.'[86] The Twentieth Century Fund then agreed that school should return to the academics it used to teach, emphasizing literacy in Standard English over bilingualism and bi-dialecticalism, through new federal policy for quality programs.[87] Hunt and the NSB also pushed for selective funding of 'excellence,' but the most strident racial rhetoric came from the new right journal *Heritage Today*:

> The most damaging blows to science and mathematics education have come from Washington. For the past 20 years, federal mandates have favored 'disadvantaged' pupils at the expense of those who have the highest potential to contribute positively to society. . . . By catering to the demands of special interest groups – racial minorities, the handicapped, women and non-English speaking students – America's public schools have successfully competed for government funds, but they have done so at the expense of education as a whole.[88]

The indictment of special interest groups like minorities, for ruining educational quality, depended on a distorted reading of test scores, much like the fake Literacy Crisis earlier erupted from a skewed report on basic skills. For ten years up to 1983, black achievement scores were showing gains while white scores showed significant losses. There is no such thing as 'the average student' or 'the average graduate' in American education. Hunt and the NSB referred to these 'averages' to prove that the *whole* education system had become mediocre. In fact, school performance in an unequal society breaks down radically according to class, race, sex, region and course of study (academic or occupational, which is another reading of class, sex and race). SAT scores, for example, historically show black students scoring one standard deviation below whites; women scoring higher than men in the verbal section and lower in the math; education majors and career education students scoring below liberal arts majors, and so on. The fake 'average student' teaches us nothing about the real conditions of American education. If we look closely at the racial breakdown of achievement in the 1970s, the *white mediocrity* alarming the official commissions becomes more apparent.

The improving minority position vis à vis white scores could be noted from the fabled SAT itself. In a 1982 press release on the sudden turn-around that year in the SAT decline, the College Board reported that

> The increase in average test scores for the nations's college-bound seniors on the SAT . . . was due significantly to improvements in minority group scores, despite the relatively low numbers of minority SAT-test-takers. . . . For most minority groups, the improvement from 1981 to 1982 was larger than the overall national gain and was largest for blacks, whose verbal scores rose nine points and mathematical scores rose four points, compared to a two-point gain in verbal and no gain in math for the white majority. . . . Over the past six years . . . the gap between minorities and whites is narrowing at a fairly steady pace. . . . Between 1976 and 1982, when scores for whites declined from 451 to 444 on the verbal section and from 493 to 483 on the math section, scores for most minority groups rose.[89]

The College Board President, George Hanford, concluded that 'The increase in scores for most minority groups also coincided with an increase in the number of minority students taking the test. This is an encouraging sign since an enlarged population of test-takers is often associated with a decline in scores.'

Hunt, in *Action for Excellence*, noted improving minority scores and took this as a sign that we need to move on to 'quality' because the task of 'equality' has been won:

> There were improvements in basic skills among the lowest-performing 25 per cent of students. Black students as a group . . . showed actual improvements in their performance of basic tests of reading, writing, and computing – which suggests that our efforts over the past two decades to improve educational opportunities for these young people have had real impact. . . . The largest drop-offs in achievement occurred in the most able students. This suggests that we may be regressing from the standard of literacy which was considered adequate 15 years ago.[90]

Hunt read black gains and white losses as an *overall* decline in the standard of literacy. Boyer objected to this kind of measurement, insisting that equality had to be defined as a chapter of American education still to be written, not finished in the past. He noted in *High School* the decline of the black drop-out rate, from 13 per cent in 1970 to 6.5 per cent in 1980.[91]

Ironically, the most extensive discussion of the black-white split came in a background paper to the most aggressive report against federal policy for the disadvantaged. Paul Peterson from the University of Chicago was commissioned to write a lengthy statistical policy study for the Twentieth Century Fund agenda, *Making the Grade*. While the report's majority tilted for quality against equality, and the noisy minority appended footnote after footnote dissenting in the name of equity, Peterson's paper refused to fault federal compensatory programs. From his research, he not only avoided the fiction of 'the average student,' but he also could not support the Fund's declaration that a serious decline in education had occurred. He concluded on the opposite trends in racial scores that

> The difference in educational performance between blacks and white noticeably declined among both the younger and older age groups. Black nine-year-olds made modest gains in mathematics, while the test scores of white nine-year-olds slipped. Among the thirteen-year-olds, the gap between blacks and whites narrowed in both reading and mathematics. Among seventeen-year-olds, the performances of both white and black students in mathematics and science fell, but the slippage among white students was greater. In reading, the performance of blacks improved, while white students' test scores fell.[92]

Peterson drew on NAEP achievement test summaries through the 1970s and from results tabulated by the National Center for Educational Statistics. The rising performance of blacks in education was consistent with Richard Freeman's earlier analysis of the differential impact of overeducation on students.[93] Those groups with lower aspirations would find schooling more attractive even as the job market clout of degrees declined. Elite, white males who historically had the most advantages in society would feel the downwardly-mobile effects of a stagnant economy more. Thus, in the 1970s, Freeman found that college students from more-advantaged homes were more likely to drop out than those from lower-class backgrounds, a reversal of historical trends.

What Freeman failed to assess was the social support to equality still operative from the liberal reforms and protest movements of the 1960s. Neither he nor the restorationists of the third phase were willing to include the protest period as a social support to the educational performance of women and minorities. An even thornier problem for those interested in justifying inequality and adjusting people to settle for less, is the difficulty blacks had in translating educational gains into economic gains. If they were improving in basic skills through the very period of the Literacy Crisis, why was the black economic picture not advancing along with the brighter educational one? The answer is racism and inequality, but this would point a critical finger at the system. To explain away the discrepancy between black educational gains and black economic regression, the theme of 'the new basics' and of academic-computer study for the twenty-first century entered. This ideologized inequality into a problem of student deficits. The black student may have basic skills, but now she or he needed ultra-competence in white English, and computer fluency. Without these and the academics traditionally kept from dominated groups, success was not yet theirs to hold.

The third phase could only justify inequality and make people settle for less if it defined the white mediocrity crisis as a *general* crisis of student-teacher underachievement. The world was described from the point of view of the privileged whose partisan programs disguised the failure of the economy to provide equality. This maneuver through consciousness held the fate of the system in its hands. If blacks and others could not be convinced that *they* were the problem, the built-in inequality of society would be threatened with exposure for the system it is, a complex structure giving the advantaged more advantages.

Under the Pentagon: subterranean homesick blues

If the crisis in white mediocrity was limited only to segregating and motivating the deactivated white elite students, the third phase might have had an easier time of it. The problem of animating the high-achievers was equal to the problem of motivating the great middle. While the official reports noted that the traditionally high-achievers were not taking enough math, science and foreign language courses, and scoring lower on the SAT, they also drew a sorry picture of larger youth alienation. Peterson's vexation was typical:

> While it seems to be the case that students, especially white students, are learning less in their adolescent years, it is not clear whether this is due to lower educational standards in high schools; less respect for teacher authority among students; less parental instruction as children enter adulthood; increasing restlessness and anomie within a youth culture pervaded by drugs, alcohol, and premarital sex; lower expectations for success in adult life; or all of these.[94]

Sizer recognized student alienation as well as the power of youth to resist schooling: 'these were considerable people, ones who would play the game adult educators asked them to play only when and how they wanted to. . . . In this sense, kids run schools.'[95] While Sizer joined Goodlad and Leonard in seeing schools as a boring offense to student intelligence, the official reports interpreted youth resistance in a negative light. They drew from the Peterson model of student social pathology: drop-outs, underachievers, endless remediation thanks to student illiteracy, alcoholism, absenteeism, VD epidemics, out-of-wedlock babies, and cruising through school on soft electives.

The burden of official diagnosis is that students still cannot read, write, add, speak or follow instructions. They took their undisciplined minds and behaviors into the job world and into the military after school. They were choking college with remedial work that should have been taken care of in high school. The military consequences of this pathology were noted as much as the business price. The NCEE said in *A Nation at Risk*:

> Business and military leaders complain that they are required to spend millions of dollars on costly remedial education and training programs in such basic skills as reading, writing, spelling, and computation. The Department of the Navy, for example, reported to the Commission that one-quarter of its recent recruits cannot read at the ninth-grade level, the minimum needed simply to understand written safety instructions. Without remedial work, they cannot even begin,

much less complete, the sophisticated training essential in much of the modern military.[96]

The Hunt report agreed that 'In the armed forces, sophisticated weapons systems require more sophisticated skills.' The National Science Board report concurred that more sophisticated knowledge and less remediation were needed for military security. In the heat of this debate, the Congressional chair of a bi-partisan task force on education appealed for more money in terms of education for defense:

> How can we have a strong defense, how can we have people operating the weapons and designing new weapons, how can we have a strong leadership, how can we have a strong industrial base, how can we provide more and more jobs and an expanding economy . . . if the President is going to cut money for education?[97]

The schools were accused of poorly preparing the manpower sent on to the military and to industry. Principals, teachers and parents were instructed to get tough on students. While it was up to school and the family to properly socialize the next generation of soldiers and workers, it was up to government to pursue the fiscal policies favorable to business and the arms race. In this regard, the military had no complaints. Its budgets began climbing in the later Carter years and then soared with Reagan. Schools were not targeted for more federal funds, despite the great flurry of reports examining educational failures. Something other than a federal finance strategy was intended for public education. Money would not be directed away from corporate profits and from the military, so where would the funds necessary to restore educational quality come from? Remember that ten years of economic stagnation had left every major institution in a depression, not just the schools. If twenty major studies had been carried out in 1983 on housing, transport, roads, bridges, health care, family farms, the courts, the jails, the credit structure, as many alarms would have been raised there as were flung around over public education. The system was generally eroding, in far weaker shape than in the 1960s. Some privileged sectors of the economy were developing in the midst of general decline – high-tech, the military, finance institutions. Which of the many disintegrating social

spheres would be or could be reformed? Education got a leg up
on all the others probably because it is the single largest constituency. Also, it is the place where the adjustment of future labor
to 'settling for less' in a high-tech society had to be achieved.
Economic recovery through rearmament required people to live
with guns instead of butter.

Schooling was recruited in 1983 to help the adjustment to the
austerity of the arms race. Even if there was doubtful payoff at
the end of the school road, you were still required to behave and
study hard. An unequal and exhausted job market promised you
relief in the twenty-first century. For now, students and teachers
were required to shape up. This explains why 'discipline' became
such a key theme in 1983. The less tangible the rewards from
following the rules, the more you have to impose authority to get
people to perform. The call for autocracy in school principals in
1983 marked the anti-democratic drift of the new economics.
One concrete strategy to get people to shape up without tangible
rewards is called 'jawboning.' Jawboning requires a strongman or
strongwoman at the top who knows how to lecture people. This
meets the official appeal for 'leadership.' Jawboning is the
cheapest way to break a performance strike. It raises productivity
by cajoling, embarrassing and regimenting people. The rules are
carefully and publicly detailed by a visible, imposing figure. There
is no debate and no dissent permitted on the rules. It is a take-
it-or-leave-it proposition. After the rules are announced, it helps
for the strongman to make an example out of some people to
demonstrate that he or she means business. Following this punitive
episode, the jawboner has to continue lecturing students and
teachers while maintaining minute surveillance of their activities.
The importance of jawboning as a cheap, anti-democratic method
of reform was highlighted by media coverage of strong principals,
especially Joe Clark, mentioned previously, the black ex-drill
sergeant praised by Reagan and on TV several times.[98] He
expelled 10 per cent of the students soon after he took over
East Patterson High School. The military became the model of
excellence in an economy wildly tilted towards military
production.

A conservative jawboner at the university level was Chester
Finn, one member of the commission producing *Making the*

Grade. He looked out on the reform fever sweeping the nation after 1983 and wrote that

> Most remarkable of all is the fact that the qualitative reforms now underway in American education coincide with a period of grave financial distress for many schools and colleges. . . . How, one may ask, is it possible to witness all these signs of educational revitalization even when so many of our schools and colleges are in such straitened fiscal circumstances? . . . The society appears to have shelved the long-established notion that doing something better necessarily means doing it more expensively. . . . We tended to forget how much can be achieved through intelligent application of energy, resolve, and common sense. Now, we are remembering it.[99]

Finn and other restorationists did not apply the do-more-with-less idea to the military. The transfer of wealth to the private sector and to the new arms race required an ideology *denying* that wealth mattered for excellence! Indeed, the most excellent were those who did most with less, thanks to their aptitude and intelligence. Those who said money was the answer were weaklings and cheats. Golden Age simplicity thus put liberal social programs and demands from the disadvantaged on the defensive. The jawboners reached back into their American Heritage for rugged individualism and pioneer simplicity. This spartan challenge was directed only at the groups activated by the 1960s and of course did not apply to the rich, to the major corporations or to the military.

The new austerity said 'do more with less' and 'pay for anything more out of your own pocket.' This spared government from cutting the military budget and from raising corporate taxes. Financing official reforms from the bottom up took several shapes – regressive taxation, donations and merit pay/master teacher plans for the schools. This scenario unfolded gradually after 1983.

First it was necessary for the authorities to reach consensus on what to do with curriculum. They did this through a succession of interlocking groups and commissions from Paideia in 1982 onward. Next, it was necessary to issue grave alarms from each group. The prestige of the official commissions guaranteed sympathetic and widespread media coverage of the alarms. The consensus agenda, the sheer volume of similar alarms, the great media attention, the promulgation of local and state reform groups as spin-offs, all created a climate of crisis defined from the top. This managed discourse identified student-teacher mediocrity as the cause of educational and economic malaise and then set out concrete plans to turn the ship around. We would lose the Trade War, the Cold War and the chance for prosperity unless we all worked together fast. The alarms raised anxiety which the spectacle of strong leadership soothed. As is usual, strong action often wins early public approval, because weary people keep looking for someone to do something about the mess we are in.

Massive press coverage convinced the public that the new jawboners meant business. Once public acceptance of the crisis and of official solutions emerged, it was time to present the bill. Regressive taxes were identified as the source of funds to finance school excellence. Small increases in sales, income and property taxes on householders were suggested, as polls indicated growing public willingness to pay higher taxes for quality schools. Ten years of hard times made everyone resist any new taxes. Also, the reputation of public schooling was low, so people did not want to throw more money that way. Further, the credibility of politicians and businessmen was declining, so their appeals for higher taxes usually fell on deaf ears. The 1983 crisis scenario changed this. The low opinion of public education was ironically used to create the crisis climate. That climate engineered a high opinion of the official reform wave, thus permitting new taxation. Tax-increase plans spread from state to state as the official movement gained momentum.[100] This strategy generated new revenues from the bottom in hard times, while protecting key constituencies at the top – the military-industrial complex, high-tech corporate profits, the rich and their tax loopholes, tax abatements for corporate construction in local areas, the oil depletion allowance, etc. The education crisis and regressive bottom-taxation thus distracted from the real economic crisis rooted in the economy. Businesses in the third-phase plan were called upon to 'do their part,' by getting more involved in schools, adopting poor districts like orphans, donating over-age equipment, offering excess supplies and furniture, and by lending experts to short-staffed departments. All this generosity was tax-deductible. Citizens were encouraged to follow the generosity of business by donating their time and their resources to local schools. It was national bake-sale time for excellence in education.

A second mechanism to get the bottom to finance the reform plan invented by the top came through the merit pay/master teacher plan. This scheme promised to make teacher-pay performance-based and meritocratic. The best would be rewarded, at last. A career-ladder would give teachers quality-marks to shoot for. Underneath these surface claims, the subterranean issues involved the problem of attracting more math-science teachers, raising entry-level salaries from their dismal low place, so that higher-achieving and hence more white candidates would choose education as a career, and, lastly, how to discipline new teachers and old ones, in the face of the stubborn performance strike now underway and in the face of tenure held by most of the teachers currently in-service. Each of these problems was complicated by the presence of two giant teachers unions which interfered with management's ability to adjust pay scales and curriculum.

The wage package is the big-ticket item for any sector of the economy. It is the first place management looks when it wants to cut costs or raise profits. The 2.2 million public schoolteachers are paid poorly for their hard work but they do have one of the most democratic wage scales of any laboring group. The scales rise in small steps based on seniority. They are negotiated collectively in an across-the-board, everybody's-in-the-same-boat manner. This encourages solidarity. Such collectivity stands in the way of management's desire for 'differential pay.' The NSB in its report called bluntly for differential pay, higher wages for math, science and engineering teachers, and damn the torpedoes. The power of the two giant teachers unions forced the authorities to engage in a more complex maneuver called merit pay/master teacher plans, which disguise naked management control with the themes of career-ladder, 'teacher recognition', and meritocratic, value-free standards.

Management wanted to reallocate selectively the teacher wage package so that math and science teachers were paid more, out of a seemingly neutral, merit-based system. The overall wage package would increase slightly, financed by regressive taxation on sales, income and property of householders. But the extra wages would be distributed differentially and inequitably. Those teachers in subjects more easily quantified would have an advantage over those subjects less easily measured for 'effective' teaching. It was simply easier to go into a math, science or tech course and measure cognitive skills in students, and hence determine that 'meritorious' teaching had occurred there. Humanistic subjects taking holistic approaches were bound to lose out in such an arrangement. Money could then be tilted to raising entry-level salaries and to extra pay for the tech contingents. The symmetry was ideal: new tax monies raised unequally from citizens will be distributed unequally to teachers.

Raising entry-level salaries was as important as differentially paying math and science teachers more. The teaching profession was no longer desirable by 1983, thanks to declining wages, lowered prestige and decaying schools. Students coming through the vocationalized, basics-depressed schools of the 1970s could hardly be expected to choose teaching for a career. The 1983 reports noted how education majors were being drawn from lower-achieving student groups. This was on the eve of a new baby boom which would dramatically raise the demand for teachers in the coming two decades. As a disabled profession, teaching was vulnerable to minority penetration in the 1980s, even though as of 1983 only 8 per cent of the teacher force was non-white.[101] Suspiciously, part of the third phase reform included new competency tests for pre-service teachers. They were tested in standard usage and in their subject areas prior to licensing. Many black candidates began failing these exams, thus opening spaces for whites.[102] Even a depressed profession still offered upward mobility for minorities, so the sudden appearance of competency exams just when the pay, prestige and demand for teachers were about to rise can only be interpreted for the racist impact it had. The effect was to expel people of color already in the pipeline to teaching. This impact was consistent with the curricular reforms which would benefit the already advantaged, those familiar with Standard English and those with computers at home to practice on.

Besides controlling the future color of the teacher corps, the pre-service competency tests fit the same management discipline intended from merit pay plans. A get-tough management had to condition new teachers and old ones to jump at the crack of the whip. It also had to bully them into cracking their own whips over the students' heads. The big changes were being imposed rather than negotiated, so an autocratic atmosphere of performance-testing put teachers on the defensive. This was especially important given the performance strike out of which new teachers and old ones would have to be shaken. The undisciplined new teachers would have to get the word fast even before they began work. The old teachers, an aging corps of tenured people who could not be disciplined with the threat of dismissal, would be managed by the threat of pay raises for only some.

These official maneuvers were more than an erosion of democracy. They were also an insult to the reasons so many teachers entered education. For many, it was a calling, not for money or fame, but rather for public service and social dedication. The most stirring rewards of teaching come from the human potential liberated in a classroom. The austerity and the arms race degraded this gift of labor through one devious regimen after another, carrots and sticks, divide and conquer, depressant curricula, more surveillance, jawboning, in a growing desperation to get students and teachers performing.

A society that refuses to direct available resources to education must use tough authority to get students and teachers to perform. Rules and punishment substitute for prosperity and democracy. Instead of merit pay schemes, teachers need big pay increases across-the-board. They should establish their own mechanisms for rewarding peers they admire. Also, there should be mechanisms by which students and the community both reward and challenge teachers, for their devotion and for their lapses. These interactions should be self-organizing and mutual, based in support rather than punishment or unequal rewards. Even more than higher pay, teachers need shorter hours, smaller classes and better working conditions. Both Boyer and Goodlad suggested the four-hour course load per day. To this should be added the four-day work week. This will require hiring many more teachers to take on the fifth day and the students in small classes. Most of all, teachers need a pedagogy of reconciliation with their students. Sizer recommended less administration and a simpler curriculum, which permitted students to leave high school after mastering basic literacy or after mastering an advanced course of study. The grand structure of curriculum matters less than the learning process in each classroom. In this regard, Goodlad understood best the need for an active, participant classroom. His call for an end to teacher-talk education built on Herb Kohl's program for a humanizing pedagogy through basic skills, published a year before the great crisis of 1983, but not getting the attention it deserved in the conservative climate of the time.[103] Without an empowering pedagogy, no agenda for school reform can work. Students will only be more alienated and will clearly sabotage the best-designed plans. Disempowering agendas are self-defeating because they force students into sabotage or non-cooperation. Students will animate themselves only for a humanizing, inspiring classroom, which joins learning to experience, which makes every day interesting, and which nurtures their link to society and to the future. Budget cuts, discipline, tests, requirements, remote academics and computer-rites will eventually fall to their resistance.

Big brother's small problems

The short-run is more promising for the third-wavers. Regressive taxation proved acceptable to several constituencies. Merit pay made some progress against teacher-union opposition. Tough new requirements changed the curriculum from state to state. Computers poured into schools and colleges. Teacher-training computer seminars sprouted up in ways similar to the promotion of career education a decade earlier. The authorities made a powerful initiative in 1983 and successfully defined the terrain of battle. The world was turned upside down as education was blamed for the economic crisis. The long-term prospect was less hopeful, not only because an austerity program was bound to provoke student resistance, but also because the sheer costs of the new regime would be beyond what could be raised from regressive taxation and bake-sale contributions. Excellence simply cost a lot more than the authorities would budget for universal quality.

Some of the third-phase reports dared to estimate the cost of excellence. Boyer's cost-accounting indicated that simply repairing the degraded school buildings in the nation would cost some $25 billion. The price of extending the school year to 220 days added another $20 billion to the education bill. Extending the school day from 6.5 to 8 hours would cost $20 billion as well. A master teacher plan would eventually require $5 billion a year, according to the Twentieth Century Fund. *Time* estimated, in its cover-story on the 1983 crisis, that enough computer hardware for each student to spend 30 minutes a day with hands-on practice would cost $4.5 billion plus twice that amount for teacher-training. A modest $5,000 pay increase for teacher salaries equaled $11 billion annually. The National Science Board report indicated that designating only one in every forty schools as a pilot project in excellence would cost at least $829 million every year. Annual school costs in 1983 were running at about $130 billion, so the price of the third-phase reforms was simply astronomical. If these called-for changes were not financed, and if the job market still did not reward graduates, then the official campaign could not sustain its offensive. It will erode because it cannot deliver the promises it made, which will only make its discipline demands more intolerable.

Student resistance to arbitrary authority, and the money shortage, were two probable saboteurs of the third phase, but so was the teacher shortage. The arms race and the growth of high-tech industries drained math, science and engineering teachers from the schools into the private sector. Up to half of the new math teachers in schools were dragooned from other fields. Where would the teachers come from to teach all the new required courses in math, science and even English? If they found the teachers, where would they find the money to pay them? If they required more writing and more homework, how would English teachers possibly cope, given that their current class sizes were too large already? If class sizes were lowered, then more teachers would have to be hired, and more money would have to be found to pay for larger staffs, and larger staffs of new teachers would be harder to police with a mandated curriculum.

From the high school students' point of view, most of what came down from the authorities was bound to be bad news. 'The new basics' would be more of the talky courses which bore them to death. Such a 'new' curriculum also left out the item most important to them: sex. Even the liberal undercurrent in Goodlad, Boyer and Sizer kept hands off this subject. Boyer wondered how school could be so out of touch with student interests, but left his remarks at that. Goodlad saw the remoteness of school from student life creating a tension about to explode, but he left sexuality out of his curriculum themes. Sizer spoke at length about the importance of sex to adolescents, yet his streamlining of curriculum and administration did not include addressing the

sexual conditions of students. Even the more adventurous critics
of third-phase schooling – from Kohl and Leonard to Andrew
Hacker and Joel Spring – did not take on the question of sex.[104]
Everyone recognized the centrality of this theme in student life
and few said anything constructive about it. Why this silence? Is
it prudishness? Is it unacknowledged confusion about how to
deal with it? Is it a self-censoring surrender to the power of the
restoration, whose new right wing made sex education into a
devil? Is it a politic silence, so that teachers, parents, citizens and
policy-makers will take all their other criticisms seriously, without
the disturbing issue of sex getting in the way? What chance did
the official reform have with students as long as it denied sex?
What chance would *alternate* education have if it also denied
student sexuality? There is no glib answer to this issue. Students
have a right to sexuality in the same way that they have a right
to speak their own voices and to co-participate in curriculum
design. Sexual themes and democratic governance will have to be
tested in the real situations of each school, student group and
community. Ignoring sex and preventing democracy make
education impossible. But fake forms of each are equally destructive. Laundered sex education only confuses the issue. The denial
of humanizing discussion of sex guarantees its exploitation in films,
music and print media. It also guarantees the sullen alienation of
students.

Another sabotaging feature built into the third-phase agenda is
the collision of Standard English with minority students. The
percentage of non-white students in public schools will continue
to grow while the new plan is to cut back on bilingual and bi-
dialectical programs. This racial imposition of correct usage will
create more failure as well as more hostility in the schools. Such
disorder will help discredit the official plans.

Sex and order in the Golden Age

In the Golden Age of the 1950s, a great cry was not raised about
sex, but there were grave concerns for the basics, for the Cold
War and even for 'excellence.' *Life* magazine declared in 1958,
soon after Sputnik, that 'the outcome of the arms race will depend
eventually on our schools and those of the Russians. . . . It is

hard to deny that America's schools, which were supposed to reflect one of history's noblest dreams . . . have degenerated into a system for coddling and entertaining the mediocre.'[105] In that year, John Gardner produced his study *The Pursuit of Excellence*. A far more influential post-Sputnik report was Conant's *The American High School Today* (1959), an early Carnegie study on education.[106] Conant's twenty-one recommendations for curriculum reform were almost identical to the academic agenda of the 1983 reports, minus computer education.

The graveyard of the 1950s provided conservative ways of seeing the world as well as concrete reform agendas. Conant was out from his Harvard base in 1959 when he visited high schools for his study. He found that 'the majority of bright boys and girls were not working hard enough. The academically talented student is not being sufficiently challenged . . . and his program of academic subjects is not of sufficient range. . . . From the 15 per cent of the youth who are academically talented will come the future professional men and women.'[107] He comfortably promoted academics only for an elite. In the good old days, the best were the best and schools should get on with the job of selecting excellence. Conant was confident that this could be done effectively. 'No radical alteration in the basic pattern of education is necessary to improve our public high schools,' he wrote.[108] The model of school as an information delivery-system was already in place. It only needed to be tuned up. Compare Conant's assurance to the alarms and overhauls in the third phase of the restoration. The closing note of the NCEE's *A Nation at Risk* captured the urgency of 1983:

> Our final word, perhaps better characterized as a plea, is that all segments of our population give attention to the implementation of our recommendations. Our present plight did not appear overnight, and the responsibility for our current situation is widespread. Reform of our educational system will take time and unwavering commitment. . . . It is by our willingness to take up the challenge and see it through that America's place in the world will either be secured or forfeited.[109]

The stakes have grown higher, the problems more tangled, the opposing forces more complex since Conant's tour.

Conant's junior colleague from Harvard, Jerome Bruner, was also on a tour of American schools back then. He found there 'the passivity of knowledge-getting' and 'the embarrassment of passion.'[110] From his observations, and in an influential small book called *The Process of Education* (1960),[111] Bruner raised issues of learning process that eluded Conant. Twenty-five years later, Goodlad made the sorry discovery that classrooms were as passive and as unemotional as they were in the Golden Age of the 1950s. Twenty-five years from now, we may make the same charge, if the third-phase agenda carries the day.

The years since Sputnik have marked a monumental passage in the great arc of history. A comfortable age in the 1950s was swept into the vortex of Sputnik and then into the upheavals of the 1960s. In response to the egalitarian surge from below, authorities in the 1970s and 1980s reached back in time for models of education. Yet the restoration in school and society had trouble putting all the pieces back together again. The 1983 project was the most ambitious and risky of all the initiatives. Its backward ideas and false promises can produce even greater student resistance. If consensus is not engineered successfully for the official plans, more decay in the schools will result as well as more resistance. That resistance may yet become its own angel of reform. If students move from negative sabotage to positive change, they will invent their own agenda in place of settling for less. This future of 'more' needs teachers, students and citizens defining democratic forms of excellence.

5 The hinge of 1983
Answers rise like angels:
agendas for transformation

There is always space for education to act. The question is to
find out what are the limits of this space.

Paulo Freire, 1981 seminar

Those who feel more class time and homework is the answer
are not treating the cause of the problem but the symptom.

Remedial writing student, 1983

How do you expect a kid to sit down and write an essay when
he doesn't have a desk to write it at and the teacher doesn't
have paper?

New York teacher, 1984

Most schools are dreary, boring places. Perhaps it is time to
encourage educators to take risks, to try out new ideas.

George Leonard, 'The Great School Reform Hoax' (1984)

Paradise locks

The gates of heaven have many locks and the keys invented here
on planet earth do not always fit. Among the many earth angels
working on the locks, there was Mortimer Adler in 1982,
convinced that a bookish Paideia was the key to turning America

into an earthly paradise. But frustration has been more common than divine success from traditional agendas. One telling moment of frustration came from Henry Chauncey, the President of the Educational Testing Service (ETS) in the mid–1950s. He complained that 'although some 1,400 studies in the teaching of arithmetic alone had been made up to 1946, we still know little of a definitive nature about how mathematics should be taught.'[1]

Chauncey was impatient to find in 1955 that many scholarly students avoided math and science in high school. They chose non-academic general courses instead. This student resistance would perplex Sidney Marland in 1971 and would infuriate the National Commission on Excellence in Education (NCEE) in 1983. Marland wanted less resistance to occupational courses. The NCEE agreed with Chauncey on the need for more student attention to math, science and academics. Thirty years ago, policy-makers like Chauncey felt that *too little college material* was going on to college. In the 1970s and 1980s, they concluded that *too much non-college material* was going on to college. This vexing reversal was like the irony of producing 'over-education' and 'underachievement' at the same time.

Ironies of another kind also dogged Marland's vast labors in the restoration. He had hoped to absorb academic and general courses into a single career program for high school and college: 'We need to break down the barriers that divide our educational system into parochial enclaves. We must blend our curricula and our students into one flexible, comprehensive system.'[2] The third-phase agendas turned his scheme on its head by absorbing careerism into academics instead. Rather than occupationalism being the dominant theme for all courses and students, academics would be the core curriculum for all. The Dupont report of 1984, *High Schools and the Changing Workplace*, noted this stunning reversal with some embarrassment: 'The assertion that high school graduates who proceed directly to the workplace need the same education in the core competencies as those going on to college may seem startling, but the panel believes such education to be essential.'[3]

An unstable restoration thus exchanged heresies from its first to its third phase. The career heresy of work-themes for all violated the tracking-out of the job-bound mass from the college-bound elite. The 'excellence' heresy of academics for all equally violated this sorting function of the schools. While careerism offered too little to inspire students, the new academic mystique promised everyone too much. With academics for all, schools promoted 'an ideology of social mobility that is at odds with high levels of unemployment and the overabundance of qualified workers,' in Henry Giroux's words.[4] The new academics may simply flunk out all those who had been tracked out before. But this will only create more discrediting failure for the school system and more student alienation. Here was a teetering rearrangement swung open by the great hinge of 1983.

Double hinge: reversing the reversal

Can the current crises in school and society be solved without economic restructuring? Can school policy and classroom pedagogy have a significant effect on social transformation? A range of opposition answers to these questions have been proposed in the recent period. However, before considering some of these alternate agendas, it helps to notice that major reconstruction is already underway from the right. The issue of whether society needs fundamental restructuring has already been preempted by the restoration. The demise of liberal arts in the university and of liberalism in society are two signs of this conservative overhaul. By 1983, the reversal of the 1960s matured into plans to redefine society generally. The agendas have been panoramic – from high school to graduate school, from reorganized home mortgages to restructured telephone service, from a reinvented 'square' tomato to the computerized home, from robots replacing workers to financial control boards replacing elected officials, from industry deregulation to breaking the minimum wage for teenagers.

A new social contract was being written from above with little debate at the bottom. At stake were the standard of living, the quality of work and education, and the political rights of average Americans. These were the sacrifices required to solve at last the long business crisis. That crisis itself was used as an opportunity to overcome the stalemate. A promise of economic recovery was the carrot justifying the stick of austerity. A similar promise of recovery through rearmament also legitimized the new arms race.

The carrots were promises but the sticks were real clubs thrown at the tough problem of building conservative consensus.

Weak consensus for austerity slowed the drift to the right in the 1970s and 1980s. However, the greater strength of conservatism was in the decline of opposition; 1983 kept the opposition on the defensive while broadening the territory for official consensus. Dissenting voices were forced to react to the most manufactured crisis since Sputnik. The commissions occupied center stage. Other points of view ran around the circle trying to catch up with them. Seizing the initiative is an ideal strategy for winning battles, but winning the war is another thing. On the one hand, the comprehensive overhaul revealed the unstable position of authority no less than it showed an opening to the right. On the other hand, the great debate rehabilitated the defensive opposition even as it kept democratic dissent at the margins. Official consensus at the top was forged in a public arena including the renewal of divergent opinions.

The dangers of this two-way street equal the opportunities. If the overhaul fails to restore performance in classrooms, productivity in workplaces, and prosperity in society, the groups that launched it will be further discredited, at a time when establishment legitimacy is low. Given that school reform cannot provoke economic recovery and that academics are the talky courses students flee from, the chances for failure are lively. This will create more openings for opposition culture. That new opposition will find a strident establishment busily remaking society. With restoration forces on the offensive, it will be necessary to insert opposition in the cracks of the official project. Wedged in the large terrain of contradictions, it is possible to rouse more debate, to reveal the consequences of the agendas, to exert a counter-pull away from the brave new world settling into place.

Alpha plans and gamma dramas: keys for the cracks

Opposition culture has a number of resources to draw on for responses to the restoration. There remained in this period a remarkable amount of protest, most visible in anti-nuclear, anti-apartheid and anti-intervention politics. The number of marches, teach-ins, sit-ins, civil disobedience, dissident publications, politicized art, film, dance and theater has been extraordinary for a conservative age. At the same time, the economic crisis made life harder for people, creating more unorganized alienation from the system. Dissident groups have a large base of popular grievances to speak to. The unpopular austerity hastened the decline of social institutions since the 1960s. In turn, institutional decay meant unmet needs, and those needs translated into declining legitimacy for the authorities. Restoring legitimacy is one point at which curriculum and economics meet, so the relation of school reform to social change became urgent after 1983. To develop an alternate agenda for this change, a look at some key opposition proposals is helpful.

One important statement from the left was Christopher Jencks's study *Inequality* (1972). When he asked if schools were effective agents for social change, he reached some dismal conclusions. The liberal reforms of the 1960s produced little egalitarian change in social hierarchy, he found:

> None of the evidence we have reviewed suggests that school reform can be expected to bring about significant social changes outside schools. . . . Equalizing educational opportunity would do very little to make adults more equal [because] children seem to be far more influenced by what happens at home than by what happens in school. They may also be more influenced by what happens on the streets and by what they see on television. Second, reformers have very little control over those aspects of school life that affect children. Reallocating resources, reassigning pupils, and rewriting curriculum seldom change the way teachers and students actually treat each other minute by minute. Third, even when a school exerts an unusual influence on children, the resulting changes are not likely to persist into adulthood. . . . A school's output depends largely on a single input, namely the character of the entering children.[5]

These findings raised many awkward problems. They were consistent with the 1966 Coleman study which found minority students performing better in desegregated schools, but which still defined family background as the fateful variable in school success. From a conservative point of view, the small cognitive gains from integration and compensatory education did not justify the costs.

165

From an egalitarian point of view, the limits of education reform only posed the need for larger structural changes in school and society. The effects of race, class and environment could only be reversed by a major equality program in society at large, according to Jencks. On the other hand, traditional pedagogy contradicted the meliorative intentions of compensatory programs. This suggested that curriculum needed as much transformation as any other part of society.

Jencks's findings led him to look away from education, but he turned lively egalitarian eyes on the social structure. Such a political turn showed the advance of protest culture from the 1960s. This advance of reform to the economic system made the intervention of the restoration timely. Just before the early restoration turned the tide against protest culture, Jencks proposed ideas for the democratization of society:

- Wage levels within occupations should be equalized. This would localize the thrust for equality into single job areas and institutions. Such 'micropolitics' would give individuals in lower ranks more power directly at the workplace. National redistribution of income would be more remote.
- Jobs within occupational sectors should be rotated so that expertise is democratically distributed rather than monopolized by an elite. Access to training within your occupation would encourage higher aspirations at the bottom and more changeover at the top.
- Tax the beneficiaries of public education higher rates to pay for schooling. Upper-income white males benefit the most from their years of education, so they should pay proportionately more for the advantages education confers on them. The present tax system is a resource-transfer from the lower groups to the upper ones, because the less successful wage-earner gets less education.
- Mobilize mass support for an egalitarian agenda where such support does not now exist.

As education reforms, Jencks made the following suggestions:

- Hindrances to aspiration should be removed. Entry-testing and college academic requirements punish people for past failures instead of encouraging future success. Open admissions to college can reverse the downward effects of family origins.

- Use judicial rulings and busing where necessary to break the tradition of racial segregation.
- Use open enrollment in school districts to prevent race and class segregation, and to out-flank the ability of rich areas to spend more on students.
- End separate college and non-college tracks in high school. Tracking depresses the aspirations of students who could , succeed in scholastic work.
- Support experimental programs to test the transformative effects of non-traditional methods.

In regard to transformative pedagogy, Jencks understood the lacuna in his study. About the hole on classroom teaching, he said:

We have not tried to explore the effects of the handful of schools that differ drastically from the American norm. We have focused on the differences among the public schools attended by large numbers of children. This means we cannot say much about the theoretical limits of what can be done in a place called school. . . . If schools used their resources differently, additional resources might conceivably have larger payoffs.[6]

A few years later, Wayne Jennings and Joe Nathan addressed the outcomes of experimental curricula: 'For more than 50 years now, studies have been documenting the effectiveness of non-traditional school programs in the United States. This research should cause us to question 95 per cent of current educational practice.'[7] Their report on the accomplishments of deviant approaches to learning was taken from 'startling/disturbing' research largely ignored for decades. When they published their findings, Goodlad was in the field, observing a thousand instances of 'a place called school,' from which he concluded that only experimental methods could uncover the potential of classroom learning.

Jencks's focus on expenditures, test scores and family background tilted his study away from considering the political effects of traditional teaching as well as the potential effects of non-traditional pedagogy. He called for equal spending in rich and poor districts simply because the happiness of all children is of equal importance right now, whether or not budgets affect future test scores and adult incomes. He wrote, 'It is bad for children to be hungry whether or not hunger produces brain damage and it is bad for children to be miserable or bored in school, regardless of whether misery and boredom in school lead to misery and boredom in adult life.' These humane sentiments are worthy of an egalitarian program. What Jencks failed to consider was the function of school spending in the political socialization of students. Plush environments and small classes for the wealthy let them know that they are the dominant class. The social sphere outside the home confirms what is taught in the home. The Standard English approved in school echoes the correct usage of the upper-income family. Conversely, shabby, crowded classrooms impose disrespect on lower-income students. They learn that they are the dominated sector of society. Squalor and indignity in school confirms the message of disempowerment learned in the home. In language, their colloquial speech or slang is an outlaw idiom disapproved by teachers, texts and tests.

The internalizing of dominant and dominated consciousness is the affective heart of schooling. Expenditures and testing are parts of the construction of variant consciousnesses. Education is functional or dysfunctional to society at any instance to the degree it prepares student attitudes appropriate to the needs of an unequal social order. The breakdown in school socialization was a crisis in the 1960s spilling over into the 1980s. The 'better' students became disaffected along with the others. Each restoration campaign after the 1960s set up *cognitive* programs as means to restore the *affective* performance of curriculum. The difficulty of this cognitive/affective transfer was apparent in the great eruption of 1983. The attitude-formation role of schooling has been referred to as 'the hidden curriculum,' though Boyer wryly remarked in *High School* (1983) that there was nothing hidden about it, given all the bells ringing for the change of class.

The hidden curriculum: out of sight, into mind

The debate on school and social change was intense at the moment Jencks issued *Inequality*, a work whose title announced a key

theme of the critical 1960s. Then, the severest critic of domestic-
ating education was Ivan Illich. Unlike Jencks, he did not propose
reforming public schools or any mainstream institution. Illich
denied that any official education could be egalitarian. Large
structures were by definition bureaucratic and manipulative. He
proposed instead small units created and controlled by the learners
themselves.

Illich complained in *Deschooling Society* (1970) that

> the hidden curriculum of schooling initiates the citizen to the
> myth that bureaucracies guided by scientific knowledge are
> efficient and benevolent. . . . And everywhere it develops the
> habit of self-defeating consumption of services and alienating
> production, the tolerance for institutional dependence, and
> the recognition of institutional rankings.[8]

The hidden socialization into hierarchy saturated all aspects of
life, according to Illich, but education was special in attitude-
formation:

> The hidden curriculum of family life, draft, health care, so-
> called professionalism, or of the media, play an important
> part in the institutional manipulation of man's world-vision,
> language and demands. But school enslaves more profoundly
> and more systematically . . . by making learning about oneself,
> about others, and about nature depend on a pre-packaged
> process.[9]

Illich declared that 'most learning requires no teaching.' In
breaking with authority, each of us was 'personally responsible
for his or her own deschooling.' These radically egalitarian ideas
challenged the logic of the schools with the same force that
Jencks's income-leveling plan challenged the economy. Illich
accompanied his analysis with practical proposals for building
alternatives outside official institutions.

Deschooling pointed to the self-organization of 'learning webs'
and 'convivial networks.' The imagery of webs and networks was
a visually democratic antagonist to the mainstream pictures of
school as funnels, channels, tracks, factories and delivery-systems.
Illich sketched four means for achieving a deschooled society:

– *Reference Services to Educational Objects*: Learners will

169

need computer-assisted directories to the things, places, and processes needed for study, such as books, labs, theaters, etc.

- *Skill Exchanges*: This reference service connects people to situations through which they can acquire a self-identified valuable skill.
- *Peer-Matching*: This communications networking assists peers in locating partners for a learning project.
- *Reference Services to Educators-at-Large*: This is a self-described directory of 'professionals, para-professionals and free-lancers,' including recommendations from former clients.

Besides computer-assistance, such small-scale networking required posters, ads and newsletters. As another policy question, Illich proposed tax-credits for parents to allow them to deschool their children. These vouchers could be used for any educational program, not only for ones certified by the state. Ironically, tuition tax-credits emerged as a conservative plank in the restoration. Conservative ideas for tax-credits aimed at supporting private sector schools that were even more authority-dependent than public schools. However, in the debate following his deschooling thesis, Illich saw that uncritical and opportunistic withdrawals from public education could lead in a distorted direction.[10]

Another of his ideas made an ironic re-emergence in restoration clothing. Illich campaigned hard for lower levels of consumption. This call to live with less became, unexpectedly, a key conservative theme. 'Settling for less' in the 1970s and 1980s downwardly adjusted people's aspirations. Illich viewed manipulated high levels of buying as basic to the power of big organizations. Over-consuming goods and services from large structures made people dependent on official delivery-systems. By needing less, you could detach yourself from the tyranny of market forces. What Illich could not foresee was the official campaign to manipulate lower living standards. The depressed 1970s were a dramatically different experience from the fat times of the 1960s. Politically, the manipulated loss of 'the good life' became an exposed flank of the restoration. Austerity and the denial of the American Dream weakened the chance for a strong conservative consensus. This downward dive in the standard of living was not what Illich had in mind when he proposed a self-empowering, egalitarian withdrawal from consumerism. Opposition strategy in the changing winds of culture war thus required an adaptation beyond Illich's call for living with less. To contradict official policy, opposition forces have to encourage high aspirations and the legitimate demand for *more*.

The terms on which 'more' is demanded define whether high expectations restore bureaucratic control or contradict it with egalitarianism. This is a delicate moment in culture war, because consumer consciousness is so basic to sustaining the manipulative status quo. On the one hand, people have the right to material rewards from lives of hard work. On the other hand, groups like minorities, the underemployed young and senior citizens have not historically had material comfort. They live now with unmet needs. Material security cannot be taken for granted, even if we define it as subsistence levels of food, clothing, shelter and medical care. Because goods and services are unequally distributed now, an opposition agenda for 'more' could be empowering if it won a redistribution of income and services. The problem here is not to get the same old delivery-system delivering more of its degraded products and dependent services. Even more complicated in this reconstruction, the environmental movement since the 1960s has been redefining production and consumption in relation to personal health, to world equity, to ecological damage, and to global resource reserves. Opposition agendas cannot simply accept the forced decline in the popular standard of living while wealth continues to accumulate at the top. Neither can they endorse the reckless consumption of unhealthy goods and services. Thus, 'the good life' in the new age will have to go hand-in-hand with redefining security and plenty, as well as a program to see that they are equally distributed. This is a point of policy where self-organization against bureaucracy needs to be coordinated with ecological/egalitarian control of large structures.

Such a redefinition of production and distribution will not be simple because a powerful model of 'the good life' has already been inserted into culture through the consumer marketplace. The old model of consumption will erode more quickly when opposition culture takes the offensive again with new programs. Those new understandings are maturing slowly in the margins of a traditionalist age. The psychological hold of consumerism is not invincible, as the 1960s' 'dressing-down' mystique showed. Among the opposition demands for 'more,' material and spiritual needs will be addressed. The decline in the quality of working and living is an unmet need which old-fashioned consumerism cannot touch. The spiritual dimension of satisfying social life is another exposed flank in the restoration. Austerity spreads harshness rather than rewarding experiences.

Since 1970, a great number of skill-exchanges and learning webs sprang up.[11] This non-formal activity is a political question-mark in a time when tax-credits and lower living standards moved to the right as themes. Deschooling and free-schooling often became havens for an elite, as Illich, Kozol and others noted a decade ago. There is ample room in this society for 'parallel politics' – small-scale alternates coexisting with official institutions without a political contention between them. As long as networks are not in active opposition, they take their place as another part of the market, a voluntary sector, hors de combat. The restoration has lived with a great deal of alternate education, so detached structures are not synonymous with growing opposition. The school system itself created up to 10,000 alternate units enrolling up to 7 per cent of the students.[12] Many keep alive the anti-authority elan of the 1960s, while others are either traditionalist enclaves for back-to-basics advocates, or sanctuaries for white students avoiding integration, or places for problem-students too hard to handle in the regular program.

Still, this picture of parallel-politics is not enough. The opposition value of deschooling is more complicated. Culture war is dynamic. It is not a collision of fixed forces. Each episode changes the political climate and the elements involved. What we observe at any moment can be transformed by the ongoing engagement. This is how a lower living standard and tax-vouchers could move to the right as themes in a few short years after Illich's brilliant interventions. In the restoration, skill-exchanges and alternate schools are not functioning as an active opposition. Yet they may do so when culture war swings back to egalitarian activism. As it stands in the mid-1980s, the lattice of learning webs is more alive than the moribund public schools. In some ways, they take the heat off the mainstream institutions where the bulk of the problems and the people remain. They can also be interpreted as an erosion of traditional legitimacy. The alternate sphere at least shows unofficial ways of doing things. It provides practice in self-organization and safe corners for experimental ideas driven out of the mainstream. As such, the networks and alternate spaces provide sanctuary for retreating opposition where it can maintain some level of maturing activity until conditions are better for an advance from the margins to the center. The dangers here, of course, are that the habits of opposition are most easily corrupted in the margins, while the habits of opposition are left unexercised at the center. The full meaning of these politics will become clearer as the climate of culture war evolves.

Climatology

From a different method and in a wholly different idiom, Illich wound up agreeing with Jencks that the public school system was not a place to produce an egalitarian society. Jencks proposed income-redistribution and job-rotation as the high road to equality, with school policy secondary. Illich's visionary demand was to desert the society altogether and build the alternative outside. Another important variety of opposition which differed from both Jencks and Illich was offered by Samuel Bowles and Herbert Gintis in *Schooling in Capitalist America* (1976).[13]

Bowles and Gintis agreed with Jencks that schools do not originate and cannot cure economic inequality. They analyzed schooling in terms of a 'correspondence principle,' through which schools reproduce social inequality. They agreed with Illich that schools are manipulative. But their departures were key. While Bowles and Gintis strongly developed Jencks's concluding note on socialist reform, they proposed a broad-based transformation through opposition *within* schools and within other mainstream structures. They did not agree with Jencks that schools were marginal to the struggle for equality and they did not agree with Illich that schools were hopelessly controlled instruments.

In their model for opposition, politics within regular schools and large structures mattered most because that was where most people were. They did not expect the system to fall of its own weight or from voluntary desertion for alternatives. To them, deschooling and free-schooling were potential distractions from the tasks of institutional opposition. In a critique of Illich spec-

173

ifically, Gintis argued that bureaucracy itself could be transformed if the logic of the system was opposed.[14] The logic of domination inserted itself in the many institutions of a market economy whose foundations rested in inequality. Cracks, openings, contradictions and unmet needs prevented the logic of domination from being seamless, they proposed, so there were opportunities inside schools and colleges as well as inside all official arenas for organizing transformation.

Their proposals for opposition thus valued public education in ways denied by both Jencks and Illich. A program for joint action in school and society can be extracted from their mid-restoration work:

- Educational alternatives must face the economic roots of school problems, pointing to larger social change outside the classroom, in the corporate economy.
- Balance short-term and long-range objectives.
- Equalize education through open admissions to college, equal school district expenditures, compensatory programs, no tracking and free college tuition.
- Link opposition inside school to groups outside who are oppressed or who take action for social change.
- Curriculum should: undermine inequality; prepare youth for participation in economic democracy; create understanding of how to fight oppression; balance self-development with directed teaching; develop awareness of worker-control experiments and of class-consciousness; inspire a sense of power and mutual respect; discuss and show humane alternatives.
- Councils of teachers, students, parents and community members should be set up to discuss school problems, solutions and policies.

In a later work, *Beyond the Wasteland* (1983), Bowles and other collaborators repeated the call for free undergraduate education and added the idea of low-interest loans to graduate students.[15] This would strengthen equal access to higher education. They argued for more money for public schools, as well as for public investment in libraries, museums and community cultural centers. These centers would act as 'decentralized networks of information-sharing,' a description close to Illich's ideas for learning webs.

Such a shift towards deschooled learning indicated a changing appreciation of non-formal study by Bowles and his co-researchers, David Gordon and Thomas Weiskopf. In the earlier book, Bowles and Gintis had dismissed too quickly the value of alternate units. Some of this formal bias remained in *Beyond the Wasteland*, especially in the proposal that 'paid free time' for workers should be used at degree-granting colleges and in high-school equivalency programs. Their idea would certainly help adults go back to school, but their greater interest was in unstructured learning. To this end, they proposed the museums, libraries and centers with information services. Still more was needed, they contended, in the domain of public parks. These publicly-developed parks could offer inspiring cultural settings for free time. Bowles's transition from doubting free schools to supporting the educational value of parks was significant.

The shift from 1976 to 1983 in the two books also showed his declining interest in educational reform per se. He and his co-authors focused on economic restructuring. The analysis avoided the earlier socialist-marxist idiom and chose a democratic framework. The program still pointed to the egalitarian transfer of wealth and power from the top to the bottom. But this would be accomplished by ending the loopholes and wastes of the present economy and by public investment in social production ignored in the current market. These changes were appropriate to the new conditions of culture war. The advancing restoration drove socialism off the agenda. The conservative reversal of the 1960s chilled the radicalizing themes of the protest era. Further, conservative economic policy had produced a disastrous stagnation. 'Hard times' was a popular issue waiting for the opposition. The proposals to end waste, end loopholes, and end the market-domination of investment, filled a vulnerable vacuum. Lastly, the peremptory, authoritarian politics of the restoration after Reagan broadened the need to defend democracy. The expanding terrain for opposition lay in the direction of democratic rights and recovery through social investment. They wisely found the cracks in the walls of authority and situated themselves in the open space for opposition.

Widening the cracks

To help situate opposition in the cracks and openings available, it matters to know whose shoulders you are standing on and in what directions you might look. The previous review of some opposition analyses offered several models for egalitarian counter-agendas. Varieties of opposition develop in relation to the main themes of a period. In the restoration, the themes underlying the campaigns for careerism, for back-to-basics and for excellence have been:

- restoring authority and reversing mass movements
- restoring the good names of business and the military
- adjusting people to 'settling for less' in activism and aspirations and to accepting a new arms race
- justifying inequality through testing and language regimes
- disguising inequality as excellence
- disguising job-training as computer literacy
- glamorizing the cheap-labor future of high-tech
- concentrating administrative power through merit-pay plans and through new required testing and courses for students
- selectively pushing math and science under general cover of academics for all
- controlling critical learning in liberal arts through career and basic skill programs
- financing school reform through regressive taxation
- tilting school funds away from compensatory programs, in the name of excellence
- using Standard English, correct usage and 'American Heritage'[16] core curricula to tilt curriculum away from bilingual, bidialectical, interdisciplinary, women's and minority studies
- using preservice licensing exams in literacy to screen out minority candidates and attract more whites to teaching, on the eve of a new baby boom in the 1980s.

This program for culture war was accompanied by structured silences on a number of key questions. The silences allowed restoration forces in the comprehensive overhaul of 1983 to stay mute on the seamy effects of conservative policy. Among the issues ignored in the 1983 reports were:

- library and textbook censorship
- creation science challenging evolution
- attacks on secular humanism, sex education, busing, affirmative action, gay rights
- school budget cuts and military budget increases
- rising test scores among black students
- high unemployment despite careerism in schools and colleges
- the disabling of liberal arts by careerism and back-to-basics
- unequal spending between rich and poor districts
- unequal spending between university and community campuses
- the deskilling of jobs from automation and computerization
- declining entry-level wages for new graduates
- limited job-prospects from high-tech
- increasing worker-alienation, student resistance and teacher performance strikes.

An opposition agenda inserted into these themes could be divided into several parts. The first section could address the reversal of the larger political and economic themes of the restoration. A second agenda could relate to the domain of education specifically. The larger social counter-themes could be defined as follows:

- question authority to promote democracy
- expose inequalities in sex, race, age and class
- encourage high aspirations and the demand for more
- keep opposition visible and active, suited to conditions
- universalize high-quality social services including education
- transfer resources through taxes from the private sector to public programs
- convert military spending to social investment
- promote trade union organizing and strike support
- create jobs through public industries and community projects.

A strategy for education reform could begin by listing larger policy questions:

- unrestricted open admissions to college
- free tuition for higher education

- vigorous affirmative action in college admissions and in faculty hiring
- overfund poor school districts and community colleges through a special federal tax on the top 20 per cent income brackets
- raise public schoolteachers' pay to the equivalents of engineers' salaries for comparable degrees and years of service
- reduce administrative personnel and budgets 50 per cent
- incorporate students and community members in school governance and curriculum planning
- develop joint councils of students, parents, teachers and administrators to examine merit and demerit in each constituency and to determine rewards and corrections for each group
- special funding for bilingual and bidialectical programs
- support students' rights to their own language against the mechanical study of correct usage
- no customized work-training in schools or colleges
- no tracking out of the college-bound and the non-academic student
- Students' Rights to Know and Teachers' Rights to Teach: free access to all books, materials, and ideas, as well as unhindered discussion of all subjects.

An agenda of specific education reforms could begin with several suggestions made by Boyer, Goodlad and Sizer, the liberal troika dissenting from the austerity programs of 1983:

- a four-class load per day for teachers in public school
- classes limited to twenty students
- start public school at four and end at sixteen (Goodlad)
- absorb computers as a subject in humanities (Boyer)
- simplify, reduce the bureaucracy surrounding the classroom
- test less, and replace the 'talking teacher' pedagogy with active discussion classes and field projects (Goodlad's strong point and Herb Kohl's program in *Basic Skills*).

To these specific reforms, the following items could be added:

- a four-day work-week for public schoolteachers

- a fifth-day 'field project' for students working with specially-hired project-teachers
- graduation from high school at sixteen, into a *community mentor network* funded publicly and organized locally. The network's units would include one recent 16-year-old graduate, plus three community members – an 18-year-old, another about 25, and a third in her or his 40s. The new graduate would be in a mentor group for two years, after which she or he would become an 18-year-old member of a new mentor group, for a second two-year term. This community 'paideia' could develop young people's plans for work, community service, travel, artistic growth, further study and social life. New graduates in the network could attend college while being mentored but it would be wise to put off that decision for a while in favor of development through mentor channels.
- curriculum in school and discussions in the mentor groups should include sexual subjects appropriate to the student's culture, language, interests and age
- curriculum should address other non-traditional subjects besides sexuality: war and peace, Utopia, folk culture, labor history, women's and minority studies, socialism and capitalism, etc.
- the student's voice in its own idiom should be emphasized in class discussion and writing
- intuition, imagination and art-making should be major parts of the curriculum
- students and teachers should meet to design plans for the physical renovation of their school or college.

These reforms speak to some unmet needs of students and teachers, so they will have an appeal to those groups. Such a democratic agenda will also meet resistance from existing authorities. Thus, it will take skilled maneuvering to build support from the bottom which can win concessions from the top. The democratic agenda will also be costly: small classes, shorter work-week, fewer course-assignments and more pay raises for teachers, a mentor-network, etc. Reducing high school by two to three years can redirect funds to financing reform. Also, the current budgets have a great deal of waste in terms of top-heavy administrative

179

salaries and in huge purchases of textbooks and tests. Herb Kohl proposed an anti-waste plan for reallocating the funds already available to schools, based in less bureaucratic management.[17] This can release money now tied up at the top in staff wages and in unnecessary purchases. Still, more funds will be needed. Universal, high-quality education presents costs that drove the official reports and the dissenting statements of 1983 into fiscal silence. The cost of major reform begs the question of the economy: can a major reallocation of resources for education occur without reform in the corporate-military control of the economy? The answer is no. Without economic reform, school changes will be financed minimally by monies raised the wrong way – by regressive taxation and by pitting teachers against each other via merit pay plans. Democratic reform in education needs egalitarian policies in society. Such school and social reform accompanied each other in the 1960s, enhancing the power of each. Many reformers assume that social and economic issues only distract from or discredit educational programs. The lasting influence of the 1960s showed the force of reform pursued inside and outside school at the same time.

One river, two streams: the self-directed school

The open points for democratic opposition can be located at the various intersections of school and society. One crossing-point involves school as a public institution – underfunded and over-regulated, an unstable arrangement. Schools not only have an acknowledged claim on public funds but they also have a right to secular, constitutional and democratic freedoms. This territory offers two openings into school finance and governance: the right to demand adequate funding and the right to greater independence. At another intersection of education and the economy, schools can be defined as paid labor for teachers and unpaid labor for students. This sphere of work is micro-managed and underproductive. Top-heavy administrations are a glaring argument against bureaucracy, against waste, and for autonomy. In making this argument, schools are in a strong position, thanks to their ethos of public service work for teachers and human development for students: two social ideals worthy of tax funds.

From another point of view on the social activity of schooling, it can be argued that education is an open arena for business marketing. Schools consume goods and services which support the economy, but how does this consuming help learning? Education is for learning and not for buying, so there is room to question the costly purchases of tests, texts, furniture, computer hardware and software, and audio-visual teaching aids. These commercial habits of school spending strengthen the power of bureaucracy which decides how to spend the money and what materials will dominate the classroom. Questioning expenditures is thus a way to question authority and pedagogy at the same time, in the name of efficiency and learning.

Yet another problematic intersection with the economy involves education being a training-ground for the job market. Educators hardly know what jobs will be needed down the road, but they still hear a dominating question – what does business want from schooling? The job market is as predictable as the weather and is as comfortable for students as a briar patch. But, even if occupational openings could be pinned down, there are old and strong arguments against narrow job-training in school. Education is broadly perceived as generally developmental, so the dominance of narrow vocational goals is vulnerable. The long-term uncertainty of the business future led the 1983 agendas to promote 'flexibility' and 'adaptability' as key goals for student development. Now, business wants employees who tolerate work at the going wages, or unemployment at unpredictable intervals, or changes in work at the whim of management. An unstable business climate requires non-specific education into 'flexibility.' Management power at the workplace can be more easily exerted over a 'flexible' worker, but such a need gives liberal education a chance to push back narrow careerism. The call for general over vocational education after 1983 presented an opportunity to renew humanistic learning.

Some strong sentiments for humanistic education, for less bureaucracy, and for more autonomy, informed the liberal dissents to the 1983 agendas. Goodlad was convinced that decentralization of command was crucial for making schools work: 'The guiding principle being put forward here is that school must become largely self-directing. The people connected with it must

181

develop a capacity for effecting renewal and establish mechanisms for doing this.'[18] Sizer pointed in the same direction:

> Giving teachers and students room to take full advantage of the variety among them implies that there must be substantial authority in each school. . . . This means the decentralization of power from central headquarters to the individual schools. For state authorities, it demands the forswearing of detailed regulations on how schools should be operated.[19]

State responses after 1983 went in exactly the opposite direction, mandating more detailed requirements. Liberalism was still out in the cold.

However, the eventual failure of the austerity overhaul may make Goodlad and Sizer prophets-before-their-time. In preparing for that moment, the goal of the self-directing school can be placed in a social program for autonomy: education needs full autonomy from business; schools need autonomy from state and district micro-management; teachers need autonomy from principals and supervisors; students need autonomy from teacher-talk, testing regimes, back-to-basics and bookish syllabi. Progress at any of these levels can have an effect on the others. However, Goodlad and Sizer proposed autonomy only for principals and teachers. Such an idea can be self-sabotaging. If a strong wave of autonomy fails to change the student-teacher relationship, students will resist even well-meaning reforms.

Oceans of resistance

The vast alienation of students from school and society can drown any plan that does not empower them to transform reality, to study their culture critically and to remake it. Teachers were token participants in the official agendas of 1983, while students were entirely excluded. This exclusion troubled Boyer when he reflected on the first anniversary of the NCEE's famous alarm on the 'rising tide of mediocrity':

> Simply stated, schools have less to do with 'standards' than with people, and I am disappointed that teachers and students are not adequately involved in the current push. . . .

America has a *youth* problem – not just a school problem.
Indeed, students were hardly mentioned in *A Nation at
Risk*. . . . Can we 'fix' the schools without dealing with our
larger social problems? Can we have healthy schools if students
feel confined and uninvolved?[20]

Boyer also noted the absence of concern for disadvantaged
students in reports nominally endorsing equity with excellence.

Students will resist any process that disempowers them.
Unequal, disabling education is symbolic violence against them,
which they answer with their own skills of resistance – silence,
disruption, non-performance, cheating, lateness, absence,
vandalism, etc. Very familiar school routines produce this alienation: teacher-talk, passive instruction in pre-set materials, punitive testing, moronic back-to-basics and mechanical drills, imper-
sonal and shabby classrooms, tracking, the denial of sexual themes
and other subjects important to them, the exclusion of student
co-participation in curriculum design and governance, and the
outlawing of popular idioms in favor of correct usage.
Accompanying student resistance to school regimens is their withdrawal into the youth culture, where they invest all the subjective
energies denied in the classroom. The self-directed school can
hope to reverse these conditions only with an empowering, critical
pedagogy. Any curriculum opaquing reality instead of illuminating
it, against student equality and aspirations, will sink in an ocean
of rejection.

The self-directed classroom is a pedagogy for *desocialization*.
This kind of learning reconstructs the conditioned habits of domination and resistance in teachers and students. Mutual desocialization was certainly not a learning goal discussed in 'the great
debate' of 1983. It has been a familiar part of liberatory education,
especially in the work of Paulo Freire, who speaks of education
for transformation and empowerment in his work among illiterate
peasants in Latin America:

From the beginning, we rejected the hypothesis of a purely
mechanistic literacy program and considered the problem of
teaching adults how to read in relation to the awakening of
their consciousness. . . . We wanted a literacy program which
would be an introduction to the democratization of culture, a
program which itself would be an act of creation, capable of

releasing other creative acts, one in which the students would
develop the impatience and vivacity which characterize
search and invention.[21]

To Freire, the logic of alienating education was in a 'banking'
concept, where teachers made information-deposits into the
empty accounts of their students' brains. This passive paradigm
drives students into silence or angry resistance. The counter-alienation model is based in 'conscientization,' or the desocialization
of students from learned roles. Conscientization is critical awareness of the forces making society, the part students play in the
making of that society, and the powers people have to *remake* the
conditions they self-define.

This framework exchanges an authoritarian model for an egalitarian process. It contradicts the logic of domination needed to
reproduce dominant ideology in students. Through egalitarian
learning, teachers and students begin their desocialization because
they immediately reconstruct education. In that reconstruction,
the conditions producing resistance decline while the conditions
for critical awareness are created. This reversal liberates potentials
for learning which were unknown or held back in a dominated
classroom. Such desocialization prefigures an egalitarian society.
Still, the process is not simple, direct or automatic. It requires
patient experimenting in a field of unknowns over a period of
time. Facing successes and failures in this effort, teachers have to
initiate desocialization and direct it even though they have few
models to draw on and few chances to experience it.[22]

The democratic teacher most often learns how to do it on the
job. Besides the great demands of an in-class training-period,
there is the accompanying difficulty of absorbing mandated
material – like history, biology, or economics – or of teaching to
a required standard test imposed at the end of the course from
the outside. Other interferences to desocialization come from the
old habits of the teachers and students themselves. The
empowering class is constantly under regressive pressure from the
force of the past. The old script of teacher-talk and student silence
is a formidable presence which needs constant counter-practice
for reversal. Besides these habits among the class participants,
there is also outside surveillance of the course. Authorities in the
school, college, department or community resist education outside

traditional forms of knowing. This official pressure to conform to banking education indicates that there is no such thing as the isolated classroom here and 'the real world' out there. Society is always in the classroom and the classroom is always in society. This mutuality can be a strong interference to transformation, but it can also give education a potential for social change. Desocialization through schooling can raise questions about power and hierarchy everywhere else. The critical consciousness spreading through the campuses and high schools of the 1960s became a political crisis for the whole society, not an isolated education problem.

The ideology of education as an ivory-tower separate from 'the real world' is a partisan notion disguising the real power of this immense social sphere. If education were truly powerless to affect society, schooling would be more ignored and less troubled than it is. Because schools and colleges are in fact at the center of society, they have a potential to unsettle the culture which requires constant official supervision. This was a lesson not lost on the authorities after the 1960s. The amount of official scrutiny and control since the 1960s reflected the need to monitor the outcomes of a powerful social agency. Education reform then is unavoidably social reform, whether or not the reformers choose to acknowledge the politics and economics of curriculum.

At the very least, education involves tens of millions of people and tens of billions of dollars. The people come there from all corners of daily life. The graduates and the drop-outs leave for all corners of the economy. The unsettling reach of this activity is confirmed every time a campus eruption interferes with Washington's foreign policy. Such post-1960s dissent continues as one force for desocialization. Another force of equal importance is transformative pedagogy, for the classroom heart of education.

A change of hearts

Teachers must initiate desocialization in their courses because students are not able to do it for themselves. After this initiation, teachers will be responsible for directing the process for some time to come, because it will take an unpredictable series of exercises before students accept self-government of their own learning. In many classes, the mix of students and the conditions for learning may make it impossible for students to desocialize from authority-dependence. The teacher who intends empowerment will then ironically find herself or himself forced back into traditional roles by student resistance. Students may refuse to cooperate with any project, disabling or enabling. Illich proposed that people had to liberate themselves. Deschooling suggested that liberation was individual and inevitable, not in need of organized desocialization. This Utopian hope seems unlikely. Symbolic violence in school and society powerfully conditions students into negative alienation. They reject the goals of authority as well as rejecting their own powers of reconstruction. Their resistance shows some remarkable shrewdness, but little remaking of the culture around them. Giroux commented on student alienation that

> some working-class students either resist or reject the notion
> of book learning and other forms of literacy in favor of
> subversive school behavior and a celebration of physicality and
> manual labor. In doing so, these students may undermine
> one of the fundamental ideologies of the school, but they do
> so at the cost of rejecting the possibility for developing modes
> of critical literacy that could be crucial to their own
> liberation.[23]

Barney Glasser put the issue in a psychological idiom: 'If a person cannot develop an identity through the two pathways of love and self-worth, he attempts to do so through two other pathways, delinquency and withdrawal.'[24] The reversal of delinquent withdrawal requires the teacher to reconstruct the classroom with values that create the conditions for critical literacy.

The first task of the teacher in this reconstruction is to desocialize herself or himself from the banking model of the educator. Teachers who stop delivering pre-packaged batches of knowledge to their students overcome the professionalized practice of educating, but they do so with some risk of career suicide. They are simply expected to behave like professionals who implement the official syllabus. Each teacher needs to calculate the risks involved in reforming his or her middle-management role. The passive model of instruction dominates the schools not because it is a superior, neutral form of learning, but rather because it conditions students to absorb hierarchy, official ideology and the professional separation of the teacher from the student. This is what makes pedagogy a terrain of culture war. The form of teaching is a political question no matter what method a teacher winds up using.

The forms in use so far remain traditional, which is why inertia greets every new reform. Goodlad observed teacher-talk pedagogy dominating the thousand classrooms selected in his eight-year study:

> Teachers appear to teach within a very limited repertoire of pedagogical alternatives, emphazing their own talk and the monitoring of seatwork. This customary pedagogy places the teacher very much in control. Few activities call for or even permit active student planning, follow-through and evaluation. . . . Students listened; they responded when called on to do so; they read short sections or chose from alternative responses in quizzes. But they rarely planned or initiated anything.[25]

Boyer found the same passive instruction dominating the schools chosen for his 1983 report:

> Students suffer from information overload – not to mention boredom. Some pass notes to each other; others doze in the heat of the afternoon, heads down on the desk. Nevertheless, the teacher believes it has been a successful class. He has 'covered' the material and there have been no serious disruptions.[26]

Boyer's discovery of 'banking' education was not news, but his insistence that students suffer from *too much information* contradicted the mediocrity claims of official panels.

The saturation of students with official information provokes their resistance to intellectual work. This saturation depends on the collaboration of teachers, who administer official knowledge in every classroom. These teacherly commitments to the standard syllabus should have given Goodlad, Boyer and Sizer pause for thought when they suggested decentering authority into the hands of teachers and principals. They proposed that, with higher pay, more recognition, fewer students and courses and less administration, teachers would take to active, experimental and participatory pedagogy. For teachers who now talk some 70 per cent of the time in class, according to Goodlad, while engaging only 1 per cent of the hour for unstructured student discussion, this may not be so easy. A self-conscious desocialization is needed to ease the transition.

An agenda of values for this transition can be drawn from the Freirean approach to liberating education:

- *Empowerment*: The pedagogy develops student powers on several levels: inquiry, social perception, self-knowledge, peer-relations, constructive engagement of the teacher, reflection on the making and remaking of knowledge and culture.
- *Reconciliation*: Students and teachers reconcile the habitual separation between them, reduce hostility, discover common goals. Students also reconcile their own horizontal divisions based in sex, race, age, religion, region or kinds of labor. Students reconciled with each other and with the teacher will experience solidarity instead of alienation, and more willingly take part in reconstruction.
- *Co-intentionality*: Teachers initiate a desocializing study which includes student co-determination of the subject matter and the governance/evaluation of the class. The teacher is the director of the process who adjusts the studies according to student input.
- *Dialogue*: The basic learning method is dialogue, a problem-posing discussion format in conversational idiom led by the teacher. The dialogue successively deepens an inquiry into key themes from student culture or key questions from a subject-area related to student interests. The class study is in critical, conceptual and conversational idioms, merging academic language with concrete student experience, treating student speech with respect.
- *Situated Study*: The pedagogy is situated in the idiom, themes, expressed consciousness and levels of cognitive development of the students. Developmental exercises emerge from previous ones, linked to actual student engagement of the objects for study, rather than fixed rigidly into a syllabus. The teacher does not lecture for the sake of transferring knowledge for the students to memorize.

– *Creative/Experimental Process*: Intuition, imagination and experimentation are valued methods of learning. Knowledge is not fixed to be swallowed whole. It is invented new in each class. The excitement of learning is the 'making of meaning'.[27] The class learns by subjectively interacting with the objects of study. It expresses its knowledge in its own words. The methods to provoke this learning are open to the needs of the class – interdisciplinary, group work, field projects, etc. Creative and critical writing, written and visual materials, are integrated to stimulate imaginative reconstruction of knowledge.

Inventing the reinvention: critical literacy

The above values for desocialization need absorption into day-to-day teaching methods. One operational goal for the classroom is critical literacy. This form of language-learning acknowledges the culture war in education. It accepts alienation as the primary learning problem of students and reverses the unequal power relations which cause that alienation. By revealing the politics of learning, this kind of speaking, reading, writing and thinking can be defined separately from other forms of literacy in the recent period:

– *Basic Literacy*: the minimal skill of decoding a printed passage and of encoding spoken words into written language.
– *Functional Literacy*: The ability to interact with political, legal, commercial, occupational and social demands in daily life, such as voting, filing tax returns, applying for work, signing leases and contracts, following printed instructions, passing a driver's written exam, balancing a checkbook, comprehending instructions in a phone book or in an employee benefit plan, etc.
– *Higher-Order Literacy*: The ability to work out multi-step problems on your own, to follow complex procedures through a series of operations, to trouble-shoot malfunctions of equipment or processes, to start and finish projects on your own with the ability to match unknown data, to do

unsupervised research, to look up information in books, catalogues and retrieval systems, etc.

- *Cultural Literacy*: The ability to speak, write, read and make references within the elite idiom; Standard English, correct usage, lexicons and accents inside the wordworld of high culture. Idioms without such cultivation are signs of social inferiority.
- *Computer Literacy*: Familiarity with digital keyboards and electronic operations; understanding how to follow program commands; recognizing when a system is following or deviating from a program; knowledge of a basic computer language and the special vocabulary referring to hardware, software, etc.

Critical literacy does not inject students with dominant ideology. It does not place cultivated expression on a pedestal. Neither does it present traditional subject matter as the fixed form of wisdom. The most-valued forms of speaking and knowing are not universal standards of excellence but are themselves products of power and inequality. They have come down through the ages from societies which never provided equal learning to all their members. A desocializing classroom examines all idioms and all objects of study with critical intentions, with democratic interests to challenge domination.

Critical literacy begins at the levels of knowledge currently displayed by students. Situated inside student speaking and knowing, the class frees students from having to resist the worship of upper-class speech and official information. Neither does it worship their own idiom or knowledge. Student idioms and perceptions are simply the ground from which transformative pedagogy begins. This approach also liberates the classroom from mechanical training in occupational literacy. The critical literacy class does not stop at teaching narrow job skills or learning how to restart a down computer. Minimal career goals depress aspirations. They also leave untouched the critical and creative resources all students possess. All career goals and technical training and job skills are taught along with a critical view of these very needs for the job market.

One approach to these questions was situated in the reality of culture war by Robert Pattison in *On Literacy* (1982). He defined literacy as 'the passionate awakening of the mind.'[28] To achieve this awakening, the literacy class needed to make students articulate users of the language they already possess. Further, it had to reveal the current problems of using language in a divided society. To Pattison, self-conscious literacy was not a mechanical reading and writing skill. Neither was it the teacher's presentation of correct usage. It was, instead, the activated voice, hand, eye and mind self-defining value in the world. He suggested that the autodidactic prisoner, like Malcolm X, showed the convergence of literacy and the passion for knowledge. Knowing was where literacy and power met.

The problems of using language did not come from the illiteracy or the mediocrity of students. They rested, for Pattison, in the political clash of idioms – official versus colloquial. Correct usage to him was a key to opening up valuable works of tradition. However, he saw it mystified into a universal standard, when it was simply a 'middle-class' idiom for the elite domination of society. To demystify correct usage, Pattison proposed studying Standard English as a second language, an egalitarian idea discussed in Chapter Three on the Literacy Crisis. Pattison's Utopian hope was for the end of culture war, for the peaceful coexistence of daily speech and standard form. He did not discuss social and economic reforms needed to accomplish this transition. His appeal was to the classroom where the clash of idioms now made education impossible.

His visionary insights pointed to an eventually bilingual, multi-dialectic egalitarian society. This happy evolution may not be possible without accompanying social reform. The class domination in standard usage was placed in political context by Noelle Bisseret in her history of language and power:

Dominant and dominated languages are the inevitable result of the existing social system but also the scene of a power struggle. Pejorative words of popular origins which designate the act of talking ('to rattle on,' 'to jabber') allow one to suppose that words are suspected by the dominated. They unconsciously know that the dominant impose their own definitions of the world order through the totality of their practices, including verbal practices, and thereby justify their power.[29]

These political battles through language emerged before the school system itself was created. Mass education absorbed the structure of language and power already existing in society at large. By now, society and education are so enmeshed with each other that they have to be known together, an insight Pattison shared with Bisseret, but which left Pattison mute on the social change needed to consolidate education reforms.

Critical literacy and desocialization accept the intersection of the verbal and the political, the self and society. This is the same merging of subjectivity and politics which made the historic crack of the 1960s so potent. The critical, desocializing classroom not only stands on the shoulders of the 1960s in general, but in particular it is indebted to 'the open classroom' ideas emerging in the earlier decade.[30] Open education in the protest period called for democratic, student-centered, experiential and experimental classrooms. Since then, the explosion of 'open' and 'alternate' experiments has been contained, but they can be found maturing in the low-profile margins of the restoration. Individual teachers have experimented with open as well as Freirean approaches.[31] Signs of a maturing pedagogy can be found in the reflection on learning process, domination, language and thought, subjective empowerment, alienation, political extension of subject matter to daily life, sexual divisions and race, and the problem of student resistance to transformation as well as to official knowledge. Pioneering work on these questions was begun by Freire, Illich, Kohl and Kozol, and the terrain is still a frontier.

The transformative project is filled with advances, setbacks, inspirations, frustrations, surprises and anxieties. In such a formative period, teachers often experience more transformation than they see in their students. The search for methods is also a search for a new society. The act of learning is strong enough to challenge as well as confirm the dominating culture we inherit. The potential of transformative education was experienced by Kohl in his experiments with open classrooms:

> I became involved in creating things in the classroom – in doing research on myths and numbers, in learning from the experience of the students. My students and I resembled a community much more than a class, and I enjoyed being with them. We worked together in an open environment which

often spilled out of the school building into the streets, the neighborhood, and the city itself.[32]

Another witness was Illich, who reported on a visit to a village where Freirean educators worked:

> Freire discovered that any adult can learn to read in a matter of forty hours if the first words he deciphers are charged with political meaning. Freire trains his teachers to move into a village and to discover the words which designate current important issues, such as access to a well or to the compound interest on the debts to the *patron*. In the evening, the villagers meet for the discussion of these key words. . . . I have frequently witnessed how discussants grow in social awareness and how they are impelled to take political action as fast as they learn to read. They seem to take reality into their hands as fast as they write it down.[33]

These changes have costs and risks. Kohl wrote that he quit his school without changing its overall authoritarian milieu. Freire was arrested in the Brazilian coup of 1964 and forced into exile until 1980. Education is a tough and inviting medium at the heart of culture war.

Imagine a long restoration which never closed the egalitarian opening of the 1960s. Consider the deepening Legitimacy Crisis, the unsolved economic crisis, the weak consensus for austerity, and the prospects for a waning of conservative culture. In that transition, learning can approach student alienation, transforming sullen disregard into passionate discourse. That changing of resistance to empowerment points to a society without war or inequality.

The roads there have been built over decades by many hands. They are being built again now, with often invisible labors, despite an age of restored domination. When the ideals of equality and Utopia stride history again, and when the pending crises open wide, the terrain for transformation can grow surprisingly fast in school and society. Students and teachers will then be able to claim the forbidden and the forgotten, to act on needs unmet and learning denied. They will speak of art and inquiry in rich and equal voices, all good idioms for writing epics on battles won and lost in culture war.

Notes

1 The hinge of 1969

1 Herbert Kohl, *36 Children* (New York, 1967) and *The Open Class-room* (New York, 1969); Jonathan Kozol, *Death at an Early Age* (New York, 1967); George Dennison, *The Lives of Children* (New York, 1969); George Leonard, *Education and Ecstasy* (New York, 1968); James Herndon, *The Way it Spozed to Be* (New York, 1968); Charles Silberman, *Crisis in the Classroom* (New York, 1970).
2 Silberman, *Crisis in the Classroom, op. cit.*, p. vii.
3 Ivan Illich, *Deschooling Society* (New York, 1970), p. 148.
4 Herbert Marcuse's *One Dimensional Man* (1964) appeared on the very eve of the campus explosions. In later works like *An Essay on Liberation* (1969) and *Counter-revolution and Revolt* (1972) his analysis caught up to the upheavals which adopted him as a mentor.
5 C. Wright Mills wrote in 1963 that the task of the liberal college was '*to keep us from being overwhelmed.*' He went on to say that 'Its first and continuing task is to help produce the disciplined and informed mind that cannot be overwhelmed by the burdens of modern life. . . . He must see the frustration of idea, of intellect, by the present organiz-ation of society, if he is to meet the tasks now confronting the intelli-gent citizen.' (*Power, Politics, and People*, ed. Irving Horowitz, New York, 1963, p. 363.)
6 Diane Ravitch, *The Troubled Crusade: American Education, 1945–1980* (New York, 1983), p. 182.
7 In *The Confidence Gap* (New York, 1983), Seymour Martin Lipset and William Schneider surveyed the decline of public confidence in all major institutions since 1964. Not one industry or institution improved its reputation from the 1960s to the 1980s, despite the intense conservative campaigns in the last years. Business, military and education suffered lowered legitimacy.
8 The premier school crisis report of 1983, *A Nation at Risk: The Imperative for Educational Reform* from the National Commission on Excellence in Education made it clear that the consent of the governed was a problem for the 1980s. It said, 'For our country to function,

citizens must be able to reach some common understandings on complex issues, often on short notice and on the basis of conflicting or incomplete evidence' (p. 7). The credibility of business, government and military authorities was crucial to their ability to win public consent. The absence of consensus was a problem focused on by the second most important crisis report, *Action for Excellence*, put out by the Education Commission of the States. Further, the Business-Higher Education Forum also pleaded for consensus in its report, *America's Competitive Challenge*, during the alarming parade of panels in 1983.

9 As the marines retreated from Beirut in February 1984, Secretary Schultz explained away the disaster by blaming public debate for weakening the White House's foreign policy. See the report on Schultz's jawboning of Congress in the *New York Times*, 5 February 1984.

10 See the remarks of Dr Joan Raymond, chief of the Yonkers public schools, in 'President's Campaign on Discipline,' *New York Times*, 2 March 1984.

11 Dr Ruth Love, superintendent of the Chicago schools and prominent member of the Paideia group, lost a lawsuit challenging her right to exclude anti-military groups from schools while allowing in military recruiters. See 'Judge Rules Anti-War Group Has Right to Advise Students,' *New York Times*, 25 January 1984.

12 Paulo Freire's *Pedagogy of the Oppressed* (New York, 1970) gained more and more popularity in the 1970s and 1980s. This interest in liberatory education grew despite the larger drift towards more traditional curricula in schooling. Freire's visits to US campuses occasioned standing-room crowds in the late 1970s and 1980s.

13 See H. Bruce Franklin's 'Teaching Vietnam Now: Who Won and Why?,' in *The Chronicle of Higher Education*, 4 November 1981. It was followed in the weeks afterwards by a flood of letters, especially the 9 and 16 December issues of *The Chronicle*. There was another hot exchange on teaching methods which recalled the debates of the 1960s, following Steven M. Weiss's 'I Remember Max,' in *The Chronicle* of 10 February 1982, with dissenting letters in the 24 February issue. Another good place to see ongoing polemics around the 1960s is *The American Educator*, the professional journal of the American Federation of Teachers. The Winter 1983 number had an essay by Robert Erwin on 'What Happened to Respectability?,' arguing that 'The cultural revolutions of the sixties and seventies have overthrown that reliable social norm, respectability, and left in their wake a moral wilderness.'

14 See Arnold Beichman's long jeremiad, 'Is Higher Education in the Dark Ages?,' *New York Times* magazine, 16 November 1983, pp. 46–90.

15 Christopher Lasch, *The Culture of Narcissism* (New York, 1979), p. 17.

16 For some discussion of the decade-long attack on open admissions at

the City University of New York, see the 'Introduction' to my book
Critical Teaching and Everyday Life (Boston, 1980). For more background, see 'The Case for Open Admissions: A Status Report,' by
Timothy Healy, Ed Quinn, Alexander Astin and Jack Rossman,
Change, Summer 1973, pp. 24–37. The conditions that led to the
demise of free tuition were well-researched in Sherry Gorelick's 'City
College: Rise and Fall of the Free Academy,' *Radical America*, Vol.
14, No. 5, Sept.-Oct. 1980, pp. 21–35.
17 Robert L. Ebel, 'The Case for Minimum Competency Testing,' *Phi
Delta Kappan*, April 1978, p. 547.
18 *Ibid.*, p. 547.
19 Peter Brimelow, 'What to Do About America's Schools,' *Fortune*, 19
September 1983, pp. 60–4. Brimelow proposes a laissez-faire solution,
favoring tuition vouchers so that public education's monopoly on tax
funds will be broken. That issue of *Fortune* also highlighted vocational
training programs that work in preparing students with skills that
business wants. The major flaw is that these programs were in special
industries like aerospace, which are dynamic sectors of the economy.
Further, the programs are handsomely funded exceptions to the
vocational school picture.
20 *Time*, 10 October 1983, cover-story on education, p. 61. *Time* decided
to declare the great school crisis of 1983 already on the way to
solution, thanks to tough, no-nonsense principals in some exemplary
schools.
21 Beichman, *op. cit.*
22 D. Richard Little, 'Legacy of the '60s – declining quality,' *The Christian Science Monitor*, 17 January 1977, p. B12. Little echoes the key
restoration theme of putting authority back in control. He saw the
1960s raising some right questions with the wrong answers: '. . . the
faculty must reassert its responsibility for the curriculum and turn
away from the aimless diversity that attaches equal educational value
to every course in which students are willing to enroll.' The word
'diversity' is key to the restoration search for authority through a 'core
curriculum,' where students have fewer electives to choose from and
where non-traditional and outlaw ideas from the 1960s are erased as
curricular offerings.
23 Steven M. Cahn, 'Restoring the House of Intellect,' *The American
Teacher*, Fall 1981, pp. 8–9. Cahn repeats the importance of faculty
assertion in the realm of curriculum requirements (see note 22). This
essay's important restoration themes led to it being reprinted in the
same year in *The New Republic* and in *The American Educator*. See
also Cahn's promotion of traditional pedagogy in 'The Authority of
the Teacher,' *Academe*, May-June 1982, pp. 13–14. *Academe* is the
journal of the American Association of University Professors.
24 Quoted in Cahn, 'Restoring the House of Intellect,' *op. cit.*, p. 9.
25 Merrill Sheils, 'Why Johnny Can't Write,' the cover-story on the
Literacy Crisis, *Newsweek*, 8 December 1975, p. 58.
26 See Angus Mackenzie, 'Sabotaging the Dissident Press: The Untold

Story of the Secret Offensive Waged by the U.S. Government Against Anti-War Publications,' *Columbia Journalism Review*, March–April 1981, pp. 57–63. In the same area of government repression, see Nelson Blackstock, *Cointelpro: The FBI's Secret War on Political Freedom* (New York, 1975).

27 Richard Ohmann, 'The Literacy Crisis is a Fiction, if Not a Hoax,' *The Chronicle of Higher Education*, 25 October 1976. This is one of the earliest and clearest opposition statements on the Literacy Crisis.

28 *Declining Test Scores: A Conference Report*, ed. Evelyn Stern Silver, National Institute of Education, Washington, D.C., February 1976. The Conference itself was held on 19–21 June 1975 in Washington.

29 Albert Shanker, 'American Schools Are Envy of the World,' speech reported in the United Federation of Teachers' newspaper, the *New York Teacher*, 24 January 1982, p. 16.

30 Henry Steele Commager, in remarks during a keynote address, Conference on Critical Thinking and the Moral Individual, Sonoma, California, 17 August 1983. Commager wondered how a nation of 200 million people could produce such dismal presidents in its last six elections, while a small nation of some 4 million in 1790 could produce such statesmen in its first six presidents.

31 See Irwin Gross, 'Public Relations Isn't Kid Glove Stuff at Mobil,' *Fortune*, September 1976, p. 202, and *What's Wrong With the U.S. Economy?*, Institute for Labor Education and Research (Boston, 1982), p. xiii. For a jubilant defense of business image campaigns in the restoration, see Burton Yale Pines, *Back to Basics*, New York, 1982, Chapters I and II, 'A Free Enterprise Counter Offensive,' and 'Evangelizing for Capitalism,' pp. 31–65.

32 Paul L. Montgomery, 'Business Institutes on the Rise,' *New York Times*, 31 March 1981.

33 Quote from *What's Wrong With the U.S. Economy?*, *op. cit.*, p. xiii.

34 *U.S. News and World Report*, cover-story, 'Marxism in U.S. Classrooms,' 8 January 1982, pp. 42–5.

35 Upton Sinclair produced two critical studies of schooling in the 1920s, *The Goose-Step: A Study of American Education* (1922), and *The Goslings: A Study of the American Schools* (1924).

36 Corporate film-making in the 1970s is discussed in *What's Wrong With the U.S. Economy?*, *op. cit.*, pp. xii–xiii.

37 Sheila Harty, 'Hucksters in the Classroom,' *Social Policy*, Vol. 12, No. 2, 1981, pp. 38–9.

38 *Ibid.*, p. 39.

39 For a penetrating study of official definitions of 'literacy' and 'illiteracy' see James Donald, 'How Illiteracy Became a Problem (and Literacy Stopped Being One),' *Journal of Education*, Vol. 165, 1983, pp. 35–52. Donald studied the period from 1790–1870, during which formal education was legislated in Britain. He compared radical literacy among the self-educated in 1790 to official literacy among the schooled of 1870. The politics of reading, writing and speaking determined evaluations of who is literate.

40 John Dewey, *Democracy and Education* [1916], Free Press edn (New York, 1967), p. 13.
41 For an extensive analysis of the recent profits crisis in both economic and political terms, see Samuel Bowles and Herbert Gintis, 'The Crisis of Liberal Democratic Capitalism: The Case of the United States,' *Politics and Society*, Vol. 11, No. 1, 1982, pp. 51–93. Bowles joined with David Gordon and Tom Weiskopf in 1983 to extend the analysis and develop an alternate agenda in *Beyond the Wasteland*. For further background on the profits crisis underlying the new austerity see also James O'Connor, *The Fiscal Crisis of the State* (New York, 1963). For critical perspectives on the politics of governing in an age of decline, see Jurgen Habermas's *Legitimation Crisis* (Boston, 1969).
42 The Grove College decision came in a week filled with restoration themes in the news. The Reagan Administration was pushing its school prayer amendment again in Congress, as the primary season heralded an election year catching up on the new right social agenda. In addition, the Supreme Court, on 6 March 1984, approved the use of Christmas creches in public places. For a report on the Grove College case, see the *New York Times* report on this item, 7 March 1984.
43 See Fred M. Hechinger, 'Censorship Rises in the Nation's Public Schools,' *New York Times*, 3 January 1984. For a detailed account of censorship battles in the 1970s by one of the anti-censor combatants, see Edward B. Jenkinson's *Censors in the Classroom* (New York, 1979). Jenkinson chronicled some of the most notorious incidents of censorship as it spread from district to district, in a decade when some 200 pressure groups targeted books and curriculum for conservative attacks. See also Michael S. Littleford, 'Censorship, Academic Freedom and the Public School Teacher', *Journal of Curriculum Theorizing*, Vol. 5, No. 3, Summer 1983, pp. 98–132, for a strong statement on the problem.
44 Fred Pincus, 'Book-Banning and the New Right: Censorship in the Public Schools,' *Educational Forum*, 1984, in press. Pincus's extensive research on conservative forces in the 1970s and 1980s included a paper on 'The Heritage Foundation and Federal Education Policy,' *Radical Teacher*, November 1983, pp. 1–6. That paper discussed the conservative think-tank most influential on Reagan's school policies. In a more general inquiry into restoration themes, Pincus published 'From Equity to Excellence: The Rebirth of Educational Conservatism,' *Social Policy*, Vol. 14, No. 3, Winter 1984, pp. 50–6.
45 Dena Kleiman, 'Influential Couple Scrutinize Books for Anti-Americanism,' *New York Times*, 13 July 1981. For the Gablers' own voice on these issues, see their 'Mind Control Through Textbooks,' *Phi Delta Kappan*, October 1982, p. 97.
46 Frances Fitzgerald, *America Revised* (New York, 1979); William Griffin and John Marciano, *Teaching the Vietnam War* (Montclair,

1979); Jean Anyon, 'Ideology and United States History Textbooks,' *Harvard Educational Review*, Vol. 49, No. 3, 1979, pp. 361–86.

47 For a fine example of authority-based pedagogy in the lecture-model, see Mortimer Adler, *The Paideia Proposal* (New York, 1982), and Adler's *Paideia: Problems and Possibilities* (New York, 1983). Adler has promoted 'Great Books' education for most of this century. His 'core curriculum' in *Paideia* goes back to the laundered reading lists of the 1950s, selecting historical documents, for example, which exclude women's studies, black or Latin studies, labor studies or revisionist history, all of which bloomed after the 1960s.

48 See Diane Wang and Cindy Jaquith, *FBI vs. Women* (New York, 1977); Julian Jaffe, *Crusade Against Radicalism, 1919–1929* (New York, 1972); and Robert K. Murray, *The Red Scare: A Study in National Hysteria, 1919–1920* (Minneapolis, 1975) for some background on anti-communism in US political life.

49 For studies on student attitudes in the post-1960s generation, see 'Fewer Liberals, More Moderates Among This Year's Freshmen,' *The Chronicle of Higher Education*, 9 February 1981, p. 5; Alexander Astin, *The American Freshman: National Norms for Fall 1980* (Los Angeles, 1981); and Dean R. Hoge, Cynthia L. Luna and David K. Miller, 'Trends in College Students' Values Between 1952 and 1979: A Return to the Fifties?,' *Sociology of Education*, Vol. 54, No. 4, October 1981, pp. 263–74. The noticeable return of student activism in the 1980s was reported in 'America's Youth in Search of a Cause,' *U.S. News*, 16 April 1984.

50 Richard Freeman's *The Overeducated American* (New York, 1976) was the most discussed treatment of this phenomenon. For another view, see Russell Rumberger, 'The Rising Incidence of Overeducation in the U.S. Labor Market,' *Economics of Education Review*, Vol. 1, No. 3 (Summer 1981), pp. 293–314. Rumberger's discussion of how overeducation tends to affect whites more than blacks fits into Freeman's findings that white men and white students from upper-income homes were more likely to drop out of college in this period. This white-black divergence is the background for understanding the racial aspects of the 'mediocrity' crisis of 1983, in Chapter 4. The phrases 'over-aspiring American' and 'over-aspiring worker' became media buzz-words after a giant career education conference in Houston in 1977.

2 *Settling for less, 1971–5: the war for 'careerism'*

1 The unpopularity of occupational programs in community colleges came to the attention of two key observers early in the two-year college movement: Leland Medsker in *The Junior College: Progress and Prospects* (New York, 1960) and Burton Clark in *The Open-Door College* (New York, 1960). These two Carnegie-supported studies are good companion pieces for the dilemmas of the new mass colleges,

because Medsker surveyed the broad development while Clark focused his case-study on a single institution. Both noticed the apparent student preference for the transfer programs over the two-year terminal degrees. This caused some confusion among the early administrations which wound up with faculty skewed towards the under-enrolled career programs. The answer to this predicament was also studied by Clark in his seminal essay 'The Cooling-Out Function in Higher Education,' *American Journal of Sociology*, Vol. 65, May 1960, pp. 569–76. The 'cooling-out' controversy hung over the community colleges. For Clark's own retrospective on the issue of downwardly-manipulating student goals, see his piece 'The Cooling-Out Function Revisited,' in *New Directions for Community Colleges: Questioning the Community College Role*, ed. G. B. Vaughan (San Francisco, 1980). Essentially, Clark endorses 'cooling-out' as a necessary evil in a democracy with a limited occupational hierarchy. He sees no other choice for two-year colleges other than adjusting students to the shape of the economy. Yet, in his 1960 book he criticized the imposition of elite college curriculum onto the community colleges.

2 *Work in America: Report of a Special Task Force to the Secretary of Health, Education and Welfare* (Cambridge, 1973). This widely-read study went through two printings each year in the mid–1970s.

3 Sidney P. Marland, *Career Education* (New York, 1974), p. 8. This is Marland's magnum opus and most complete statement of his 'career education' visions. It is also an unforgettable excursion into a Dickensian character. My distillation of his career philosophy comes from this work plus some of Marland's ancillary writings: 'The Condition of Education in the Nation,' *American Education 7*, No. 3, April 1971, p. 4; 'Career Education and the Two-Year Colleges,' *American Education 8*, No. 2, March 1972, p. 11; 'The Endless Renaissance,' *American Education 8*, No. 3, April 1972, p. 9; 'The School's Role in Career Development,' *Educational Leadership 30*, No. 3, December 1972; with Harold Licthenwald and Ralph Burke, 'Career Education, Texas Style,' *Phi Delta Kappan*, May 1975, pp. 616–20, 635.

4 Marland, *Career Education, op. cit.*, p. 8.

5 See Kenneth Hoyt, Rupert Evans, Edward Mackin and Garth Mangun, *Career Education: What It Is and How To Do It* (Salt Lake City, 1972), and Kenneth Hoyt, Nancy Pinson, Darryl Laramore and Garth Mangun, *Career Education and the Elementary School Teacher* (Salt Lake City, 1973). Marland's Associate Director at the US Office of Education also helped in the development of curricular models: Robert M. Worthington, 'A Home-Community Based Career Education Model,' *Educational Leadership 30*, No. 3, December 1972, p. 213.

6 Most of the major 1983 reform reports downplay vocationalism, but the most persuasive anti-vocational or anti-career statements can be found in Mortimer Adler, *The Paideia Proposal* (New York, 1982);

Ernest L. Boyer, *High School* (New York, 1983); John I. Goodlad, *A Place Called School* (New York, 1983); and Theodore Sizer, *Horace's Compromise* (Boston, 1984). The crisis wave from 1982–4 reacted strongly against careerism, promoting an academic curriculum, especially science and math. This was a remarkable and even desperate turn-around from the curricular thrusts of the 1970s.

7 James Bryant Conant, *The American High School Today* (New York, 1959). Bryant favored two precise outcomes from high school, an elite of perhaps 15–20 per cent aimed at further university academics and a mass ready to leave high school and go to work, suitably prepared, or else on to a two-year college for advanced occupational courses. However, he disapproved of the anti-democratic image such tracking conjured up, so he suggested abolishing formal designation of academic and vocational tracks. To give the vocationals some pride, he thought that an honors list for non-academic students should be established. Conant's 1959 curriculum is almost identical to the academic reforms proposed in the 1982–4 reports.

8 Marland, *Career Education, op. cit.*, p. 122.

9 For some discussion of official interference with labor organizing, see Jeremy Brecher, *Strike!* (New York, 1974); *Rank and File: Personal Histories of Working Class Organizers* (Boston, 1974), eds Alice Lynd and Staughton Lynd; *The Autobiography of Big Bill Haywood* (New York, 1974); Richard Boyer and Herbert Morais, *Labor's Untold Story* (New York, 1973).

10 Marland, *Career Education, op. cit.*, p. 253.

11 *Work in America, op. cit.* The chairman of this study, respected manpower expert James O'Toole, expressed little enthusiasm for the career education idea. O'Toole later turned up as a member of the very anti-careerist *Paideia* group convened by Mortimer Adler.

12 *Work in America, op. cit.*, p. 138.

13 *Work in America, op. cit.*, p. 139.

14 J. T. Grasso and J. R. Shea, *Vocational Education and Training: Impact on Youth*, Carnegie Council on Policy Studies in Higher Education (Berkeley, 1979).

15 Medsker, *The Junior College, op. cit.* Medsker's tone as he considered the dilemmas of vocationalism was quite perplexed.

16 Fred Pincus, 'The False Promises of Community Colleges: Class Conflict and Vocational Education,' *Harvard Educational Review*, Vol. 50, No. 4, August 1980, p. 353. Unlike Medsker, Pincus took an ideological point of view to the contradictions of occupationalism.

17 *Ibid.*, pp. 353–4.

18 W. Norton Grubb and Marvin Lazerson, 'Rally 'Round the Workplace: Continuities and Fallacies in Career Education,' *Harvard Educational Review*, Vol. 45, No. 4, November 1975, p. 473. Like Pincus, Grubb and Lazerson took a 'revisionist' point of view to analyzing careerism. They placed the new Marland offensive in the historical context of the old occupational education.

19 Marland, *Career Education, op. cit.*, p. 42. Marland's unbelievable

celebration of working-below-your-training simply hid the reality of underemployment since the 1970s, which has made the return on educational investment lower than it has historically been.

20 See Joel Spring, *The Sorting Machine: National Education Policy Since 1945* (New York, 1975), p. 233, for a discussion of the early funding of careerism. Spring's chapter on career education in this book is a detailed narrative of the evolution of Marland's and Nixon's program for education in the wake of the 1960s.

21 For an extensive tabulation of education expenditures at the federal level in the 1960s and 1970s, see Paul E. Peterson's 'Background Paper' to *Making the Grade: Report of the Twentieth Century Fund Task Force on Federal Elementary and Secondary Education Policy* (New York, 1983), especially Chapter Two, 'Trends in American Education.' In addition, Jerome Karabel in 'Community Colleges and Social Stratification,' in the *Harvard Educational Review*, Vol. 42, No. 4, November 1972, pp. 521–61, cites the extensive occupational investments of the 1972 education bills sent to Congress by the Nixon Administration.

22 Peterson, 'Background Paper,' *op. cit.*, p. 65. Peterson's funding charts are especially helpful because they tabulate expenditures for the 1960s and 1970s in both real and constant dollars.

23 Grubb and Lazerson, 'Rally 'Round the Workplace,' *op. cit.*, p. 452.

24 Arthur M. Cohen and Florence Brawer, *The American Community College* (San Francisco, 1982). This is a comprehensive retrospective by two critical 'insiders' who have been long-time students of the community college movement. Their assessment of three decades of two-year college growth painted a rather low-key picture of giant expansion, mass attendance, huge drop-out rates, and low percentages of degrees awarded.

25 Spring, *The Sorting Machine, op. cit.*, Chapter Six, pp. 233–4.

26 See Sidney P. Marland, 'Career Education and the Two-Year Colleges,' *American Education 8*, No. 2, March 1972, p. 11.

27 James Bright, 'Does Automation Raise Skill Requirements?,' *Harvard Business Review*, July-August 1958, pp. 85–98. Bright found the changeover phase, when new technology is first introduced, to be a *temporary* period demanding skilled attention. After the break-in period, line workers have decreasing skill-demands placed on them. In addition, automated systems displaced more workers than they required for maintenance and operation after the new technology was implemented. The speed of technology turnover in the 1980s may mean that the temporary changeover periods occur with more frequency than in the past, thus explaining the recurring demand for education to train more 'flexible,' more 'adaptive' workers. The famous 1983 school reform commissions spoke often about the need for today's employees to adjust to changing work conditions.

28 James Bright, 'The Relationship of Increasing Automation to Skill Requirements,' in *The Employment Impact of Technological Change*, Vol. II, National Commission on Technology, Automation and Eco-

nomic Progress, pp. –II–207–221, US Government Printing Office, Washington D.C., 1966.

29 Ivar Berg, *Education and Jobs: The Great Training Robbery* (Boston, 1971), pp. 24, 87. Berg observed the schooling-employment dysfunction in the 1970s from an essentially sympathetic point of view towards business.

30 Richard Freeman, *The Overeducated American* (New York, 1976), pp. 186–9. Freeman expressed animosity towards and fear of the protest era in the 1960s. He was also gloomy about employment prospects for graduates in the near future, as he predicted no easing of the college labor market until the mid-1990s. His analysis of the 'cobwebbing effect' helped explain how college education helps destabilize an irrational labor market, guaranteeing an oversupply of workers in any field five years after that field declares a labor shortage. People rush into college programs to get trained for the shortage that now exists, and five years later an oversupply is graduated into a sector which has been filling its ranks year by year and needs fewer employees.

31 Russell W. Rumberger, 'The Changing Skill Requirements of Jobs in the US Economy,' *Industrial and Labor Relations Review*, No. 34, July 1981, pp. 578–90. See also Rumberger's consideration of the 'overeducation' problem, in 'The Rising Incidence of Overeducation in the US Labor Market,' *Economics of Education Review*, Vol. 1, No. 3, Summer 1981, pp. 293–314. Rumberger provides more sophisticated econometric models than did Freeman, in developing the different experiences with 'overeducation' based on sex and race. Essentially, he confirmed Freeman's determination that non-whites and women would experience downward mobility less severely in the current economic period than would white males. This occurred because white males began with the most privileged position and hence the highest aspirations in a period of depressed opportunities.

32 Graham Staines, 'Is Worker Dissatisfaction Rising?,' *Challenge*, May-June 1979. Staines directed a US Department of Labor study on Labor Quality. He wrote in the *Challenge* article that 'Workers in virtually all occupational and demographic categories evidenced appreciable, unmistakable manifestations of rising discontent.'

33 Cohen and Brawer, *The American Community College, op. cit.*, discuss the peculiar reversal of function between the terminal and the transfer tracks in two-year colleges. They wrote that 'By 1980, more students who completed career programs were transferring to universities than those who completed collegiate programs' (p. 24). While this emptied and demoralized the nominally transfer-track liberal arts, it offered an upward rather than downward avenue through which students could outmaneuver the institution.

34 David Nasaw, *Schooled to Order: A Social History of Public Schooling in the United States* (New York, 1979), p. 131.

35 Charles Silberman, *Crisis in the Classroom: The Remaking of American Education* (New York, 1970), p. 23.

36 W. Norton Grubb and Marvin Lazerson (eds.), *American Education and Vocationalism: A Documentary History, 1870–1970* (New York, 1974), 'Introduction,' pp. 19, 20. The issue of business advocacy of vocationalism even made it into Ernest Boyer's 1983 Carnegie Report, *High School*, p. 47.

37 Joel Spring, *Education and the Rise of the Corporate State* (Boston, 1973), p. 42.

38 *Ibid.*, p. 42.

39 Diane Ravitch, *The Great School Wars: New York City, 1805–1973* (New York, 1974), p. 191.

40 Nasaw, *Schooled to Order, op. cit.*, p. 123.

41 Michael Katz, *Class, Bureaucracy and Schools: The Illusion of Educational Change in America* (New York, 1975), p. 121.

42 See Lawrence Cremin's narrative of the labor-management compromise *vis à vis* industrial education in the pre-World War I era, in *The Transformation of the School: Progressivism in American Education, 1876–1957* (New York, 1964), 'Education and Industry,' especially pp. 36–41.

43 Quoted in Karabel, 'Community Colleges and Social Stratification,' *op. cit.*, p. 550.

44 John Dewey, 'An Undemocratic Proposal,' in Grubb and Lazerson (eds.), *American Education and Vocationalism, op. cit.*, p. 144.

45 John Dewey, *Democracy and Education* [1916] (New York, 1967), p. 316.

46 *Ibid.*, pp. 318–19.

47 For a report on sexual politics and education after the 1960s, see Roberta M. Hall, 'The Classroom Climate: A Chilly One for Women?,' Project on the Status and Education of Women, Association of American Colleges, Washington, 1982.

48 Gunnar Myrdal, *An American Dilemma* [1944] (New York, 1962), p. 950.

49 *Ibid.*, p. 950.

50 *Ibid.*, p. 949.

51 John I. Goodlad, *A Place Called School: Prospects for the Future* (New York, 1983), pp. 145–6.

52 Spring, *The Sorting Machine, op. cit.*, p. 236.

53 Frank Riessman, 'The Vocationalization of Higher Education: Duping the Poor,' *Social Policy*, Vol. 2, May-June 1971, pp. 3–4.

54 *Ibid.*, p. 4.

55 *Ibid.*

56 See Cohen and Brawer, *The American Community College, op. cit.*, pp. 8–9, remarks on community colleges as 'buffer institutions.' Clark's elaboration of 'cooling-out' mechanisms certainly defines the downward mission of the community college ('The Cooling-Out Function in Higher Education,' *op. cit.*). For further discussion of inequality in mass higher education, see L. Steven Zwerling, *Second Best* (New York, 1976) and Ira Shor, *Critical Teaching and Everyday Life* (Boston, 1980).

57 *The Open-Door Colleges*, Carnegie Commission on Higher Education, New York, 1970; *The Second Newman Report: National Policy and Higher Education, Report of a Special Task Force to the Secretary of Health, Education and Welfare* (Cambridge, 1972).

58 Karabel in 'Community Colleges and Social Stratification,' cites a $275 million allocation for construction in the two-year network compared to an $850 million authorization for occupational education.

59 Marland, *Career Education, op. cit.*, p. 20.

60 See a report of a speech by Reagan's Secretary of Education, T. H. Bell, by Malcolm Scully, 'Bell Condemns Careerism in Colleges,' *The Chronicle of Higher Education*, 19 October 1983, pp. 1, 21. Reagan's economic and educational policies, however, have been encouraging the very vocationalism Bell criticized. See Fred Pincus, 'Class Conflict and Community Colleges: Vocational Education During the Reagan Years,' *The Review and Proceedings of the Community College Humanities Association*, No. 4, February 1983, pp. 3–18.

61 Dewey, *Democracy and Education, op. cit.*, p. 283.

62 George Dieter, 'The Big Shift in Students' Majors: Its Impact on Colleges and Society,' *The Chronicle of Higher Education*, 20 October 1980, p. 56. Dieter accused the liberal arts of being low-quality and foggy, while professional and tech programs were high-quality ways to go about problem-solving.

63 Robert McClintock, 'The Dynamics of Decline: Why Education Can No Longer Be Liberal,' *Phi Delta Kappan*, May 1979, p. 638.

64 Maxine Greene, 'Reply,' *Phi Delta Kappan*, May 1979, p. 634.

65 Clark speaks about the inappropriateness of university standards being imported into community colleges from other, more elite colleges (*The Open-Door College*, 1960). K. Patricia Cross in *Beyond the Open Door* (San Francisco, 1971) makes the point even more forcefully that the traditional liberal arts had not served community college students well. Cohen and Brawer raised the issue again in their discussion of the demise of liberal studies on two-year campuses in the 1970s, in 'The Community College as College: Should the Liberal Arts Survive in Community Colleges?,' *Change*, March 1982, pp. 39–42. Shor in *Critical Teaching and Everyday Life* (1980) made a distinction between traditional and liberatory humanities.

66 The establishment of the Community College Humanities Association in 1978, and such conferences as 'The Liberal Arts in Crisis,' at the State University of New York, New Paltz, January 1981, the Cohen and Brawer article cited in note 65 above suggesting interdisciplinary reformulations of the liberal arts, and the forum offered for this revaluation by *Liberal Education* magazine, especially in its Summer 1982 number, indicated some of the ferment attending the resurgent interest in traditional and reconstructed liberal arts education.

67 Marland, *Career Education, op. cit.*, pp. 40–1. Marland's description of this scene is one of the wonderful moments in his book. He reports how Richardson habitually doodled on a big pad while his subordinates spoke to him. Marland's news of some 6.5 million college gradu-

ates surplus to the labor force by 1980 was shocking enough to make Richardson stop doodling and look up, yelling for his savior.

68 Christopher Jencks, *Inequality: A Reassessment of the Effects of Family and Schooling in America* (New York, 1973), p. 183.
69 Cohen and Brawer, *The American Community College, op. cit.*, p. 8. They pointedly repeat James Bryant Conant's insistence that only an occasional transfer student out of the community colleges into the universities should be permitted. The segregation of levels was conscious and determined as social policy in the 1950s.
70 James Bryant Conant, *The Citadel of Learning* (New Haven, 1956), pp. 71–2.
71 For a discussion of the GI Bill and Conant's role, see Diane Ravitch's *The Troubled Crusade: American Education, 1945–1980* (New York, 1983), pp. 13–14.
72 Cohen and Brawer, *The American Community College, op. cit.*, p. 27.
73 Jencks, *Inequality, op. cit.*, p. 27.
74 For a booster's picture of the Career Palaces that 'democratized' higher education, see Edmund Gleazer's *This is the Community College!* (New York, 1968). Gleazer, past President of the American Association of Junior and Community Colleges, bathed the two-year campuses in an ultra-marketing glow.

3 Settling for less, 1975–82: the war on 'illiteracy'

1 See Stephen Judy's discussion of the emerging SAT/CB crisis over score declines in *The ABCs of Literacy* (New York, 1980), especially pp. 25–32. Judy is critical of the CB's blank endorsement of the Literacy Crisis claims, and ridicules the back-to-basics thrust as 'on to the future looking backward all the way', a Golden Age, good-old-days episode.
2 'Back-to-Basics in the Schools,' *Newsweek*, 21 October 1974, pp. 87–95.
3 Marland referred to his own press release of 1975 in his opening statement to the Wirtz report: 'No topic related to the programs of the College Boards has received more attention in recent years than the unexplained decline in scores earned on the Scholastic Aptitude Test.' (Prefatory Note, p. iii, *On Further Examination*, the report of the Wirtz panel, College Board, 1977.) In the year before the big SAT decline of 1975, a very critical article on the CB and ETS (Educational Testing Service) appeared by Stephen Brill, 'The Secrecy Behind the College Boards,' *New York*, 7 October 1974, pp. 67–83. The new mass constituency for the SAT, the unbroken decline in scores and public attention forced critical scrutiny of the once unchallenged CB. That scrutiny was neatly reversed into an indictment of student illiteracy, allowing the testing industry to come away with clean hands and bigger sales of tests to all the new remedial programs.
4 See *Declining Test Scores: A Conference Report*, ed. Evelyn Stein

Silver, Lawrence Jonson Associates, Washington, D.C., National Institute of Education, February 1976. At the same time, the National Academy of Education issued *Towards a Literate Society*, eds. John B. Carroll and Jeanne S. Chall (New York, 1975), a further indication of the growing attention to the literacy theme. The Richfield, Minnesota school district claimed to be the first in the nation to institute minimum competency criteria in reading for its students in 1973 (*Educators Look at Reading Results*, Richfield Public Schools, 1975).

5 For a longitudinal tabulation of the SAT declines up to 1977, see the Wirtz report, *On Further Examination: Report of an Advisory Panel on the Scholastic Aptitude Score Decline*, College Board, New York, 1977, pp. 6–7. For a lucid presentation of SAT declines and other test scores up to 1982, see Chapter Two of Ernest L. Boyer's *High School* (New York, 1983), the major Carnegie Foundation contribution to the great excellence debate after 1983.

6 Merill Sheils, 'Why Johnny Can't Write,' *Newsweek*, 8 December 1975, p. 58.

7 See two NAEP reports on ten years of reading and writing trends, *Writing Achievement, 1969–1979* (Education Commission of the States, Denver, December 1980), and *Three National Assessments of Reading: Changes in Performance, 1970–1980* (Education Commission of the States, Denver, April 1981). The mixed NAEP achievement results showed some gains and some losses. This up and down picture was mentioned in numerous places, including Wirtz, Richard Ohmann, Ernest Boyer, Paul Peterson, Stephen Judy, Christopher Jencks and the newsletter of the Union for Radical Political Economy, *Dollars and Sense* (No. 87, May-June 1983, 'High Tech and the Schools'). Yet, the reality of mixed test scores did not make a dent in the claims of illiteracy.

8 *Students Rights to Their Own Language* (National Council of Teachers of English, Urbana, 1974). This policy statement was under attack in the early 1980s.

9 *Newsweek*, 8 December 1975, p. 63.

10 See Richard Ohmann, *English in America* (New York, 1975); James Sledd, *A Short Introduction to English Grammar* (Chicago, 1959); and Basil Bernstein, *Class, Codes and Control* (London, 1977).

11 Christopher Jencks, 'What's Behind the Drop in Test Scores?,' *Working Papers*, July-August 1978, p. 30.

12 *Newsweek*, *op. cit.*, p. 60.

13 Donna Woolfolk Cross, *Word Abuse* (New York, 1979). For an even stronger example of the conservative theme against the 1960s, see Paul Copperman's *The Literacy Hoax* (New York, 1978). It broadly indicts the political and curricular upheavals of the 1960s for their creation of illiteracy in the 1970s. The displacement of traditional with egalitarian and experimental courses is the key villain to Copperman. The most strident statement of conservatism in the restoration, though, is Burton Yale Pines, *Back to Basics* (New York, 1982) which applies the basics theme to literacy and society.

14 Richard D. Little, 'Legacy of the '60s: Declining Quality,' *The Christian Science Monitor*, 17 January 1977.
15 Michael F. Shugrue, *English in a Decade of Change* (New York, 1968), pp. 186, 175. Shugrue surveys the efforts from within the education system to reform itself. The resistance to liberal reform from within gives some indication of the resistance to reform from a radical opposition.
16 James R. Squire, *A Study of English Programs in Selected High Schools Which Consistently Educate Outstanding Students in English* (Urbana, 1966), cited in Shugrue, *op. cit.*, p. 161. The traditional pedagogy that produced outstanding students was also the traditional pedagogy that elsewhere was producing students who failed. A discussion of class and race is needed to account for the impact of pedagogy. See also John Goodlad, 'The Schools vs. Education,' *Saturday Review*, 19 April 1969, and Goodlad's 'Curriculum: A Janus Look,' *Teachers College Record*, vol. 70, no. 2, November 1968.
17 John I. Goodlad, *A Place Called School* (New York, 1983), p. 229. Goodlad found teacher-talk dominating the classroom far more than Squire reported in his 1966 study. While Squire recorded about 44 per cent teacher-dominated lecture-recitation, Goodlad found about 70 per cent of the classroom talk going from teacher to student. He observed *less than 1 per cent* of classroom discourse calling for unstructured opinion or reasoning by students. Goodlad concluded from his team's site visits to over one thousand classrooms that 'If teachers in the talking mode and students in the listening mode is what we want, rest assured that we have it.' The persistence of traditionalism in English classes can be seen from Candida Gillis's informal survey, 'The English Classroom, 1977,' *English Journal*, vol. 66, September 1977, pp. 20–6.
18 Jencks, 'What's Behind the Drop in Test Scores?,' *op. cit.*, p. 38.
19 *On Further Examination, op. cit.*, p. 41.
20 See, for example, the remarkable comments by Reagan's Secretary of Education, T. H. Bell, as reported by Malcolm G. Scully in *The Chronicle of Higher Education*, 'Bell Condemns "Careerism" in Colleges: Emphasis on Jobs Seen Causing Decline in Literacy,' 19 October 1983. The connection of illiteracy to occupationalism was not made in the first decade of the restoration by resurgent traditionalists. Bell declared that 'We must beware of the crowding out of student time for the liberal arts because of the professional schools' propensity to demand more and more time of students.' Job-related education might lead to intellectual incompetence, he warned. Such statements were some indication of the political distance traveled in ten years of conservative policy-making. The aggressive careerism of the Nixon-Marland phase had done its work so well that a bone could now be thrown to the ailing liberal arts.
21 Ivan Illich, *Deschooling Society* (New York, 1971). See also Jonathan Kozol, *Death at an Early Age* (New York, 1968) and *Free Schools* (New York, 1972); Herbert Kohl, *The Open Classroom* (New York,

1970); Ronald Gross and Beatrice Gross, *Radical School Reform* (New York, 1970); Charles Silberman, *Crisis in the Classroom* (New York, 1970); and Allen Graubard, *Free the Children: Radical Reform and the Free School Movement* (New York, 1972). The 'deschooling' controversy at that time can be surveyed in *After Deschooling, What?*, eds. Alan Gartner, Colin Greer and Frank Riessman (New York, 1973).

22 Christopher Lasch, *The Culture of Narcissism* (New York, 1979), Chapter Six, 'Schooling and the New Illiteracy,' pp. 257–8. Lasch took a traditional and dismal view of both open admissions and the protest era of the 1960s. For another perspective on open admissions and literacy, see Thomas C. Wheeler's *The Great American Writing Block: Causes and Cures of the New Illiteracy* (New York, 1979). Even though Wheeler uses the vocabulary of 'the new illiteracy,' he offers a revealing insight into his own education as an English teacher for open admissions students in the City University of New York. Wheeler's sensitive, optimistic and helpful accounts of his teaching practice contrast sharply with Lasch's olympian despair.

23 Lasch, *op. cit.*, pp. 257–8.

24 See Ronald Gross and Beatrice Gross, *Independent Scholarship: Promise, Problems, and Prospects* (College Board, New York, 1983). There is also another important democratic trend towards 'participatory research,' as an alternative to traditional, academic models. The Participatory Research Group (386 Bloor Street West, Toronto, Ontario, Canada, M5S 1X4) publishes a newsletter and materials on this form of inquiry.

25 Richard Ohmann, 'The Literacy Crisis is a Fiction, if Not a Hoax,' *The Chronicle of Higher Education*, 25 October 1976.

26 Goodlad, *A Place Called School*, *op. cit.*, p. 13. From what he observed, Goodlad concluded that in the 1960s and 1970s, most teachers had never left the basics. The back-to-basics movement did not have a pedagogical revolt by teachers to contend with. Goodlad saw school environments that differed from place to place, but he found remarkable uniformity in the schooling process. The normative pedagogy of the schools was a passive one, a teacher talking information to the students.

27 *On Further Examination, op. cit.*, p. 27.

28 Christopher Jencks and James Crouse, 'Aptitude vs. Achievement: Should we Replace the SAT?,' *The Public Interest*, No. 67, Spring 1982, pp. 26–7. For more discussion of the non-objective nature of the SAT, see Chapter Two of Wheeler's *The Great American Writing Block*, 'The Failure of Objectivity.' Wheeler offers some close analysis of sample SAT questions, discusses the absence of writing samples on the SAT, and some insight into reading exams as well.

29 Jencks and Crouse, 'Aptitude vs. Achievement,' *op. cit.*, p. 26.

30 Ernest L. Boyer, *High School: A Report on Secondary Education in America* (Carnegie Foundation, New York, 1983). Boyer devoted a chapter to reviewing the test-score declines, preferring the NAEP to

the SAT as a more authentic index of student skills. As expected, NAEP showed no literacy collapse. Boyer was also skeptical of the rush to computer education.

31 See Fred M. Hechinger, 'To Know the Schools, It Seems, Is to Like Them,' *New York Times*, 13 December 1983. Hechinger was referring to simplistic answers for school reform, in terms of raised SAT scores not being synonymous with raised school quality. He refers to Gregory Anrig, ETS President, who denounced the use of SAT scores to judge school quality. The National Association of Secondary School Principals had done just that in commissioning a study of high school curriculum to find out what schools were doing where SAT scores were stable. See note 50 below.

32 'High School Weak Link in Chain,' *USA Today*, 13 May 1983.

33 *On Further Examination, op. cit.*, p. 9. The predictive ability of the SAT was .39 for the math part and .42 for the verbal section.

34 *On Further Examination, op. cit.*, p. 1. Compare Wirtz's bald and dismal conclusion about student speaking skills with Thomas Wheeler's comments on writing and speaking in his open admissions class:

> Students, however illiterate, I had begun to realize, often spoke in complete sentences. I could hear in their speech the form they left out of their writing. I had become more and more convinced that students of writing needed to begin from the way they talked.
> Students have been told not to write as they talk so often that writing becomes an awkward act, like walking on stilts. If English teachers would only get their students talking about subjects that interest them, they would hear feats of grammar performed in mid-air.
>
> *The Great American Writing Block* (p. 73)

The accusation that students can barely speak and hardly write violates the reality of their performance in classes where they feel respected. Also, the conservative thesis on student illiteracy ignores the rich language students share among their peers when bosses, teachers and superiors are not overseeing them. Silence is part of their resistance to alienating situations.

35 *On Further Examination, op. cit.*, p. 23.

36 *On Further Examination, op. cit.*, pp. 13–24.

37 Ohmann, 'The Literacy Crisis is a Fiction, if Not a Hoax,' *op. cit.*, p. 32.

38 Gerard Bracey, 'Some Reservation About Minimum Competency Testing,' *Phi Delta Kappan*, April 1978, p. 550.

39 Stephen Judy, review of *On Further Examination, English Journal*, Vol. 66, No. 8, November 1977, p. 5. Judy expanded his criticism of illiteracy into *The ABC's of Literacy: A Guide for Parents and Educators* (New York, 1980).

40 John Dewey, *School and Society* [1900] (Chicago, 1956), pp. 55–6. Dewey recommended beginning any study with the least academic

machinery possible and the closest approach to student experience. The artificial language of schooling was one alienating factor creating student withdrawal, but the constant academic or vocational preparation for some vague future (getting into college or getting a job) also made students passive in Dewey's estimation. Dewey's critique of passive preparation for the future extended from *Moral Principles in Education* (1909) to *Experience and Education* (1938). In each case, he indicted curriculum and teaching methods for producing student resistance and silence, rather than blaming the students for illiteracy.

41 See Paulo Freire's *Pedagogy of the Oppressed* (New York, 1970) and *Cultural Action for Freedom* (Baltimore, 1972). He wrote of the peasants among whom he worked in Brazil before the military coup of 1964:

> Illiterates know they are concrete men. They know that they do things. What they do not know in the culture of silence is that men's actions as such are transforming, creative and re-creative. . . . Prevented from having a 'structural perception' of the facts involving them, they do not know that they cannot 'have a voice,' that is, that they cannot exercise the right to participate consciously in the socio-historical transformation of their society.
>
> *Cultural Action for Freedom* (p. 30)

42 Anthony Wolk, 'Review,' *College English*, Vol. 41, No. 4, December 1979, pp. 448–60. Wolk was part of the continuing opposition to the depressant literacy campaigns. He was editor of a newsletter published by the Conference on Language and Composition, a dissenting caucus within the larger Conference on College Composition and Communication, a large professional organization of writing teachers affiliated with the National Council of Teachers of English.

43 Leo A. Munday, 'Changing Test Scores, Especially Since 1970,' *Phi Delta Kappan*, March 1979, p. 496. See also Munday's follow-up in the May 1979 *Kappan*. The upswing Munday saw coming took place in 1982. Like many long views of the test-score situation, he did not see cause for alarm.

44 Anne Hulbert, 'S.A.T.s Aren't So Smart,' *The New Republic*, 20 December 1982, p. 12. The sub-title of her essay was 'It's time for the test's reign to end.'

45 *Ibid.*, p. 14. A sidebar to Hulbert's article in *The New Republic* ('Test Prep Panic by Peter Spiro') discussed the sleazy big business erupting in preparing students for professional school tests. Students moved in with money and determination when they had to pass a test that meant a great deal to them, like admission to medical or law school.

46 Edmund Farrell, 'The Vice/Vise of Standardized Testing: National

Depreciation by Qualification,' *English Journal*, Vol. 65, No. 7, October 1976, p. 10.
47 James S. Coleman, *Equality of Educational Opportunity* (Office of Education, Washington D.C., 1966); Christopher Jencks *et al.*, *Inequality* (New York, 1972).
48 Farrell, 'The Vice/Vise of Standardized Testing,' *op. cit.*, p. 10.
49 Silberman asked in *Crisis in the Classroom* (1970): 'What is education for? What kind of human beings and what kind of society do we want to produce? What method of instruction and classroom organization, as well as what subject matter, do we need to produce these results? What knowledge is of most worth?' (p. 182).
50 See John A. Black, 'When is a Study Not a Study? An Examination of "Guidelines for Improving SAT Scores",' *Phi Delta Kappan*, March 1979, pp. 487–9. Black charged that the NASSP prepared the study to show that traditional courses boosted SAT scores. This was at a time when electives and experimental courses were under conservative pressure. A weak rejoinder to his charges was offered in the same *Kappan* by NASSP Deputy Director Scott Thomson, 'When a Criticism is Not a Criticism.'
51 For a discussion of the prairie-fire spread of competency-testing programs, see Ben Brodinsky, 'Back-to-Basics: The Movement and Its Meaning,' *Phi Delta Kappan*, March 1977, pp. 522–7. Reference to the state-by-state basics steamroller can be found in Jencks, 'What's Behind the Drop in Test Scores?' and in Boyer's *High School*, *op. cit.*
52 Brodinsky, 'Back-to-Basics,' *op. cit.*, p. 522. See also Brodinsky's later assessment of 'The New Right: The Movement and Its Impact,' *Phi Delta Kappan*, October 1982, pp. 87–94.
53 Brodinsky, 'Back-to-Basics,' *op. cit.*, p. 522.
54 Jencks, 'What's Behind the Drop in Test Scores?,' *op. cit.*, wrote that

> If minimum standards have any effect, it will be to make high schools devote more attention to basic skills. But these are precisely the skills that have *not* declined in recent years. Test score declines, as I argued earlier, have involved more complicated skills, as well as the kinds of information that flow from such skills. If we want to reverse this trend, we must find ways of motivating students to go beyond the basics. . . . This is not a matter of establishing 'minimum standards.' It is a matter of creating respect for 'maximum standards.' (p. 41)

55 Ohmann, 'The Literacy Crisis is a Fiction, if Not a Hoax,' *op. cit.*, asked

> What would it take, by way of social change, to create full literacy? Why isn't this happening? Do those who control our economic and educational systems really want a totally literate workforce, given that there are too few jobs to go around,

and too few intelligent jobs, for the literate and capable workers who now exist? (p. 32)

56 Jencks, 'What's Behind the Drop in Test Scores?,' *op. cit.*, p. 32.
57 *Ibid.*, p. 39.
58 Lasch, *Culture of Narcissism, op. cit.*, p. 245.
59 Boyer, *High School, op. cit.*, pp. 16, 144.
60 Theodore Sizer, *Horace's Compromise: The Dilemma of the American High School* (Boston, 1984), p. 156. Sizer noted that rich school-children still have about twice as much money spent on their educat-ions as do poor kids, yet 'social class' is not a theme in high school curricula. Sizer did not delve into the 'class conspiracy' for the least education for the mass of students.
61 *Ibid.*, p. 140.
62 Jencks, 'What's Behind the Drop in Test Scores?,' *op. cit.*, pp. 40–1. Jencks recommended a tough attitude towards disruptive students who sabotaged the intellectual seriousness of the class.
63 Henry Levin, 'Back-to-Basics and the Economy,' *Radical Teacher*, No. 21, 1981, p. 9. Levin, in association with Russell Rumberger, has done extensive research on education, economics and high-tech through the Institute on the Finance and Governance of Education, Stanford University.
64 *Ibid.*, p. 9.
65 Murray Milner, *The Illusion of Equality* (San Francisco, 1972), wrote that 'The past expansion of education has had no apparent effect on mobility, and consequently, the degree of income inequality and inequality of opportunity have remained roughly constant. . . . We have labored too long under the illusion that the structure of inequality can be significantly changed by dabbling with the education system' (pp. 73, 144). Jencks reached essentially the same conclusion in his massive review of education and status, *Inequality* (1972). Despite the vast expansion of educational access in this century, the distribution of income has remained the same. Diane Ravitch quarrels with this view on education and inequality in *The Revisionists Revised* (New York, 1978). She found some inter-class mobility which rescues the equalizing myth of school.
66 Ernest J. Sternglass and Steven Bell, 'Fall-out and SAT Scores: Evidence for Cognitive Damage During Early Infancy,' *Phi Delta Kappan*, April 1983, pp. 539–45. Their earlier predictions can be found in 'The Nuclear Radiation/SAT Decline Connection,' *Phi Delta Kappan*, November 1979, pp. 184–8.
67 Sternglass and Bell, 'Fallout and SAT Scores,' *op. cit.*, p. 539.
68 *Ibid.*, p. 544.
69 For a visual tabulation of Iowa tests from 1962 to 1981, see Chapter Two of Ernest L. Boyer, *High School* (1983). Boyer offers a composite scaling for grades nine through twelve in reading, math, social studies and science achievement tests (p. 32).

70 *Ibid.*, 'Report Card: How Schools Are Doing,' p. 25, scales the long-term decline of ACT scores.
71 Shugrue, *English in A Decade of Change* (1968); Silberman, *Crisis in the Classroom* (1970); Goodlad, *A Place Called School* (1983).
72 Alfred Kitzhaber, *Themes, Theories and Therapies* (New York, 1963), pp. 6, 7, 144. Kitzhaber looked at writing instruction mostly from the elite university perspective, working as he was at Dartmouth. That teaching is a 'situated' art was confirmed in the open admissions setting by such books as Thomas Wheeler's above-cited *The Great American Writing Block* (1979) and by Mina Shaugnessy's *Errors and Expectations* (New York, 1978), both products of the vast experimental years in City University's remedial programs. See also the pedagogical chapters of my book *Critical Teaching and Everyday Life* (Boston, 1980).
73 *College English*, the journal of the National Council of Teachers of English, for higher education, was under the editorship of Richard Ohmann from 1968–78. During that period it was a rich source of creative and critical methods for writing classes. See the May 1974 and December 1977 numbers of *College English* for examples of non-minimal approaches to basic writing classes. The *Radical Teacher* magazine in the later 1970s and early 1980s was another good source of teaching models. A good sample of its offerings can be seen in No. 20 (Fall 1981), the special issue on back-to-basics. The work of Ken Bruffee at Brooklyn College was another instance of pedagogical experimentation rejecting minimal goals. See Ronnie Dugger's report on Bruffee, 'Cooperative Learning in a Writing Community,' *Change*, July 1976, pp. 20–3. Peter Elbow's *Writing Without Teachers* (New York, 1973) and Bill Bernhardt's *Just Writing* (New York, 1978) were creative and non-authoritarian approaches to self-education in writing, quite against the basics thrust of the time. For a sample of a Paulo Freire-method in this period, see Nan Elsasser and Vera John-Steiner, 'An Interactionist Approach to Advancing Literacy,' *Harvard Educational Review*, Vol. 47, No. 3, August 1977, pp. 355–69. Another good example of the maximal literacy insisted on by Jencks and Ohmann can be found in Henry Giroux, 'Writing and Critical Thinking in the Social Studies,' *Curriculum Inquiry*, Vol. 8, No. 4, 1978, pp. 291–310. These few suggestions are the tip of the opposition iceberg, under which a great deal of resistance to conservative basics was kept alive. However, the dominant thrust of the age was towards conservative, traditional courses and methods. For some flavor of the intense debate around the most ambitious mass literacy project of them all, City University of New York's open admission program, see Timothy Healy, Edward Quinn, Alexander Astin and Jack Rossman, 'The Case for Open Admissions,' *Change*, Summer 1973, pp. 24–37; Martin Mayer, 'Higher Education for All?,' *Commentary*, February 1973, pp. 37–47; Jerome Karabel, 'Open Admissions: Toward Meritocracy or Democracy?,' *Change*, May 1973; Ken Libow and Ed Stuart,

'Open Admissions: An Open and Shut Case?,' *Saturday Review*, 9 December 1972, p. 54.

74 David Tyack, *Turning Points in American Education* (New York, 1967), pp. 279–80.

75 Burton R. Clark, 'The Cooling-Out Function in Higher Education,' *American Journal of Sociology*, Vol. 65, May 1960, pp. 569–76. This seminal essay on the community college's depressant functions began a tradition of critical assessment that continued in K. Patricia Cross's *Beyond the Open Door* (San Francisco, 1971), L. Steven Zwerling's *Second Best* (New York, 1976), and David Nasaw's *Schooled to Order* (New York, 1979). Clark himself offered a reassessment of the cooling-out thesis in 'The Cooling-Out Function Revisited,' in *New Directions for the Community Colleges* ed. George Vaughan (New York, 1980), pp. 15–31. Sadly enough, and with notable irritation in his voice, a defensive Clark agreed that cooling-out the aspirations of students still is an important role in the community college. He thought it was a legitimate function in a democracy with limited rewards from the job market.

76 Burton R. Clark, *The Open Door College* (New York, 1960), p. 124. This case-study of San Jose Community College should be read in tandem with Leland Medsker's *The Junior College* (New York, 1960) which is a survey of the first decade of the whole community college movement. Together, these two early Carnegie studies offer a good insight into the contradictions of inegalitarian mass higher education, then in its formative stages.

77 Chuck Halloran, 'UCLA vs. the Literacy Crisis,' *UCLA Monthly*, Vol. 12, No. 4, March-April 1982, pp. 1, 2, 4.

78 Joel Spring, *The Sorting Machine: National Educational Policy Since 1945* (New York, 1976), p. 12.

79 Gene Maeroff, *Don't Blame the Kids: The Trouble With America's Public Schools* (New York, 1982), p. 96. For the advance of conservative censorship in the schools, see also Fred M. Hechinger, 'Censorship Rises in the Nation's Public Schools,' *New York Times*, 3 January 1984.

80 Robert Lindsey, 'Home of the Future: Size Will Shrink But Not the Price,' *New York Times*, 24 January 1981.

81 'The "Affordable Home" Is Tiny and Not Really Cheap,' *Wall Street Journal*, 7 December 1983.

82 On the Nixon 'cold bath' recession, see Samuel Bowles, David Gordon and Thomas E. Weiskopf, *Beyond the Wasteland: A Democratic Alternative to Economic Decline* (New York, 1984), pp. 148ff especially.

83 For further documentation on student performance in basic skills in the 1970s, see the 1977 HEW report *What Students Know and Can Do*. It found that 90 per cent of 17-year-olds in 1974 could read a job ad in a newspaper and describe it, and 60 per cent could even understand the phone company's long-distance rate structure!

84 Mina Shaughnessy, *Errors and Expectations* (New York, 1977), p. 3.

Her unfortunate early death prevented her from going on with her work, but her influence was recognized by the Fund for the Improvement of Post-Secondary Education, which established a grant-program in her name, in 1981.

85 *Ibid.*, pp. 51, 119.
86 Stephen Judy, *The ABCs of Literacy* (New York, 1980), pp. xii-xiii.
87 *Ibid.*, p. 36.
88 *Ibid.*, pp. 82–108, 126–8.
89 Herbert Kohl, *Basic Skills* (published 1982, 1984 edn, New York), p. 4.
90 *Ibid.*, pp. 22, 19.
91 Robert Pattison, *On Literacy: The Politics of the Word from Homer to the Age of Rock* (New York, 1982). Pattison dismissed much of the illiteracy claims as the 'same old whine' of middle-class language standards.
92 *Ibid.*, p. 65.

4 Settling for less, 1982–4: the war for 'excellence' and against 'mediocrity'

1 *A Nation at Risk: The Imperative for Educational Reform*, the National Commission on Excellence in Education, Washington D.C., 1983, p. 1.
2 David P. Gardner's background in intelligence was discussed by John Ohliger in a critique of the 'excellence' campaign, 'Who Put the Question Marks in Mr Reagan's Chowder?', presented at the 1983 Annual Fall Conference of the Northern Area Adult Education Service Center, 27 October 1983, Schaumburg, Illinois. Ohliger cited Zoe Ingalls's profile in *The Chronicle of Higher Education* (9 September 1981) on Gardner, when the NCEE was first commissioned: 'Gardner Brings a Traditional View to New Federal Review of Education.' Ingalls wrote that 'From 1955 to 1957, Mr Gardner served in what he calls an "undercover capacity" for the US Army Intelligence in Japan and Korea. "That's about all I can say about it. I was part of our positive intelligence operation," he says. "Collecting information – in an unconventional fashion." '
3 The Education Commission of the States publishes updates of 'National Education Reform Reports.' These booklet-summaries offered, in the first year of the new crisis, helpful comparisons of the ten most influential studies, including ECS's own *Action for Excellence*. This is one simple reference source to view the remarkable convergence of opinion among top policy-makers at the same moment. ECS documents are available from its office at 248 Hall of the States, 444 N. Capitol Street, N.W., Washington D.C., 20001.
4 *The Confidence Gap: Business, Labor, and Government in the Public Mind*, Seymour Martin Lipset and William Schneider (New York, 1983). Lipset and Schneider concluded that the American system was

more 'brittle' now than at any time in this century. The implication is that should there be a major economic crisis or a major foreign policy setback, the chance that Americans would support a very different organization of society is increased.

5 Kenneth Keniston, 'The Mood of Americans Today,' *New York Times Book Review*, 8 November 1981, p. 44.

6 For a discussion of the economics of austerity and the politics of the conservative 'cold bath' of the early 1970s, see *Beyond the Wasteland: A Democratic Alternative to Economic Decline*, Samuel Bowles, David M. Gordon and Thomas E. Weiskopf (Garden City, 1984). For insights into the growing sophistication and aggressiveness of business in the schools, see Joel Spring, 'From Study Hall to Hiring Hall,' *The Progressive*, April 1984, pp. 30–1. Spring discussed the big business effort in the early 1980s to make schooling more securely pro-business. His report on business-school linkages updates Sheila Harty's *Hucksters in the Classroom: A Review of Industry Propaganda in the Schools*, Washington D.C., Center for the Study of Responsive Law, 1979.

7 The Chairman of the NCEE was then President-Elect of the University of California, David P. Gardner, who included only one classroom teacher in the commission with him. The composition of the ECS Task Force that produced *Action for Excellence* is even more revealing: fourteen heads of major corporations, thirteen governors, one teacher and one union leader. Professors and presidents from Harvard, Yale, Columbia and other mainline institutions were sprinkled liberally through the commissions, along with school principals and superintendents and an occasional community college president, the traditional infrastructure just under the top policy-makers through which programs achieve national distribution.

8 *Newsweek*, 9 May 1983, cover-story, 'Saving Our Schools,' pp. 50–8. The NCEE report *A Nation at Risk* received vast coverage in hundreds of newspapers, magazines and broadcast media. To see the evolving politics of the education issue, two stories are revealing: 'The Making of a Presidential Issue,' *Newsweek* (20 June 1983), and 'School is In: Making an Issue of Education,' *Time* (27 June 1983). For a critical report on the NCEE, especially its military rhetoric, see the editorial in *The Nation* (24 May 1983), 'Arming Education.'

9 *Newsweek*, 9 May 1983, p. 50.

10 *A Nation at Risk, op. cit.*, pp. 8–12.

11 For a good discussion of the difficulty comparing mass US high schools with elite European ones, see Chapter Two of Ernest L. Boyer's major 1983 crisis report, *High School: A Report on Secondary Education in America*, The Carnegie Foundation for the Advancement of Teaching, New York, 1983.

12 *A Nation at Risk, op. cit.*, pp. 17–18.

13 *Making the Grade: Report of the Twentieth Century Fund Task Force on Federal Elementary and Secondary Education Policy*, with a back-

ground paper by Paul E. Peterson, The Twentieth Century Fund, New York, 1983, pp. v, 3.

14 *Action for Excellence: A Comprehensive Plan to Improve Our Nation's Schools*, the Task Force on Education for Economic Growth, the Education Commission of the States, Washington D.C., 1983, pp. 3, 46.

15 *Ibid.*, p. 31.

16 Governor Hunt campaigned so vigorously for the new agenda that *Newsweek* used a photo from a North Carolina high school for its cover. On the inside, *Newsweek* highlighted Hunt's statewide reform efforts, especially his elite North Carolina School for Science and Mathematics, funded at three times the normal per capita budgets, as a fake demonstration model of 'excellence.' Governor Lamar Alexander of Tennessee went to battle for the new agenda also, especially the issue of merit pay, which he pushed through the state legislature against the opposition of the teachers unions. His merit pay plan passed the Tennessee State Senate on 22 February 1984, and established the ranks of probationary teacher, apprentice teacher, career level I teacher, career level II teacher and career level III teacher (*Senate Bill 1*). In California, school chief Bill Honig led an aggressive, upbeat conservative campaign for school reform and cornered Governor Deukmejian into increasing education outlays. Honig's ability to get more funds for schooling legitimized his traditional agenda for reform.

17 A national best-seller in 1984 was *In Search of Excellence: Lessons from America's Best-Run Companies*, by Thomas J. Peters and Robert H. Waterman, Jr (New York, 1983). This book's eight 'basic' principles involve how to motivate employees so that productivity increases and hence profits. It made a cult of efficiency and effective management without considering social questions such as the purpose of the business activity or the social consequences of the product. 'Excellence' indicated an efficient, motivated staff which produced what management decided should be produced.

18 *Educating Americans for the 21st Century*, National Science Board Commission on Pre-college Education in Mathematics, Science and Technology, Washington D.C., 1983, 'Executive Summary.'

19 *Ibid.*, 'Introduction.'

20 Joel Spring, 'From Study Hall to Hiring Hall,' *op. cit.*, and 'High Tech and the Schools' (*Dollars and Sense*, No. 87, May-June 1983) discuss the new penetration of curriculum by business.

21 *Action for Excellence, op. cit.*, p. 16.

22 *A Nation at Risk, op. cit.*, p. 24.

23 *Academic Preparation for College: What Students Need to Know and Be Able to Do*, The College Board, New York, 1983.

24 *The Paideia Proposal*, Mortimer Adler (New York, 1982) and *Paideia: Problems and Possibilities*, Mortimer Adler (1983); *Horace's Compromise: The Dilemmas of the American High School*, Theodore R. Sizer (New York, 1984). Sizer was a member of Adler's

Paideia Group, but his book was far more in touch with reality than Adler's. Hence Sizer had a different conception of authority-based schooling. Where Adler leaned on the authority of classic texts, Sizer turned to the wisdom of the individual teacher in a specific school setting.

25 Boyer's long report *High School* (1983) and John Goodlad's *A Place Called School* (New York, 1983) preceded Sizer's *Horace's Compromise* as a liberal dissent from the authority-computer agendas of the major commissions. Goodlad was the most sensible and progressive of the group, as he understood learning process better than Boyer or Sizer. Boyer's agenda came closest to the official plans, so his report got the most attention. Goodlad and Sizer called for less structure and more autonomy for teachers and students, an anti-authoritarian thrust quite out of tune with the main trend of the moment.

26 *The Condition of Teaching: A State by State Analysis*, C. Emily Feistritzer, The Carnegie Foundation for the Advancement of Teaching, New York, 1983. As a quantitative report, this document reveals the degradation of teaching through the conservative restoration. It is best read as the quantitative research companion to Goodlad's qualitative report, *A Place Called School*.

27 Boyer, *High School, op. cit.*, p. 1.

28 Goodlad, *A Place Called School, op. cit.*, pp. 1, 2.

29 *Signs of Trouble and Erosion: A Report on Graduate Education in America*, the National Commission on Student Financial Assistance, Graduate Education Subcommittee, John Brademas, Chairman, New York, December 1983, p. 11.

30 *America's Competitive Challenge: The Need for a National Response*, a Report to the President of the United States, from the Business-Higher Education Forum, Washington D.C., 1983, p. iv.

31 Adler's Paideia Program was a strenuous attempt to renew scholastic humanism. In the late 1970s, shortly before Paideia was issued, other efforts to renew traditional humanities took organizational form through the American Association for the Advancement of the Humanities and the Community College Humanities Association. A non-traditional 'Crisis in the Liberal Arts' Conference in January 1981 at New Paltz offered some criticism of the elite character of liberal arts historically.

32 Adler, *The Paideia Proposal, op. cit.*, frontispiece.

33 Charles Silberman, *Crisis in the Classroom: The Remaking of American Education* (New York, 1970). Silberman produced this study after four years of research under Carnegie sponsorship. This multi-million dollar effort endorsed progressive education on the very eve of the conservative counter-attack against the liberal trends of the 1960s. Silberman wrote that 'schools discourage students from developing the capacity to learn by and for themselves; they make it impossible for a youngster to take responsibility for his own education, for they are structured in such a way as to make students

totally dependent on the teachers. . . . The teacher's role must change in other and equally profound ways. There must be far less telling on the part of the teacher and far more doing on the part of the student' (pp. 135, 218). These remarks were in tune with the alternate critique of schooling current in the 1960s, and they anticipate the critique of teacher-talk education by Goodlad in the third phase of the restoration. The political distance traveled from 1970 to 1983 can be seen in the very low profile given to student-centered teaching or progressive methods in Boyer's Carnegie report *High School*, during the 1983 crisis.

34 Christopher Jencks, 'What's Behind the Drop in Test Scores?,' *Working Papers*, July-August 1978, especially pp. 39–41.

35 John Dewey, *Democracy and Education* [1916], Free Press edn (New York, 1967). Dewey asked, 'Why is it, in spite of the fact that teaching by pouring in, learning by a passive absorption, are universally condemned, that they are still entrenched in practice?' (p. 38). He complained in 1916 that the principles of active education were conceded as correct in theory and then violated in practice. He asserted that

> It is as absurd for the [teacher] to set up his own aims as the proper objects of the growth of the children as it would be for the farmer to set up an ideal of farming irrespective of conditions. . . . The vice of externally imposed ends has deep roots. Teachers receive them from superior authorities; these authorities accept them from what is current in the community. The teachers impose them on the children . . . the first approach to any subject in school, if thought is to be aroused and not words acquired, should be as unscholastic as possible. (*Democracy and Education*, pp. 107, 108, 154)

36 Adler, *The Paideia Proposal, op. cit.*, p. 5. While Dewey insisted that the educator cannot start with knowledge already worked out and then presume to ladle it out to students, Adler's Paideia and the core curriculum proponents planned traditional lectures to dominate the pedagogy. See Dewey's *Experience and Education* (1938) for Dewey's consistent critique of teaching by programmed doses of knowledge.

37 Dewey, *Democracy and Education, op. cit.*, pp. 260, 327.

38 John Dewey, *Experience and Education* [1938], Collier edn (New York, 1963), p. 67.

39 Sizer, *Horace's Compromise, op. cit.*, p. 6. Sizer understood adolescents better than any of the other third-phase observers, but he was often unable to use his knowledge, perhaps because of its radical implications. For example, he saw the crucial role of 'class' in school and the utter absence of 'class' as a theme of study in the curriculum. Yet, his own curricular recommendations included nothing in relation to 'class.' Similarly, Sizer saw how important 'sex' was to the teenagers in high school, but he did not address the theme

of 'sex' or 'sex education' as a legitimate part of the curriculum. These lacunae are political because they are the touchiest issues to address seriously while maintaining an establishment point of view. Sizer skirted class and sex in his reform proposals and thus protected his establishment credentials in a conservative age when such themes are illegitimate.

40 Adler, *The Paideia Proposal, op. cit.*, p. 79.
41 See Chester Finn's discussion of Paideia's influence on the third phase, in 'Moving Toward a Public Consensus,' *Change*, April 1983, pp. 15–22. Finn was a Vanderbilt University professor who was influential in the conservative ideology of the third phase. He served on the commission that produced the Twentieth Century Fund report *Making the Grade*. He also co-edited a follow-up volume to the 1983 crisis reports, *Against Mediocrity* (New York, 1984), especially directed towards renewing traditional liberal arts. Finn's view on the relationship of private to public schooling can be seen in 'Why Public and Private Schools Matter,' *Harvard Educational Review*, November 1981, pp. 510–14, a restoration tilt towards more help for the private sector.
42 See Charles E. Smith, 'Sputnik II – Where Are You When We Need You?,' *Change*, October 1983, pp. 7–10.
43 *Annual Report* by President Henry Chauncey, Educational Testing Service, 1954–5, Princeton, New Jersey, pp. 15ff.
44 Boyer, *High School, op. cit.*, p. 5.
45 *Life* magazine, 28 March 1958, p. 25.
46 'Education and Economic Progress: Toward a National Education Policy: The Federal Role,' 2 February 1983, p. 2 of the Conference Report published 23 March 1983 by the Carnegie Foundation in New York. This conference brought together fifty very high-level policy-makers from business, government, research universities, education organizations, including three labor executives from trade unions. Governor Hunt was one convenor of the conference. The assertion that education decline equaled 'unilateral disarmament' appeared in this conference report a month before the famous NCEE use of the slogan in *A Nation at Risk*.
47 *A Nation at Risk, op. cit.*, pp. 6–7.
48 *America's Competitive Challenge, op. cit.*, p. iv.
49 See, for example, Edward B. Fiske's extensive reporting on Japanese public education, 'Japan's Schools: Intent About the Basics,' the start of a four-part series in the *New York Times*, 10 July 1983. See also Herman Arthur's characteristic report, 'The Japan Gap,' *American Educator*, Summer 1983, pp. 38–44. *Newsweek* helped Japan's educational prestige glow with 'How the Japanese Do It,' 9 May 1983, p. 54. Japan's traditional and authoritarian society looked wonderfully efficient to third-phase reformers. The model of Japanese behavior-surveillance on the job began appearing in American car plants reopening with a new work-force.
50 *Time*, 19 October 1983, cover-story.

51 Peter Brimelow, 'What To Do About America's Schools,' *Fortune*, 19 September 1983, pp. 60–4. Brimelow concludes that 'Public education has been a curious and anomalous experiment with socialism.' That special issue of *Fortune* came out in favor of market competition in education through tuition vouchers redeemable at public or private schools. It chose to highlight as models of 'excellence' several highly-funded, special vocational high schools in dynamic areas of the economy like high-tech, restauranting and aerospace. These few training areas have a special relationship to the job market because they are still growth sectors in a generally stagnant economy. Thus, like Hunt's extra-funded 'model' school in North Carolina, they are not models of anything except inequality and deception.

52 Boyer, *High School, op. cit.*, p. 5.

53 See *Beyond the Wasteland, op. cit.* for an extensive discussion of conservative economic policy after the 1960s, and as a strategy to reverse the 1960s. Also, Samuel Bowles and Herbert Gintis offer an extensive critique of economy decline in the US since the 1960s in 'The Crisis of Liberal Democratic Capitalism: The Case of the United States,' *Politics and Society*, Vol. 11, No. 1, 1982, pp. 51–93.

54 *Signs of Trouble and Erosion, op. cit.* Brademas complained poignantly about the shabby condition of graduate research facilities. He also pointed out that the poor job market for research PhDs made the rising costs and long years of study for graduate degrees less of a good investment for prospective students.

55 The President of the University of Michigan explained his new direction in 'Retooling Colleges for the 21st Century,' *New York Times*, 15 April 1984, p. 67. President Harold T. Shapiro glamorized the prospects for refinancing graduate research towards the needs of high-tech. What he failed to mention was that the Education School, the School of Natural Resources and the Art School at the University of Michigan were being cut 30–40 per cent to finance a big thrust in high-tech and computers. This sleazy avoidance of the costs of high-tech characterized the authoritarian policy of the third phase.

56 'America's Youth in Search of a Cause,' *US News and World Report*, 16 April 1984, p. 32.

57 Goodlad, *A Place Called School, op. cit.*, p. 228.

58 George Leonard, 'The Great School Reform Hoax,' *Esquire*, April 1984, pp. 47–56. Leonard's vision of a user-friendly, computer-run teaching school raised as many questions as it answered. He is a proponent of active education and insisted that information-mastery could be handled by computer modules, but that school had to include lively teacher-student interaction.

59 Adler, *The Paideia Proposal, op. cit.*, p. 24.

60 *A Nation at Risk, op. cit.*, pp. 7, 10, 12.

61 *Making the Grade op. cit.*, pp. v, 4.

62 Academic Preparation for College, *op. cit.*, Chapter 3, 'Computer Competency: An Emerging Need'; and *Educating Americans for*

the 21st Century, op. cit., which emphasized computer training for teachers.

63 Goodlad, *A Place Called School, op. cit.*, p. 228.
64 Leonard, 'The Great School Reform Hoax,' *op. cit.*
65 Boyer, *High School, op. cit.*, p. 195.
66 Herbert Kohl, *Basic Skills* (New York, 1984), p. 32. Kohl took Goodlad's progressive themes farther into the realm of dissenting alternatives, for an explicitly democratic agenda to counter official basics.
67 'An Attack on the High-Tech High,' *San Francisco Chronicle*, 11 August 1983.
68 Henry Levin and Russell W. Rumberger, 'The Educational Implications of High Technology,' Institute for Research on Educational Finance and Governance, Stanford University, Palo Alto, February 1983, pp. 6, 10. See also Rumberger's 'The Changing Skill Requirements of Jobs in the US Economy,' *Industrial and Labor Relations Review*, No. 34, July 1981, pp. 578–90.
69 Levin and Rumberger, 'The Educational Implications of High Technology,' *op. cit.*, pp. 4, 5.
70 The Bureau of Labor Statistics estimated that high-tech accounted not only for 3.2 per cent of all employment in 1982 but will account for only 6 per cent of all employment by 1995. In addition, the BLS indicated that skill-levels needed for high-tech careers are modest. Only 25 per cent of high-tech employees hold jobs requiring advanced education. See Richard W. Riche, *et al.*, 'High Technology Today and Tomorrow: A Small Slice of the Employment Pie,' *Monthly Labor Review*, Vol. 106, November 1983, pp. 50–8, and George T. Silvestri, *et al.*, 'Occupational Employment Projections Through 1995,' *Monthly Labor Review*, Vol. 106, November 1983, pp. 37–49.
71 *High Schools and the Changing Workplace: The Employers' View*, Report of the Panel on Secondary School Education for the Changing Workplace, National Academy of Science, Washington D.C., 1984, pp., 4, 6, 9, 10.
72 William Serrin, 'Worry Grows Over Upheaval as Technology Reshapes Jobs,' *New York Times*, 4 July 1982. See also Serrin's 'High Tech Is No Jobs Panacea,' *New York Times*, 18 September 1983. He also wrote a sobering prediction of the high-tech job market, agreeing with Levin's and Rumberger's assessment (see note 68), in an article hilariously headlined 'Job Market Becomes Brighter,' *New York Times*, 16 October 1983.
73 See Amy Dru Stanley, 'High Tech Will Hurt Women,' *New York Times*, 19 September 1983. John Holusha wrote in 'The New Allure of Manufacturing' (*New York Times*, 18 December 1983) about the rise of the new 'flexible manufacturing' plants with 'continuous process production' where computers and robots predominate. Thus, the need for labor is reduced while the wages of the lower-skilled labor needed to tend robots and computers is also lowered. This new

robotic-computer arrangement may enable the runaway industries to return to the US under conditions very favorable to management and unfavorable to labor and unions. The wage-enhancing factor of unions encouraged the flight of industry to the sunbelt and abroad, but the wage-depressing features of high-tech and hard times may reverse this trend.

74 George S. Counts, *Dare the Schools Build a New Social Order* (New York, 1932), p. 33.

75 *America's Competitive Challenge, op. cit.*, p. 12.

76 Richard Freeman, *The Overeducated American* (New York, 1976). See Chapter 2, 'Responses to the Depressed Market.' Freeman wrote that 'lemming-like rushes into particular areas . . . should be avoided. When more and more students are flocking into an area, that is a good indication of possible cobweb surpluses in the future' (p. 195). Freeman not only foresaw the results of a rush to one field but he also concluded that the prestige of education had to decline in an era of overeducation, thus revealing the economic imperative governing education, a reverse of the third phase blaming educational mediocrity for the decline of the economy.

77 Sizer, *Horace's Compromise, op. cit.*, pp. 200–1.

78 Boyer, *High School, op. cit.*, pp. 5, 6.

79 See 'Bell Names Commission to Study Ways to Raise Schools' Standards,' *New York Times*, 27 August 1981.

80 *A Nation at Risk, op. cit.*, p. 47.

81 Adler, *The Paideia Proposal, op. cit.*, pp. 74–5.

82 *Academic Preparation for College, op. cit.*, p. 33.

83 See *Newsweek*'s massage of Governor Hunt's reform program, 'It's Working in North Carolina,' 9 May 1983, p. 52.

84 Edward B. Fiske's in-progress report on the rush of computers into colleges stated that women applicants dropped 13 per cent when one university *required* all new students to buy their own computers. See 'Computers in the Groves of Academe,' *New York Times* magazine, 13 May 1984, p. 90. Fiske breezed by the negative impact of the high-tech religion on women, who have historically been socialized away from science and math. He also did not consider the class and race bias in the computer explosion. It just so happened that Fiske focused on elite universities, but it did not occur to him to ask about the class of students involved and the class of those left out. Students were being asked here to finance the high-tech tilt of school and society by buying the hardware needed to train them for business. This reflected the passing on of retooling costs to the future employees and current citizens.

85 For a penetrating account of the politics of language and aptitude, see Noelle Bisseret, *Education, Class Language and Ideology* (London, 1977). Bisseret traces the social construction of dominant class standards from the sixteenth century to the present, elaborating the power relations hidden in speech, schooling and standards which are supposedly universal.

86 *A Nation at Risk, op. cit.*, p. 6.
87 *Making the Grade, op. cit.*, p. 6.
88 Eileen Gardner, 'What's Wrong With Math and Science Teaching in Our Schools,' *Heritage Today*, No. 3, May-June 1983, pp. 6–7.
89 'News from the College Board,' press release, 14 October 1982, pp. 1–2. The recognition of the narrowing gap between black-white achievement scores remained low-profile, as in the small note in the *American Educator*, Winter 1983, p. 2, 'Achievement Gap Narrows Between Blacks and Whites.'
90 *Action for Excellence, op. cit.*, p. 4.
91 Boyer, *High School, op. cit.*, p. 239.
92 Paul E. Peterson, 'Background Paper,' *Making the Grade, op. cit.*, pp. 57–8. Like others who noted the rising black achievement scores, Peterson did not speculate on why blacks were not able to translate these gains into economic advances.
93 Freeman asserted that the less-advantaged groups would have their educational goals less influenced by the overeducation phenomenon because they had more ground to make up than the more advantaged groups. Also, the declining economy would influence the aspirations of those who hoped for the most, thus resulting in higher drop-out rates from the more advantaged student groups.
94 Peterson, *op. cit.*, p. 57.
95 Sizer, *Horace's Compromise, op. cit.*, p. 140.
96 *A Nation at Risk, op. cit.*, p. 10.
97 Speech by Representative Paul Simon (D-Ill.) quoted in *The Washington Spectator*, Vol. 9, No. 20, 1 December 1983, p. 1.
98 See the *Newsweek* and *Time* cover-stories on the 1983 crisis (9 May and 19 October) to see the fond pats-on-the-back given to strong leaders. Joe Clark appeared several times on national TV, once on ABC's 'Nightline' in March 1984, and then on the Phil Donahue Show, in May 1984. He was singled out by New Jersey Governor Thomas Kean and by President Reagan for praise. Clark began his rule of East Patterson High School by expelling 400 troublemakers.
99 Chester Finn, 'Moving Towards a Public Consensus,' *op. cit.*, p. 21.
100 For a reportage on the regressive taxation which is being used to finance the official reforms, see 'Southern States Moving to Improve Schools,' *New York Times*, 11 January 1984, p. 1. This report by William E. Schmidt does not consider the bottom-financing plan while it does survey the tax developments eased in with the reform plans. Schmidt also quoted one civil rights official who thought that taxes for public education could be raised now because a conservative White House was viewed as standing against desegregation efforts. *Time*'s cover-story of 10 October 1983 also had some reporting on taxation to finance reform, as did the *New York Teacher* (paper of the New York United Teachers, AFT) of 19 March 1984, p. 11. See also 'School Desegregation Grinds to a Halt in South,' *U.S. News and World Report*, 21 May 1984, pp. 49–50.

101 See Emily Feistritzer's study, *The Condition of Teaching, op. cit.*, p. 25.
102 See Hope Aldrich, 'Few Blacks Passing Ga. Teacher Test, Study Finds,' *Education Week*, 9 November 1983. See also *Ebony* magazine's cover-story on racism in the new teacher competency tests in the April 1984 issue.
103 Herbert Kohl, *Basic Skills, op. cit.* The broad social and empowering definition Kohl gave to 'basic skills' redefined what the minimal competency movement had been doing. However, Kohl's progressive upgrading of 'the basics' was superseded by an official upgrading of the three Rs into 'the new basics' in the third phase. Essentially, the authorities also agreed that minimums were too low and a new formulation of the required basics was needed both to get students performing and to raise the credentials needed for the diminishing number of good jobs. Kohl's concept of 'the basics' is still on ice, until a transition in school and society to the left can take it off the shelf.
104 Goodlad wrote that 'potential for explosion exists, I believe, in the present disjuncture between elements of the youth culture on one hand and the orientation of teachers and conduct of school on the other.' (*A Place Called School*, p. 76.) Kohl had many good suggestions for empowering students through basic skills, but he did not discuss sex education. Leonard went into detail about how the user-friendly computer-instruction system would coordinate with great lectures and exciting seminars, but he did not discuss the theme of sex either. Andrew Hacker took a sardonic view of the new reform wave ('The Schools Flunk Out,' *The New York Review of Books*, 12 April 1984) but did not reflect on the absence of sexuality. Joel Spring focused on the advance of business into customizing school curriculum. Timothy Healey's review of several major studies on the 1983 crisis ('High Schools on the Brink,' *New York Times*, 13 May 1984) similarly ignored this key issue to adolescents.
105 Sloan Wilson, 'It's Time to Close Our Carnival: To Revitalize America's Educational Dream We Must Stop Kowtowing to the Mediocre,' *Life* magazine's special issue on the post-Sputnik education crisis, 28 March 1958, p. 37. The alarming tones and recommendations in Wilson's essay are very reminiscent of the official alarms of 1983. However, the intervening 1960s placed some limitations on the rhetoric of elitism. The 1983 reports could not talk about stupid students and had to insist that equality was as important as quality, a token gesture to acknowledge verbally the themes which protest culture permanently raised in the 1960s.
106 James Bryant Conant, *The American High School Today* (New York, 1959). This was the first in a long series of Carnegie studies in education. Conant's magisterial calm in 1959 deserted him when he next did a tour of urban black ghetto schools (*Slums and Suburbs*, 1961). He was shocked at the conditions he found, but still did not recommend integration. Two years later, he published another

education study, *The Education of the American Teacher*, which, like the 1959 high school report, provided an agenda for reform which closely paralleled the 1983 plans.

107 Conant, *The American High School Today, op. cit.*, pp. 23, 40, 60.
108 *Ibid.*, p. 40.
109 *A Nation at Risk, op. cit.*, p. 36.
110 Jerome Bruner, 'Learning and Thinking,' *Harvard Educational Review*, Vol. 29, No. 3, Summer 1959, pp. 184–92. Bruner's dismay with the passive classrooms he saw repeated Dewey's earlier frustration and Goodlad's later one.
111 Jerome Bruner, *The Process of Education* (Cambridge, 1960). This was a report on the key post-Sputnik Woods Hole conference of curriculum experts.

5 The hinge of 1983

1 *Annual Report to the Board of Trustees*, 'Report of the President,' 1954–5, Educational Testing Service, Princeton, p. 28.
2 Sidney P. Marland, *Career Education* (New York, 1974), p. 20.
3 *High Schools and the Changing Workplace: The Employers' View*, Report of the Panel on Secondary School Education for the Changing Workplace, National Academy of Sciences, National Academy of Engineering, Institute of Medicine, National Academy Press, Washington D.C., 1984, p. xii.
4 Henry A. Giroux, 'Theories of Reproduction and Resistance in the New Sociology of Education: A Critical Analysis,' *Harvard Educational Review*, Vol. 53, No. 3, August 1983, p. 278. See also Giroux's longer work on this theme in *Theory and Resistance in Education: A Pedagogy for the Opposition* (Bergin Press, South Hadley, Massachusetts, 1983).
5 Christopher Jencks *et al.*, *Inequality: A Reassessment of the Effects* of *Family and Schooling in America* (New York, 1972), pp. 255–6.
6 *Ibid.*, pp. 12, 97.
7 Wayne Jennings and Joe Nathan, 'Startling/Disturbing Research on School Program Effectiveness,' *Phi Delta Kappan*, March 1977, pp. 568–72.
8 Ivan Illich, *Deschooling Society* (New York, 1970), p. 106. For other discussions of 'the hidden curriculum' see Jean Anyon, 'Social Class and the Hidden Curriculum of Work,' *Journal of Education*, Vol. 162, Winter 1980; Michael Apple, 'The Hidden Curriculum and the Nature of Conflict,' *Interchange*, Vol. 2, No. 4, 1971; Henry Giroux and Anthony Penna, 'Social Education in the Classroom: The Dynamics of the Hidden Curriculum,' *Theory and Research in Social Education*, Vol. 7, No. 1, Spring 1979.
9 Illich, *Deschooling Society, op. cit.*, p. 68.
10 *After Deschooling, What?* eds. Alan Gartner, Colin Greer and Frank Riessman (New York, 1973), p. 20.

11 For some examples of the breadth of skill-exchanges and learning networks, see publications from The Learning Resources Network (LERN), Kansas, Manhattan; *Alternativas*, a newsletter put out for liberatory educators working in English and Spanish, ed. Blanca Facundo, Rio Piedras, Puerto Rico; *The Catalogue of Correspondence* listing peer-educators, published by Stephen Sikora of The Reader's League, PO Box 6218, Albany, California 94706; *Networking: The First Report and Directory* by Jessica Lipnack and Jeffrey Stamps (New York, Doubleday, 1982), available from The Networking Institute, PO Box 66, West Newton, Massachusetts 02165.

12 For an assessment of the first decade of growth in alternate units, see Mary Anne Raywid, 'The First Decade of Public School Alternatives,' and Robert D. Barr, 'Alternatives for the Eighties: A Second Decade of Development,' in the *Phi Delta Kappan*, April 1981. For an opposition point of view on the political value of an alternate school in a conservative time, see Carl Hedman, 'Adversaries and Models: Alternative Institutions in an Age of Scarcity,' *Radical America*, Vol. 15, No. 5, Sept.-Oct. 1981, pp. 41–50.

13 Samuel Bowles and Herbert Gintis, *Schooling in Capitalist America* (New York, 1976), especially Chapters 10 and 11, 'Educational Alternatives,' and 'Education, Socialism, and Revolution.'

14 Herbert Gintis, 'Toward a Political Economy of Education: A Radical Critique of Ivan Illich's *Deschooling Society*,' in *After Deschooling, What?, op. cit.*, pp. 29–76.

15 Samuel Bowles, David M. Gordon and Thomas E. Weiskopf, *Beyond the Wasteland: A Democratic Alternative to Economic Decline* (New York, 1983), p. 367.

16 Anxiety about the decline of the American Heritage can be found in the crisis reports of 1983, especially The Twentieth Century Fund Report, *Making the Grade*. California's dynamic conservative school chief Bill Honig spoke at length about the need to restore a core curriculum in the American Heritage at a conference on Critical Thinking, Sonoma, August 1983. The rise of protest movements in the 1960s was accompanied by non-traditional revisions of official American History, through such new disciplines as labor history, women's history, black history, etc. This diversity, as well as a growing student resistance to the official curriculum, caused numbers of restorationists to define the American Heritage as a troubled area in need of required study. One typical outcry against the dissent and diversity from the 1960s came from Sidney Hook: 'Since the 1960s, we have witnessed scenes and spectacles in academic life that would have been unheard-of in past periods. . . . What I would like to see is development of a curriculum that would make students more aware of their democratic heritage and more sensitive to the alternatives that challenge it' (*US News and World Report*, 18 June 1984, p. 38).

17 See Herb Kohl's 'Cost of Education Profile,' in *Basic Skills* (1984) for a detailed discussion of opposition strategies against administrative waste, pp. 185–96.

18 John Goodlad, *A Place Called School* (New York, 1983), p. 276.
19 Theodore Sizer, *Horace's Compromise: The Dilemmas of the American High School* (Boston, 1984), p. 214.
20 Ernest L. Boyer, 'Reflections on the Great Debate of 1983,' *New York Teacher*, 11 June 1984, pp. 10–11, reprinted from the *Phi Delta Kappan*, April 1984.
21 Paulo Freire, *Education for Critical Consciousness* (New York, 1974), p. 43. For two fine introductions to Freire's ideas, see Cynthia Brown's *Literacy in 30 Hours: Paulo Freire's Process in Northeast Brazil* (originally published in *Social Policy*, 1974, reprinted several times in booklet form and available from the Alternate Schools Network, Chicago), and Denis Collins, *Paulo Freire: His Life, Works and Thoughts* (Paulist Press, New York, 1977).
22 For two long assessments of the problems of training for liberatory teaching, see Phyllis Noble's *Formation of Freirian Facilitators* (Latino Institute, Chicago, 1983) and Blanca Facundo, *Issues for An Evaluation of Freire-Inspired Programs in the United States and Puerto Rico*, 1984, available from Alternatives, PO Box 424, Señorial Mall Station, Rio Piedras, Puerto Rico, 00926.
23 Henry A. Giroux, 'Theories of Reproduction and Resistance in the New Sociology of Education,' *op. cit.*, p. 266.
24 Barney Glasser, *Schools Without Failure* (New York, 1969), p. 15.
25 John Goodlad, 'A Study of Schooling: Some Findings and Hypotheses,' *Phi Delta Kappan*, March 1983, p. 468.
26 Ernest L. Boyer, *High School: A Report on Secondary Education in America* (Carnegie Foundation for the Advancement of Teaching, New York, 1983), p. 147.
27 See Ann Berthof's discussion of pedagogy in *The Making of Meaning* (Boynton/Cook, New Jersey, 1981).
28 Robert Pattison, *On Literacy: The Politics of the Word from Homer to the Age of Rock* (New York, 1982), pp. x, 136.
29 Noelle Bisseret, *Education, Class Language, and Ideology* (London, 1979), p. 86. For another revealing study on language, power and class, see Paul Willis's *Learning to Labor: How Working Class Kids Get Working Class Jobs* (New York, 1981).
30 Herb Kohl's *The Open Classroom* (New York, 1969) went through ten printings in its first three years. It is still a valuable introduction to student-centered teaching.
31 For some examples of the adaptation of Freire's methods to the North American context, see Marilyn Frankenstein, 'Critical Mathematics Education: An Application of Paulo Freire's Epistemology,' *Journal of Education*, Vol. 165, No. 4, 1983, pp. 315–39; Kyle Fiore and Nan Elsasser, ' "Strangers No More": A Liberatory-Literacy Curriculum,' *College English*, Vol. 44, No. 2, February 1982, pp. 115–28; Linda Shaw Finlay and Valerie Faith, 'Illiteracy and Alienation in American Colleges: Is Paulo Freire's Pedagogy Relevant?', *The Radical Teacher*, December 1979, pp. 28–40; Ira Shor, *Critical Teaching and Everyday*

Life (Boston, Southend, 1980); and Nancy Schniedewind and Ellen Davidson, *Open Minds to Equality* (Prentice-Hall New Jersey, 1983).
32 Kohl, *The Open Classroom, op. cit.*, p. 14.
33 Illich, *Deschooling Society, op. cit.*, pp. 26–7.

Index

Boyer, E. L.: on 'banking'
education, 187; on black
students' scores, 145–6; on
communism, 123–4; on
computers, 132–3, 178; on cost
of repairing schools, 156; on
decline in education, 115; on
excellence and economic
recovery, 126; on 'hidden'
curriculum, 168; on inequality,
182–3; on legitimacy of
authority, 81; and *Paideia*, 119;
on purpose of education, 104,
141; on sex education, 157; on
teaching hours, 155, 178; on
testing, 72; on vocationalism, 38,
114
Brademas, J., report, 115–16, 129
Braverman, H., 138
Brawer, F., 41–2, 44, 56–7
Bright, J., 43
Brimelow, P., 104
Brodinsky, B., 78–9, 94
Bruner, J., 160
budget: career education, 40, 52;
education cuts, 20, 106, 177; for
excellence, 151, 156–7; military,
149, 151, 177; for science
education, 111–12
Bureau of Labor Statistics (BLS),
136, 139
business: advertising, 14–18; and
curriculum, 15–18, 107;
–government links, 10, 19, 106;
international, 127; needs of,
128–9, 181; power of, 19; and
protest, 10, 14, 18; –school
links, 16–17, 117, 152; Trade
War, 124–30
Business–Higher Education
Forum, 116, 125, 139
busing, 21, 167

Cahn, S., 9–10
cancer, 87
capitalism, 53, 128, 173–5
careerism, 4, 11, 16, 29, 30–58,
176, 181; against activism,

30–58; communications
strategy, 34–6; fallacies of,
37–40; federal involvement in,
32–3, 40–2; and inequality,
47–51, 56–7; program, 33;
union resistance to, 45–8; and
work, 36–7
Carter, J., 6
censorship, 21–4, 177
Chauncey, H., 162
City University of New York, 7
Clark, B. R., 92
Clark, J., 141, 150
class, 48–9, 120–1, 133–4, 142–3,
165–6; *see also* inequality
Cohen, A., 41–2, 44, 56–7
Cold War, 122–5; *see also*
communism
Coleman, J. S., 77, 165
College Board (CB), 59–60, 72;
on decline in test scores, 62, 68,
71–3; on preparation for
college, 113–14, 142, 145
Columbia University, 9–10
Commager, H. S., 15
communications: and authority,
10–11, 25; strategy for
careerism, 34–6
communism, 24–5, 123
community colleges, 38, 41–2, 56
competencies, basic, 113–14, 116
competition, international, 104–5,
125–30
computers, 112–13, 116, 129–40
Conant, J. B., 35, 56–7, 159–60
confidence, public, in
establishment institutions, 4–5,
106
conscientization, 184
consensus, national, 4–5, 20–1,
28–9
conservative restoration, 176–7;
austerity, 1–29; and business,
10, 19, 106; careerism, 30–58;
excellence, 104–60; literacy,
59–103; Nixon administration,
3–7, 11; Reagan